T0338783

PSALMS

VOLUME 1: THE WISDOM PSALMS

KERUX COMMENTARIES

PSALMS

VOLUME 1: THE WISDOM PSALMS

———

A Commentary for Biblical Preaching and Teaching

W. CREIGHTON MARLOWE
CHARLES H. SAVELLE JR.

KREGEL MINISTRY

Psalms, Volume 1: The Wisdom Psalms: A Commentary for Biblical Preaching and Teaching

© 2021 by W. Creighton Marlowe and Charles H. Savelle Jr.

Published by Kregel Ministry, an imprint of Kregel Publications, 2450 Oak Industrial Dr. NE, Grand Rapids, MI 49505-6020.

Unless otherwise indicated, the translation of the Scripture portions used throughout the commentary is the authors' own English rendering of the original biblical languages.

Scripture quotations marked ESV are taken from The Holy Bible, English Standard Version. Copyright © 2001 by Crossway Bibles, a publishing ministry of Good News Publishers.

Scripture quotations marked NASB are taken from the New American Standard Bible® (NASB), Copyright © 1960, 1962, 1963, 1968, 1971, 1972, 1973, 1975, 1977, 1995 by The Lockman Foundation. Used by permission. www.Lockman.org

Scripture quotations marked NLT are taken from the Holy Bible, New Living Translation, copyright © 1996, 2004, 2015 by Tyndale House Foundation. Used by permission of Tyndale House Publishers, Inc., Carol Stream, Illinois 60188. All rights reserved.

Scripture quotations marked NIV are taken from the Holy Bible, New International Version®, NIV®. Copyright © 1973, 1978, 1984, 2011 by Biblica, Inc.™ Used by permission of Zondervan. All rights reserved worldwide. www.zondervan.com

Scripture quotations marked RSV are from the Revised Standard Version of the Bible, copyright © 1946, 1952, and 1971 by the National Council of the Churches of Christ in the U.S.A. Used by permission. All rights reserved.

Italics in Scripture quotations indicate emphasis added by the authors.

The Hebrew font, NewJerusalemU, and the Greek font, GraecaU, are available from www.linguistsoftware.com/lgku.htm, +1-425-775-1130.

All photos are under Creative Commons licensing, and contributors are indicated in the captions of the photos.

ISBN 978-0-8254-5846-0

Printed in the United States of America
21 22 23 24 25 / 5 4 3 2 1

Contents

PUBLISHER'S PREFACE TO THE SERIES

Since words were first uttered, people have struggled to understand one another and to know the main meaning in any verbal exchange.

The answer to what God is talking about must be understood in every context and generation; that is why Kerux (KAY-rukes) emphasizes text-based truths and bridges from the context of the original hearers and readers to the twenty-first-century world. Kerux values the message of the text, thus its name taken from the Greek *kērux*, a messenger or herald who announced the proclamations of a ruler or magistrate.

Biblical authors trumpeted all kinds of important messages in very specific situations, but a big biblical idea, grasped in its original setting and place, can transcend time. This specific, big biblical idea taken from the biblical passage embodies a single concept that bridges the gap between the author's contemporary context and the reader's world. How do the prophets perceive the writings of Moses? How does the writer of Hebrews make sense of the Old Testament? How does Clement in his second epistle, which may be the earliest sermon known outside the New Testament, adapt verses from Isaiah and also ones from the Gospels? Or what about Luther's bold use of Romans 1:17? How does Jonathan Edwards allude to Genesis 19? Who can forget Martin Luther King Jr.'s "I Have a Dream" speech and his appropriation of Amos 5:24: "No, no, we are not satisfied, and we will not be satisfied until 'justice rolls down like waters, and righteousness like a mighty stream'"? How does a preacher in your local church today apply the words of Hosea in a meaningful and life-transforming way?

What is prime in God's mind and how is that expressed to a given generation in the units of thought throughout the Bible? Answering those questions is what Kerux authors do. Based on the popular "big idea" preaching model, Kerux commentaries uniquely combine the insights of experienced Bible exegetes (trained in interpretation) and homileticians (trained in preaching). Their collaboration provides for every Bible book:

- A detailed introduction and outline
- A summary of all preaching sections with their primary exegetical, theological, and preaching ideas
- Preaching pointers that join the original context with the contemporary one
- Insights from the Hebrew and Greek text
- A thorough exposition of the text
- Sidebars of pertinent information for further background
- Appropriate charts and photographs
- A theological focus to passages
- A contemporary big idea for every preaching unit
- Present-day meaning, validity, and application of a main idea
- Creative presentations for each primary idea
- Key questions about the text for study groups

Many thanks to Jim Weaver, Kregel's former acquisitions editor, who conceived of this commentary series and further developed it with the team of Jeffrey D. Arthurs, Robert B. Chisholm, David M. Howard Jr., Darrell L. Bock, Roy E. Ciampa, and Michael J. Wilkins. We also recognize with gratitude the significant contributions of Dennis Hillman, Fred Mabie, Paul Hillman, and Herbert W. Bateman IV, who have been instrumental in the development of the series.

—Kregel Publications

PREFACE TO THE PSALTER

A commentary on the OT Psalms is nothing new. Why one more? In this case, what is special is the combination of careful exegesis with contemporary application. Every passage of Scripture is open to, and should be examined in relation to, both the author's contextual intention for his contemporaries and the readers' immediate application to their contemporary context and concerns. The Bible models this use of OT texts. When the NT apostles used Scripture for evangelistic or edificatory purposes, they sometimes appealed to what the author or speaker being quoted was saying to his audience, but often the words cited are taken out of context and the application made for those in the first-century A.D. is not exegetical but applicational. How these words were relevant for these readers' needs was more important than the original, contextual sense of those words. Since a Jewish audience initially was the target of gospel ministry, a persuasive strategy would have been to demonstrate how these OT texts supported Jesus as Messiah in conformity with Jewish hermeneutics of that time. Jewish interpretive practices, just as later Christian approaches, ranged (and sometimes fought) over both literal and figurative (or symbolic or mystical or typological, etc.) methods of deriving meaning. Both the past historical and the present homiletical values have always had currency, and over time, one at the expense of the other in successive eras of Jewish and Christian experience. One is not right and the other wrong. One is not essential and the other tangential. One is not fully rational or objective and the other fully emotional or subjective. Every Bible passage can be examined in terms of *what it meant then* and *what it means now*. Both are essential and effective, but to get to the latter we have to start with the former. We have problems when we reverse this order or skip the first step or make them interchangeable. Eisegesis (reading a foreign meaning into a text) is a problem when the audience gets the idea that the original author intended a meaning at odds with that author's own cultural and grammatical context. People today applying a text out of context have the duty to make sure their current audience understands that the applied meaning is not equivalent to (while it certainly is compatible with, or does not contradict) the original meaning (historical, contextual exegesis).

EXEGETICAL AUTHOR'S ACKNOWLEDGMENTS

To my wife, Sherry, apart from whose devotion
and support this book would remain incomplete;

Dr. Ron B. Allen, seminary OT exegesis professor, whose love of the OT Psalter
ignited my interpretive interest in them and fanned a flame of devotion; and

All who have cried out to or for God through poetry and song.

My love affair with the OT Psalter began my first year in seminary. Since I had taken Elementary Hebrew at university, I was able to jump right in to Hebrew exegesis, where my teacher (Ron Allen, a disciple of Bruce Waltke) was a Psalmatic (a term I have just coined). His enthusiasm and appreciation for the poetic and musical beauty of the OT Psalms was contagious. And having formerly been engaged with a Christian band, singing and songwriting, playing guitar (the modern lyre), and leading musical worship, the marriage of theological study and Israelite poetry and music was a natural fit. Why I did not stick with that as a specialty seems odd in retrospect. Hebrew Bible and exegesis (yet often related to OT poetry) became my vocation as a professor, and after many years by God's unmerited grace and the editors' favor (hopefully merited), I have been allowed to repent of my unfaithful straying to other disciplines and have been reunited with my first love per this opportunity to contribute to a Psalms commentary.

I have taken on this task with great delight, despite the many hours required in writing and editing, because I truly believe the Kregel series (Kerux) to which this commentary belongs is a necessary publication. Much that rolls off the evangelical presses these days does not provide the target audiences with publications that are cutting-edge. Many books play it safe, say what is expected, and mostly repeat what has been said in traditional formats with too often the same, predictable authors. All that is new is the publisher, the book cover, the font used, and maybe a new face and voice. The present series to which this first volume of the Psalter is being added is unique in enough ways to make all the effort pay off. Whether my explanations are or are not always an improvement, I have tried to challenge traditional views when warranted by the data. Beyond this, however, the Kerux format (whatever the exegesis of a given text) is arguably something new and needed by busy pastors and preachers, because it provides (digitally or in print), on the one hand, careful consideration of the meaning and translation (exegesis) of the Hebrew text; yet, on the other hand, a bountiful supply of seasoned homiletical guidance for taking each of the 150 OT psalms into the pulpit. Then, to top it off, both of these approaches to each psalm add theological reflections, hopefully with current relevance. What more could a preacher want or need?—apart from a sermonic ghost writer. For these reasons and more I am pleased to have had this part in making such a commentary series a reality.

—Creighton Marlowe

PREACHING AUTHOR'S ACKNOWLEDGMENTS

To my wife, Kathy, and our three children, Charlie, Amy, and Becky,
who mean more to me than they know;

My professors, friends, and colleagues who have left
an indelible positive imprint upon my life;

All those who do the heavy lifting of preaching to congregations
big and small, for whom I hope this book can be a blessing; and

The Triune God who loved me and saved me.

One reason many people today struggle with the incongruities between the OT author and the NT interpreter is the expectation of a universal and timeless scientific relationship between the OT text and its use in the NT. This tension disappears when we accept that often the way the NT uses the OT is in line with the Jewish expectations of NT times (that have roots in the interpretive and hermeneutical developments of the circa-four-hundred-year-long intertestamental period) rather than directly connected to all future Christians regardless of time of place. The Bible's contents were given *to* an ancient world but are useful and relevant *for* the modern world. Bridging that gap requires a good deal of cultural and hermeneutical sensitivity. The bottom line is that we always have to, or should, both interpret (historically) and then apply (homiletically) every Bible passage. This Kerux series of volumes on the Psalms is hopefully a modest step along that indispensable learning curve.

The present volume, volume 1, of this project on the OT Psalter is about the Wisdom Psalms. Wisdom is not as objective or formal a category as lament (vol. 2) or praise (vol. 3). Other studies will not include, or will add other psalms to, the psalms chosen for this wisdom volume. To some degree it was a judgment call which psalms to include, or not to include. But some objective criteria were involved in the decision-making process. While, on the one hand, wise instruction or impulses might be found in almost any psalm, those included here, on the other hand, were picked due to a thematic emphasis on the contrast between the obedient ("righteous" or "wise") and the disobedient ("wicked" or "foolish") person. This is a key element found in the OT wisdom literature (Proverbs and Ecclesiastes in particular). A second major emphasis in wisdom literature, applied to this selection of wisdom psalms, is the contrast between two roads, ways, or lifestyles: the right/godly way and the wrong/ungodly way (morally, ethically, or spiritually). Related to this are contrasting or opposite consequences leading to life or death. Those who "choose poorly" risk shorter and less productive lives. Those who "choose wisely" are not guaranteed health and wealth but push the odds in their favor toward a more safe, secure, and successful life. Wisdom Psalms featured here also resonate with OT wisdom passages that deal with divine creation and communication. Arguably other psalms could or should have been included in this volume, but what is here provides a sufficient taste of how wisdom themes can appear in and, more than that, more fully characterize a psalm.

Much gratitude is extended to all who had a part in bringing this book to fruition, especially our ever-enthusiastic editor, Herb Bateman; as well as the entire Kregel team, especially for deciding to produce this unique commentary series. Many thanks also to our colleagues for their encouragement along the way, as some unavoidable and unexpected fits and starts hampered an earlier publication date. Most of all, praise to God for continued strength, stamina, and sanity.

—Charles H. Savelle Jr.

OVERVIEW OF ALL PREACHING PASSAGES

PSALM 1

EXEGETICAL IDEA
Israelites who loved and lived by Yahweh's laws would succeed in life, but those who despised and disobeyed his ways would vanish, having a vain existence.

THEOLOGICAL FOCUS
Success in any endeavor requires fascination and familiarization with God's desired way of living, while corruption and condemnation characterize those who ridicule righteousness.

PREACHING IDEA
Successful living involves loving God's Word and understanding the implications of failing to do so.

PREACHING POINTERS
Unlike the nations surrounding Israel, worshipping and praising Yahweh was more than merely appeasing a pantheon of gods with animal sacrifices. The ancient Israelite understood that praising Yahweh involved more than the lips, and living well involved more than good intentions. The wisdom motif of Psalm 1 contrasted the lifestyle of an Israelite who did right with one who did wrong, according to the religious rules established by God through his prophets like Moses. The secret of this wisdom was delighting in the law of God, recognizing the folly of rejecting God's law, and knowing that God would judge our attitudes and actions in light of his law.

For Christ-followers today, this timeless truth remains virtually unchanged. While many in the world today value experience over truth (and some would even deny the existence of truth at all), this first psalm, then and now, reminds us of the importance of knowing God's Word. Psalm 1 uses vivid imagery from nature and farming to portray the stark contrast between the lives of the righteous and the wicked. This contrast will be noted by people as they see how one is to avoid the unrighteous (v. 1) and in how the Lord watches over the righteous (v. 6). This is an important contrast to make when the lines of right and wrong are being blurred or eliminated altogether.

PSALM 15

EXEGETICAL IDEA
The psalmist saw that the person who stood confidently in God's presence was one whose life was characterized by honesty.

THEOLOGICAL FOCUS

People who can approach God with confidence are those who live lives characterized by personal integrity.

PREACHING IDEA

Enjoying access to God is tied to doing right before God and people.

PREACHING POINTERS

The specific circumstances behind Psalm 15 are uncertain. The superscription and content provide little to go on other than its association with David and that he was concerned about personal integrity.

For many today, David's opening question ("Lord, who may dwell in your tent?") seems antiquated, maybe even irrelevant. But this question is not what is out of touch here, but rather the idea that one can approach a holy God in a careless and thoughtless way. Psalm 15 reminds us that enjoying access to God is a privilege, not a right. As a privilege it is not tied to social or economic status, gender, age, or ethnicity, but it is a privilege, nonetheless. Psalm 15 is not a call to ritual, or even doctrinal formalism. It is, however, a call to personal integrity exercised before God and with people.

PSALM 37

EXEGETICAL IDEA

The psalmist taught his readers not to worry that unlawful people had health and wealth, not to be discouraged, and not to turn to violence as an answer, but to keep trusting God because God's enemies would be defeated.

THEOLOGICAL FOCUS

God rewards those who delight in him and are dedicated to his ways, but God scoffs at and will thwart those who reject his ways.

PREACHING IDEA

Dwelling on those who do wrong can keep you from doing what is right and trusting God.

PREACHING POINTERS

The superscription of Psalm 37 is sparse on details, but many of the moral deficiencies alluded to seem to be ingrained in most societies, and Israel was no different. Later prophets such as Amos and Habakkuk would frequently condemn Israel and Judah for such sins. The psalmist faced wrongdoing head-on by encouraging his audience not to let evildoers get under their skin. Two basic reasons were given for not dwelling on the wicked. First, the success of the evildoer is temporal, and they would ultimately be judged (vv. 2, 9a, 10, 13, 15, 17, 20, 22a, 38). Second, the righteous would ultimately be delivered and blessed (vv. 6, 7, 11, 18, 22, 24, 28, 29, 33, 34, 39, 40). So, much of the rest of the psalm addresses righteous living.

Today is no different. The success of those who have cut moral and ethical corners to get where they are bothers us. More often than not, "Nice guys finish last." This often carries over into the spiritual realm. Most of us probably know of someone who was faithful in their walk with the Lord but who then was stricken with some unimaginable disease, while another person living a life of debauchery continues as a paragon of good health.

PSALM 49

EXEGETICAL IDEA
People are mortal and, like animals, must die. Not even the wealthiest is exempt or can bribe God to grant freedom from the grave, where the godly do find life.

THEOLOGICAL FOCUS
The psalmist summoned people from every economic level to remember that those who are oppressive, prideful, and prosperous should not be envied, for even the rich cannot purchase extended life.

PREACHING IDEA
The universality of death means that one must live wisely knowing that God, not wealth, delivers from the grave.

PREACHING POINTERS
The ascription of the psalm is to "the sons of Korah," of which little is certain, and the generalities of the contents make any attempt to identify a specific occasion for the song tenuous at best. But apparently, some in ancient Israel (as do many today) equated wealth with life and believed that the possession of the former somehow ensured the latter. But this was and is a fatal error. In fact, studies have been undertaken to determine whether one's wealth or the amount spent on health care has any effect on life expectancy. Research suggests that modest increases in life expectancy can be gained when there are greater financial resources available. But there are no studies that show that death can be defeated.

It is this reality of death that Psalm 49 addresses. Since death is universal and wealth cannot prevent it, what is one to do? Many Bible interpreters have recognized that Psalm 49 is a wisdom psalm. As such one would expect that there would be a heavy dose on righteous behaviors. So, one is a bit surprised to see that the psalm does not so much tell one how to live but how not to live (e.g., trusting in wealth, pride). The answer is not *what* but rather *who*, namely, the God who ransoms souls from "sheol" (לִשְׁאוֹל; v. 15). Ultimately, this will point the way forward to Christ who is the answer to the great enemy: death.

PSALM 73

EXEGETICAL IDEA
Although the ungodly seemed to succeed while the godly suffered, the psalmist was satisfied that Israel's God would bring about their downfall.

THEOLOGICAL FOCUS

While the godless person appears to prosper and godly people suffer, God will eventually judge the ungodly.

PREACHING IDEA

God is good even though bad things happen to good people and good things happen to bad people.

PREACHING POINTERS

The superscription of Psalm 73 links it to Asaph, a Levite and music leader in the time of David (1 Chr. 15:17, 19; 16:4–7; 2 Chr. 29:30). This is one of twelve psalms associated with Asaph (Psa. 50, 73–83). Whether Asaph is speaking of himself or someone else is uncertain. But the psalmist touches upon an inequity—in *Star Wars*-ian terms, "a disturbance in the force." It is a world where bad things happen to good people and good things happen to bad people. The problem is exacerbated by the knowledge that this world is ultimately ruled by a sovereign, righteous, and most importantly a good God. So, the psalmist cannot simply attribute this inequity to mere luck, fate, or fortune.

Bart Ehrman, a biblical scholar and former evangelical, left Christianity altogether over issues similar to that raised by our psalmist. As Ehrman (2008, 3) puts it, "But I came to a point where I could no longer believe. It's a very long story, but the short version is this: I realized that I could no longer reconcile the claims of faith with the facts of life. In particular, I could no longer explain how there can be a good and all-powerful God actively involved with this world, given the state of things. For many people who inhabit this planet, life is a cesspool of misery and suffering." But while the psalmist would likely acknowledge Ehrman's "cesspool of misery and suffering," he thankfully reaches a different conclusion. Rather than denying God because he does not understand him, the psalmist clings to the parts of God that he does understand, namely, his faithfulness even in the midst of trials and his ultimate judgment of the unrighteous.

PSALM 78

EXEGETICAL IDEA

The poet taught that remembering God's past interventions for Israel should strengthen present and future faithfulness.

THEOLOGICAL FOCUS

God is faithful to intervene on behalf of his people in order both to punish and preserve them.

PREACHING IDEA

History matters because rehearsing the past can expose the dangers of disobedience and also remind us of the faithfulness of God.

PREACHING POINTERS

Psalm 78 is another one of the psalms attributed to Asaph (Psa. 50, 73–83), a Levitical music leader in the time of David (1 Chr. 15:17, 19; 16:4–7; 2 Chr. 29:30). The psalm uses the generic address "my people" (v. 1) and concerns itself with passing on the faith from one generation to the next primarily through Israel's history. The appeal to this historical reiteration suggests that perhaps some in Asaph's day had either neglected or forgotten their past. This might not be all that different from today. The study of history doesn't seem to capture the imagination these days as it may have done with past generations. Just a few years ago, an article in *Forbes* magazine by J. Maureen Henderson asked the question, "Just How Clueless Are Millennials When It Comes to Popular History?" Even as this was being written, *The New Yorker* posted an article by Eric Alterman entitled "The Decline of Historical Thinking" (Feb. 4, 2019). Perhaps this decline is due in part to our being so focused on living in the moment, capturing it in a selfie, and posting it on the latest social media platform that we hardly give much of a thought to what happened last week, much less hundreds let alone thousands of years ago.

For God's people, this popular disinterest in history and the events of the past in recent times and antiquity is not only unfortunate but spiritually dangerous. It fails to understand that history is not merely about what happened to "them," but it is about what might happen to "us." This truth is at the core of the Scriptures (e.g., 1 Cor. 10:6), and Psalm 78 in particular clearly demonstrates how rehearsing the past can reveal the dangers of disobedience while reminding us of the faithfulness of God.

PSALM 127

EXEGETICAL IDEA
Israelite pilgrims rejoiced in Yahweh's essential involvement in building and protecting a city to avoid futility, and his provision of sons to ensure strength against opponents.

THEOLOGICAL FOCUS
Unless God is involved in a project, the venture is vain.

PREACHING IDEA
True security and lasting significance in life is found in God alone.

PREACHING POINTERS
It seems that security is on everybody's mind these days. The average person is concerned about pandemics, terrorism, mass shootings, global-warming, identity theft, and zombies, just to name a few. (Well, maybe not zombies!) We want to feel secure. We also want to know that our lives matter, and that our lives are significant. I suspect that this is one of the major drivers in social media. If I post frequently about my life, then it must truly matter; thus, the seemingly endless pictures of our food, clothes, friends, parties, pets, and the like are shared.

The poet of Psalm 127 (Solomon, according to the superscription) had different concerns in his day, and he wouldn't be posting "selfies," but the desire for true security and lasting significance was just as real then as it is now. As one of the psalms that would be sung on the way to the temple associated with Solomon, one would be reminded of the Lord's protection over Jerusalem and the temple, and also of their families. This song highlights the intersection point between faith and family, and the psalmist has put his finger on something that many Israelites then and many Christ-followers today have failed to realize—namely, true security and lasting significance of both faith and family are found in God alone.

PSALM 128

EXEGETICAL IDEA
God prospers prayerful Hebrew fathers who fear and follow "Yahweh" with longevity and posterity, including many sons and grandsons.

THEOLOGICAL FOCUS
Those who prayerfully fear (follow) God receive long life and many descendants.

PREACHING IDEA
A blessed life comes from fearing the Lord and prayer.

PREACHING POINTERS
Now, in the southern United States, the word "bless" in its various forms is a common feature of the vernacular. It is usually used positively like it often is in the Bible ("I'm blessed"), but occasionally "Bless their/your heart" is used to question a person's competence or intelligence or both. In any case, those who speak of being blessed commonly view blessing solely in terms of being in a good state. And being blessed is simply something that happens to you. While both these sentiments are true, the writer of Psalm 128 is most interested in relating the *how* and *what* of blessing. It is not an exhaustive treatment of the topic but a poetic reflection on it.

The standard Hebrew verb for "bless" (*barak*) occurs around eighty times in the Psalms and nearly ninety times if you count the noun form. The verb and noun forms are used around four hundred times in the Old Testament and are found in twenty-nine out of thirty-nine books. It is literally used from the very beginning as God blesses what he has created (Gen. 1:22, 28). There is little question that the word and the concept was important in the Hebrew Bible.

PSALM 133

EXEGETICAL IDEA
An Israelite pilgrim and poet celebrated the sacred nature of family fellowship and faithfulness to covenant commitments.

THEOLOGICAL FOCUS
God is pleased with and blesses family members who remain loyal to their obligations.

PREACHING IDEA
Unity of family and faith is wonderful and involves God's blessing of "life forevermore."

PREACHING POINTERS

Some of our fondest road trip memories involve snacking, stops at roadside attractions, bathroom breaks, and for many, singing. We sing as we travel (no talent required) because it helps us to pass the time and it helps us to bond. Spouses and siblings also find it harder to bicker when there is a melody to be proclaimed. Simply put, singing brings us together.

It seems Israel understood this and so the Psalms of Ascents (Psalms 120–134, aka the Pilgrim Psalms) provided a means to pass the time and bond as they traveled up to Jerusalem to worship. So, it seems fitting that one of these Psalms of Ascents, Psalm 133, pictures the blessedness of unity in family and faith. The family that walks together worships together and vice versa.

PSALM 19

EXEGETICAL IDEA

God's existence and significance was revealed in creation; and his express will was revealed in verbal communication.

THEOLOGICAL FOCUS

God wants to be known, and has made himself, and his will, known through cosmological creation and anthropological communication.

PREACHING IDEA

The revelation of God's glory and his word challenges us to evaluate the way we live.

PREACHING POINTERS

Psalm 19 is attributed to David although the particular occasion is not identified. Presumably, the idea of spiritual self-examination was as important then as it is now. You have probably witnessed one of the television exposés where a reporter armed with a blacklight inspects hotel rooms to see how clean (or unclean) they really are. The blacklight reveals spots and stains that one might not otherwise see. Presented with this unsightly and unsanitary evidence, the hotel manager often confesses that such conditions fall short of their standards, and then apologizes and pledges to correct the issues.

But, what would happen if we would examine the rooms of our lives with the divine "blacklight" of God's person and his word? What would be revealed about our thoughts, attitudes, and actions? In Psalm 19, the psalmist considers how the revelation of God's glory and his word challenges us to evaluate the way we are to live.

PSALM 91

EXEGETICAL IDEA

An Israelite psalmist in trouble placed his trust in Yahweh as his only hope and salvation, and believed that rescue could be expected from even the slightest level of harm.

THEOLOGICAL FOCUS
God promises his protection to those who trust fully in him alone as their refuge.

PREACHING IDEA
God is a refuge and source of protection for those who trust in him.

PREACHING POINTERS
Psalm 91 lacks a superscription, so identifying the specific occasion of the psalm is not possible. But the yearning for God's protection seems fairly universal.

I (Charles) used to live where there could be tornadoes and now, I live where hurricanes are a reality. Tornadoes and hurricanes are different weather phenomena, but both involve giving some thought to where to find refuge during these events. But whether we are looking for protection from natural disasters or other calamities of life, it seems we are constantly on the lookout for a place of refuge. For the author of Psalm 91, the best and ultimate storm shelter or safe room is God himself. This psalm is not a theodicy but rather an audacious declaration that God protects those who put their trust in him. For all those who are anxiety-ridden, Psalm 91 is an invitation into the divine safe room.

PSALM 111

EXEGETICAL IDEA
The worshipping community was summoned to praise Yahweh for his faithful acts of redemption on behalf of his people.

THEOLOGICAL FOCUS
God is great, glorious, and gracious; and he gives to his chosen nation both land and wise laws.

PREACHING IDEA
God's *work* in our lives should produce *worship* from our lives.

PREACHING POINTERS
The English term *hallelujah* has taken on a rather pedestrian sense and tone in today's culture. It is often used as an interjection in response to perceived good fortune: "Hallelujah, I am getting a tax refund this year." Or it is used sarcastically: "The coach finally put in a new quarterback. Hallelujah!" Even Leonard Cohen's much-covered song "Hallelujah" has almost nothing to do with God. In fact, what all these uses have in common is they really have little, if anything, to say about God.

I (Charles) suspect that this is the very reason that many modern English translations do not often use the term *hallelujah* but rather translate it as "praise the Lord" (lit., "praise Yah"). In any case, from the very first word of Psalm 111, "Hallelujah," the Israelite then and the contemporary reader now is put on notice that God will be front and center and that the Lord's *work* in our lives should produce *worship* from our lives.

PSALM 112

EXEGETICAL IDEA
This Israelite psalmist proclaimed praise because those who obey God's commands (unlike the lawless) will be prosperous, generous, confident, and celebrated.

THEOLOGICAL FOCUS
God rewards the righteous with success and satisfaction, while the wicked are dissatisfied even when their desires are obtained.

PREACHING IDEA
A blessed life is enriching, ethical, enduring, established, and even envied by the wicked.

PREACHING POINTERS
Like Psalm 111, Psalm 112 begins with a "hallelujah" ("praise the Lord") and shows that like us today, the Israelites were desiring to live a life of blessing. But what is the difference, if any, between living a charmed life versus a blessed life? According to the *Merriam-Webster's Online Dictionary*, a charmed life is "a life protected as if by magic charms: a life unusually unaffected by dangers and difficulties." Three aspects of this brief definition are noteworthy in what is omitted: (1) there is no mention of God; (2) there is no ethical component or corollary; and (3) a charmed life is one that avoids the trials and tribulations of life. On the other hand, a blessed life (at least according to the Bible) is integrally tied to God (one is not truly blessed apart from God), and ethics (a blessed person is righteous, and a righteous person is blessed), and blessedness does not avoid trials and tribulations (but is a status one has within them).

Scripture contains no promises about obtaining a charmed life, but it makes numerous proclamations about the blessed life. A charmed life is grounded in fate, luck, chance, destiny, and the like, while blessing is grounded in a sovereign God and living lives that reflect that God. So, it's great if you are living a charmed life, but if you are like the rest of us, then a blessed life is the best life. To that end, Psalm 112 helps to unpack what a blessed life looks and acts like.

PSALM 119

EXEGETICAL IDEA
This ancient Hebrew poet expressed his love for and loyalty to the laws of Yahweh with the hope that he would experience divine deliverance from a deadly foe.

THEOLOGICAL FOCUS
A life regulated by, and devoted to, God's rules has the best chance for safety and success.

PREACHING IDEA
Devotion to God's word is the proper response to the challenges of life.

PREACHING POINTERS

It is said that Eskimos have fifty (or even a hundred) words for snow, and this rich vocabulary indicates that snow is truly important for these people. Cool, but untrue. Linguistic studies have pretty much defrosted this idea. It is the Scottish, in fact, who seem to have the richest winter vocabulary. What is beyond debate is that Psalm 119 uses eight different Hebrew terms to relate to the Law, or perhaps better, the word of God. What is also true is that the psalmist takes 176 verses to adequately express his devotion to the word. In musical terms, Psalm 119 is less like a song and more like a concept album.

While little is known of this psalm's historical context, the author's devotion to God's word seems so out of step with much of the culture. Americans are becoming less and less biblically literate, or to put it negatively, more and more biblically illiterate. This is true of even some Christ-followers who regard the Bible as mostly irrelevant or even a potential hindrance to their pursuit of Christ. When you throw in a healthy dose of postmodern skepticism in the mix, it seems that the sentiments expressed by Psalm 119 are quaint and simplistic.

ABBREVIATIONS

GENERAL ABBREVIATIONS

A.D.	in the year of our Lord (*anno Domini*)
ANE	ancient Near East
B.C.	before Christ
DSS	Dead Sea Scrolls
EB	English Bible(s)
HB	Hebrew Bible
LXX	Septuagint
MT	Masoretic Text
NT	New Testament
OT	Old Testament
SP	Samaritan Pentateuch

TECHNICAL ABBREVIATIONS

absol.	absolute (free form)
acc.	accusative
aor.	aorist
appos.	appositional
ca.	circa
cf.	compare (confer)
ch(s).	chapter(s)
com.	common gender
comp.	completed by
conj.	conjunction
const.	construct (bound form)
CV	consonant–vowel (open syllable)
CVC	consonant–vowel–consonant (closed syllable)
edit.	edition
ed(s).	editor(s)
e.g.	*exempli gratia* (for example)
esp.	especially
et al.	*et alii* (and others)
etc.	*et cetera* (and the rest)
fem.	feminine
ff.	following pages
gen.	genitive
Gk.	Greek

Heb.	Hebrew
i.e.	*id est* (that is)
impf.	imperfect
impv.	imperative
inf.	infinitive
in toto	entire work
lit.	literally
masc.	masculine
ms(s).	manuscript(s)
n.	note; footnote
n.b.	*note bene* ("a good comment"; i.e., noteworthy)
neg.	negative; negation
nom.	nominal/nominative
n.p.	no page number
obj.	object
obj. gen.	objective genitive
parag.	paragraph
part.	particle
pass.	passive
perf.	perfect
pl.	plural
Ps(s).	Psalm(s)
ptc.	participle
rev.	revision
sg.	singular
subj. gen.	subjective genitive
Supp.	Supplement (in a series)
s.v.	under the word (*sub verbo*)
trans.	translator(s)
v(v).	verse(s)
vol(s).	volume(s)

BIBLICAL

Old Testament

Gen.	Genesis
Exod.	Exodus
Lev.	Leviticus
Num.	Numbers
Deut.	Deuteronomy
Josh.	Joshua
Judg.	Judges
Ruth	Ruth
1 Sam.	1 Samuel
2 Sam.	2 Samuel

Old Testament (continued)

1 Kings	1 Kings
2 Kings	2 Kings
1 Chron.	1 Chronicles
2 Chron.	2 Chronicles
Ezra	Ezra
Neh.	Nehemiah
Esther	Esther
Job	Job
Ps./Pss.	Psalm(s)
Prov.	Proverbs

Old Testament (continued)

Eccl.	Ecclesiastes
Song	Song of Songs
Isa.	Isaiah
Jer.	Jeremiah
Lam.	Lamentations
Ezek.	Ezekiel
Dan.	Daniel
Hos.	Hosea
Joel	Joel
Amos	Amos
Obad.	Obadiah
Jonah	Jonah
Mic.	Micah
Nah.	Nahum
Hab.	Habakkuk
Zeph.	Zephaniah
Hag.	Haggai
Zech.	Zechariah
Mal.	Malachi

New Testament

Matt.	Matthew
Mark	Mark
Luke	Luke

New Testament (continued)

John	John
Acts	Acts
Rom.	Romans
1 Cor.	1 Corinthians
2 Cor.	2 Corinthians
Gal.	Galatians
Eph.	Ephesians
Phil.	Philippians
Col.	Colossians
1 Thess.	1 Thessalonians
2 Thess.	2 Thessalonians
1 Tim.	1 Timothy
2 Tim.	2 Timothy
Titus	Titus
Philem.	Philemon
Heb.	Hebrews
James	James
1 Peter	1 Peter
2 Peter	2 Peter
1 John	1 John
2 John	2 John
3 John	3 John
Jude	Jude
Rev.	Revelation

HEBREW SYNTACTICAL TERMS

Verbal Stems	Function	Voice
qal	The basic stem (no particular nuance intended)	active
niphal	passive	passive
hiphil	The so-called "causative" stem; nuances of agency, repetition, etc.)	active
hophal		passive
piel	The so-called "strengthened" stem (active voice; intensity, repetition, etc.)	active
pual		passive
hithpael	Reflexive	active

Verbal States	Basic Function	Form	Tense(s)	Mood(s)
Perfect (perf.)	Completed action	Suffixed pronouns	past	Indicative; volitional
Inverted perf.	Incomplete action	Suffixed pronouns	future	Indicative; volitional

Verbal States	Basic Function	Form	Tense(s)	Mood(s)
Imperfect (impf.)	Incomplete action	Prefixed pronouns	future; present	Indicative; volitional;* precative** (jussive; cohortative)
Inverted impf.	Completed action	Prefixed pronouns	past	
Imperative (impv.)	Command	Suffixed pronouns	NA	Indicative
Infinitive (infin.)	Adverbial; purpose, et al.	Suffixed pronouns	NA	NA

*Verbs are indicative or volitional when stating certainty (it is, will be; I will do).
**Verbs are precative when stating possibility (it may/might or could/should be).

Reference

ABD	*Anchor Bible Dictionary*
ANET	*Ancient Near East Texts,* ed. Pritchard
BDB	*The Brown-Driver-Briggs Hebrew and English Lexicon*
BDBA	*The Brown-Driver-Briggs Hebrew and English Lexicon, Abridged*
BHS	*Biblia Hebraica Stuttgartensia*
CTA	*Corpus tablettes alphabetiques* (Paris 1963)
HALOT	*Hebrew and Aramaic Lexicon of the Old Testament*
NIDOTT	*New International Dictionary of Old Testament and Theology*

Bible Versions

CEB	Common English Bible
ESV	English Standard Version
HTV	[Hear] The Voice
JPS	Jewish Publication Society
KJV	King James Version
NAB	New American Bible
NASB	New American Standard Bible
NEB	New English Bible
NET	New English Translation
NETS	New English Translation of the Septuagint
NIV	New International Version
NJB	New Jerusalem Bible
NRSV	New Revised Standard Version
RSV	Revised Standard Version

Periodicals

AJ	*The Asbury Journal*
CBQ	*The Catholic Biblical Quarterly*

JBL	*Journal of Biblical Literature*
MJT	*Midwestern Theological Journal*
PTR	*Princeton Theological Review*
SJOT	*Scandinavian Journal of the Old Testament*
SJT	*Scottish Journal of Theology*
VT	*Vetus Testamentum*
WTJ	*Westminster Theological Journal*

Book Series

AB	Anchor Bible
BCOT	Baker Commentary on the Old Testament
JSOT	Journal for the Study of the Old Testament (Press)
NAC	New American Commentary
NCBC	New Century Bible Commentary
NICOT	New International Commentary on the Old Testament
NIVAC	New International Version Application Commentary
OTL	Old Testament Library
SBLDS	Society of Biblical Literature Dissertation Series
TOTC	Tyndale Old Testament Commentary Series
VTSup	Vetus Testamentum Supplement (series)

INTRODUCTION TO THE PSALTER

OVERVIEW OF INTRODUCTORY ISSUES

Author: Various Authors Assumed: David, Korah, Asaph, musical director, Moses, Solomon

Provenance: Canaan, Assyria, Babylon, Israel, Judah, Judea

Readers: Preexilic, exilic, and postexilic Jewish audiences

Date: Exodus to Exile (fifteenth to sixth century B.C.)

Historical Setting: Ancient Near Eastern culture (Canaan, Babylon)

Occasion for Writing: Events leading to praise or lament

Genre: Hebrew poetry set to music

Theological Emphasis: Praise, for God is good; lament, for life is bad at times.

AUTHORSHIP

For whatever purposes, the OT psalms were anonymous. Yet, a number of the psalms have a heading, known as a superscription, that at times may indicate authorship. Unfortunately, the information in the superscriptions, handed down with integrity and reliability in the Masoretic text (MT), were not part of the original or earliest manuscripts. They were added by later editors, who were not the authors and, therefore, not working under divine inspiration as usually accorded to the biblical books per se. When compared with the superscriptions in the ancient Greek translation of the Hebrew Bible Psalter (LXX or Septuagint), they differ. For instance, twenty-two psalms in the Septuagint lack a superscription (1, 2, 104, 105, 106, 110, 111, 112, 113, 114, 115, 116, 117, 118, 135, 136, 145–50).

Nevertheless, seventy-three superscriptions in the Masoretic text ascribe the psalm to David. The expression "of David" (לְדָוִד) in English versions can be translated (due to the prefixed preposition לְ) "to" or "about" or "for David." Authorship may be, and at times clearly is, indicated idiomatically, but other prepositions would normally be expected for "by" or "from." The rendering "by David" (לְדָוִד) is supported by the fact that it appears in the superscription to Psalm 18 (which also explains its setting as the time David escaped from Saul's sword). The psalm is repeated in 2 Samuel 22, following a discussion of David's victories. As a result, David wrote a sacred song of praise to Yahweh (יְהוָה). The content of the psalm is consistent with this event in David's career. Other individuals mentioned in various headings are Asaph, the sons of Korah, anonymous musical directors, Moses, Solomon, and others. More will be said about superscriptions below.

King David by Arent d'Arent de Gelder (ca. 1683)

This leaves us in a position to value highly what is communicated in the superscriptions, but not as authoritative. All this implies that what God wants us to derive from these psalms is not dependent on secure knowledge of authorship. In a few cases, we have an OT psalm and its traditional authorship mentioned in the NT. We may take these as secure indications of authorship, but it is possible that these NT references do not prove authorship absolutely (only the tradition), because the mention of someone like David in relation to a psalm was not done for the purpose of establishing authorship in that context, but merely to reaffirm what was commonly believed.

READERS

While the psalms often address God, they were originally written for and eventually compiled into our current Psalter for ancient Jewish people. Personal praises were intended as testimonies to be presented to a congregation (see, e.g., Ps. 22:22 and then vv. 23–31). Personal laments were probably private recordings of prayers and passions, much like a diary (see, e.g., Ps. 6). National poems or communal laments were professed publicly to God (see, e.g., Ps. 44). Although not written to us today, we are allowed to catch a glimpse into the private and public thoughts of ancient Hebrew poets/musicians as they tried to understand their sufferings, pleaded for forgiveness and salvation, and gave witness about their God, who acted when and as he saw fit yet could be trusted to answer prayer.

PLACE OF WRITING

Apart from some suggestions in the superscriptions, where a particular psalm was composed is unknown. Even if we knew relatively when and/or by whom a psalm was composed, we have no extant data that inform us about the location, other than the general understanding that these Hebrew poets were in Canaan/Israel in preexilic times, or outside (Assyria or Babylon) in exilic times, or outside or inside Judah/Judaea in postexilic times. Laments could have been composed in stages, especially since they sometimes include (seemingly) statements about experienced deliverance or mention the praise that would be offered for God's help. Whatever can be said specifically about location will be explained in the following commentary when pertinent to a particular psalm.

DATE OF WRITING

The OT Psalter or Book of Psalms, containing 150 individual psalms, cannot be dated with complete confidence or proof as to time of composition. Furthermore, the Psalter's arrangement was an editorial process that long postdates the original creation of each individual psalm. Naturally, this raises an issue of the Psalter's collection as to its divine inspiration (naturally, as all scholarship recognizes, chapters and verses and superscriptions were not part of the original texts).

Consequently, the dating of each individual psalm is based on the lives of the people associated with certain psalms by the superscriptions. Thus, the periods extend as much as eight to ten centuries from Moses (15th century B.C.) to Ezra (fifth century B.C.), depending on the school of OT chronology one follows. David certainly composed many if not all the psalms attributed to him, and all of these fall within his lifetime (early tenth century B.C.). The period most likely associated with each psalm will be explained as much as possible when each is discussed in the commentary.

Divine Inspiration, Providence, and Canon

The inspiration (divine source or substance) of the Psalms is typically tied to the nature of the autographs, which are not extant. Second Timothy 3:16 speaks of "[what is] written" ("Scripture"?) being fully "God breathed" or "inspired" ($\theta\epsilon\acute{o}\pi\nu\epsilon\upsilon\sigma\tau\sigma\varsigma$), which describes the text (as received at the time this verse was written) and not the author. This means that later, especially much later, editorial activity was not performed under divine inspiration, so there is nothing authoritative about the external order of the biblical books or the internal arrangement of chapters.

The superscriptions, however accurate in terms of faithfully maintaining a tradition, were the result of human invention and ingenuity. So, inspiration cannot be claimed for such editorial activities. Some may argue that editorial superscriptions fall under God's providence. But how far do we extend providence in relation to biblical developments following the authorial completion of other OT books (e.g., Ezra, Daniel, 2 Chronicles)? If God guided the Hebrew arrangement of the canon, how do we trump that with the Christian order? Unfortunately, the appeal to providence fails because it is too open-ended and undefined in application. In philosophical terms, if everything is subject to providence, nothing is subject to it.

OCCASION FOR WRITING

While some psalms describe the psalmist's situation, many do not, except in very general terms (e.g., "I am suffering and my enemies want my life" or "they are slandering me"). Thirteen of the psalms related to David provide background information. But only Psalm 30 has to do with a time of turmoil related to David's sins or his sense that his life was in danger or his throne threatened. Perhaps the editors felt it necessary for the reader to understand, especially in these instances, what events could explain David's emotions, accusations, and pleas. Often the reason for a psalm is not explicit, even with superscriptions, and commentaries abound with speculations.

Occasions for Psalms in the Superscriptions		
Psalm	NRSV	NETS
3	A Psalm of David, when he fled from his son Absalom.	A Psalm. Pertaining to Dauid. When he was running away from his son Abessalom.
7	A *Maskil* of David, which he sang to the Lord concerning Cush, a Benjaminite.	A Psalm pertaining to Dauid, which he sang to the Lord over the words of Chousi son of Iemeni.

Occasions for Psalms in the Superscriptions		
Psalm	**NRSV**	**NETS**
30	A Psalm. A Song at the dedication of the temple. Of David.	[29] A Psalm. Of an Ode of the dedication of the house. Pertaining to Dauid.
34	Of David, when he feigned madness before Abimelech, so that he drove him out, and he went away.	[33] Pertaining to Dauid. When he changed his face before Abimelech, and he let him go, and he went away.
51	To the leader. A Psalm of David, when the prophet Nathan came to him, after he had gone in to Bathsheba.	[50] When the prophet Nathan came to him, after he had gone into Bersabee.
52	To the leader. A *Maskil* of David, when Doeg the Edomite came to Saul and said to him, "David has come to the house of Ahimelech."	[51] When Doek the Idumean came and reported to Saoul and said to him, "Dauid came to the house of Abimelech."
54	To the leader: with stringed instruments. A *Maskil* of David, when the Ziphites went and told Saul, "David is in hiding among us."	[53] When the Ziphites came and told Saoul, "Look, is Dauid not hidden with us?"
56	To the leader: according to The Dove on Far-off Terebinths. Of David. A *Miktam*, when the Philistines seized him in Gath.	[55] Regarding completion. Over the people that are removed far away from their holy things. Pertaining to Dauid. For a stele inscription. When the allophyles seized him in Geth.
57	To the leader: Do Not Destroy. Of David. A *Miktam*, when he fled from Saul, in the cave.	[56] Regarding completion. Do Not Destroy. Pertaining to Dauid. For a stele inscription. As he was running away from before Saoul into the cave.
59	To the leader: Do Not Destroy. Of David. A *Miktam*, when Saul ordered his house to be watched in order to kill him.	[58] Regarding completion. Do Not Destroy. Pertaining to Dauid. For a stele inscription. When Saoul sent and watched his house to put him to death.
60	To the leader: according to the Lily of the Covenant. A *Miktam* of David; for instruction; when he struggled with Aram-naharaim and with Aram-zobah, and when Joab on his return killed twelve thousand Edomites in the Valley of Salt.	[59] When he set on fire Mesopotamia of Syria and Syria Soba, and Ioab returned and struck the Ravine of Salt, twelve thousand.
63	A Psalm of David, when he was in the Wilderness of Judah.	[62] A Psalm. Pertaining to Dauid. When he was in the wilderness of Judea.
142	A *Maskil* of David. When he was in the cave. A Prayer.	[141] Of understanding. Pertaining to Dauid. When he was in the cave. A Prayer.

HISTORICAL SETTING

Historically, the psalms parallel Ugaritic, Canaanite, and Egyptian poetry. Someone once said that only a Philistine could fail to love the psalms, but such poetry existed before the Hebrews made use of it. The pre-Israelite inhabitants and scribes of greater Canaan created poems about their gods, and the good and bad experiences of life, the style (but not theological substance) of which the Hebrews inherited. While worshipers in ancient Ugarit (centuries before the OT psalms) praised their chief deity (CTA 5 [67] I:1–3; cf. trans. H. L. Ginsberg; see Pritchard, 1969, 129–35; 138–42):

> Though Thou didst smite Lotan, the writing serpent /
> [Thou] didst destroy the crooked serpent //
> [Thou didst destroy] the ruler of seven heads

and (CTA 3 [regarding Anath] III:32–34),

> I muzzled Tunnanu . . .
> I crushed the writhing serpent // the ruling one of seven heads

The later Israelite author of Psalm 74:13–14 exalted Yahweh (by saying:

> It was You who shattered the sea with Your strength /
> Who smashed the heads of Tannin //
> It was You who crushed the heads of Leviathan

The OT and ANE Sea Monsters

The divided sea in Psalm 74 is not the separating of the Red Sea (actually the "reed sea" in Hebrew, in a region north of the Red Sea region). Other psalms also deal with God's battle against the "sea" (often symbolic of the Canaanite "Sea God"). In Canaanite mythology, the ancient West-Semitic word for "sea" was the same as the Hebrew םָי). The verb used for "split" in Psalm 74:13 could reference or contrast the Mesopotamian creation story (the Enuma Elish), wherein Marduk split the sea (personified as Tiamat, with consonants similar to the "deep," םֹוהְּת in Gen. 1:2). The "deep" is a typical synonym for the sea in the OT and Canaanite texts. In Psalm 93, the seas make thunderous noise, but Yahweh is mightier. In Psalm 74:13, God split "the sea" (םָי) and broke the "heads of monsters in the waters" (םִיָּמַה־לַﬠ םיִנִּנַת; cf. JPS). Was this a reference to the power of the sea literally or a stab at the Canaanite mythological creatures (Yamm and Tanin)? "Leviathan" (ןָתָיְוִל) was "Lotan" in the Canaanite literature (equivalent of ןתל). In Isaiah 27:1a, this creature is a "serpent" (שָחָנ; see Gen. 3:1), restated as the "monster/dragon of the sea" (םָּיַּב רֶשֲׁא ןיִּנַּתַה) in Isaiah 27:1b. A close connection existed between this coiling sea serpent and the twisting seven-headed serpent slain by "Baal" (לַﬠַּב). The Israelite God and an earlier Canaanite god are depicted as conquering a chaotic creature, but Yahweh (הָוהְי) is proclaimed to be the true divine Victor in the Bible (cf. the seven-headed dragon in Rev. 12, which opposes God but is vanquished).

The highly praised Canaanite god was Baal, which is evident in these following ancient Canaanite's words (CTA 2 IV [68]: 8–9):

> Now Your enemy, O Baal // Now Your enemy will You smite /
> Now will you cut off Your adversary,

The later Israelite author of Psalm 92:10 praises Yahweh.

> For behold, Your enemies, O Yahweh // For behold, Your enemies will perish /
> All lawbreakers will be dispersed.

While the Hebrew psalms are not slavish copies of Ugaritic and Canaanite poetry, they employed an established literary form and filled it with a new function, revealing Yahweh (not *Baal*) as the true God. Borrowed terminology was not the same as borrowed theology. New lessons were communicated in the established literary language of a culture in order to be understood. That the words and ways of OT psalms mirror Canaanite psalms in no way minimized the revelatory and remarkable and revolutionary message of the Israelite Psalter. But as poetic prayers and praises composed throughout ancient Israelite history, they inevitably bore the cultural characteristics (perceptions and practices) of those times, as the psalmists wrestle with and worship their God in the midst of progress, perplexities, and pain in relation to their mixed experiences in light of divine promises and punishment. It has been demonstrated that the Israelite and Canaanite traditions were not strongly linked, similarities mainly existing on the technical levels of linguistics and stylistics (Avishur, 1994, *in toto*).

Baal and the OT Psalms

In the ANE, among polytheists, the gods were often at war among themselves or with humans. In OT times, the Canaanite religion had developed to a stage where the older and traditional chief deity, El, had been ousted by Baal, a young upstart, with the help of other gods in a coup (such as Mot ["Death"] and Yamm ["Sea"] and the Sea Serpent, Lotan). This is why we read about Baal and not El in the OT. Thus, Baal, the storm god, usurped control of the Canaanite pantheon. The Ugaritic "Lotan" (= לותן) and the Hebrew "Leviathan" (לִוְיָתָן) are cognate in Semitic linguistics (i.e., note the same consonants, *L-T-N*; *t* and *th* are interchangeable and each language was written originally without vowels; the *v* in Hebrew can also be *o* at times). Baal means "Lord; master." The Hebrew words for "G/god" *are*: "El" (אֵל), "Eloah" (אֱלוֹהַ), and the plural "Elohim" (אֱלֹהִים). When used in the pagan pantheon, the latter term meant "gods." When used in connection with Yahweh (יְהוָה), the plural indicated "the greatest God." The Hebrew psalmists countered the Canaanite theologians by claiming Yahweh (יְהוָה) not "Baal" (בַּעַל) was the Creator, who

controlled creation—that the sea is just water, not a god, and only their God is truly Lord.

Canaanite Baal Figurine, Louvre

Some scholars find parallels with certain OT psalms among Mesopotamian mythology (religious texts like hymns and prayers). They argue that worship was a significant feature of OT religion (e.g., Kloos, 1986, *in toto*; see also Howard, 1999, 329–68). The OT's Royal Psalms (those that exalt Yahweh [הֹוְרִי] as king in the past, present, or future) were dubbed Enthronement Psalms by some earlier scholars (e.g., Gunkel 1998, *in toto*) because Mesopotamian kings were reaffirmed as king through a special celebration ritual or festival, so a similar ritual was assumed to have occurred in Israel in light of the context of these psalms. However, this remains speculation. Therefore, the classification Royal Psalms is preferred. More recently, attention has been paid to parallels in Ugaritic religious and poetic texts (Keel, 1978, 1997 *in toto*; for ANE prayer genres, see Longman, 2005, 41–62).

Ugaritic Language and Texts

The Ugaritic language is a Northwest Semitic Canaanite-type language, like Hebrew. Semitic languages are grouped according to similarities by regions and compass directions (North, South, East, West). Hebrew is both Semitic and Canaanite, included in the category of northwest Semitic. Ugaritic (deciphered from tablets found near Ugarit [Ras Shamra in modern Syria]) is also northwest Semitic. The Ugaritic language has been important for developing new linguistic theories about Hebrew lexicography and syntax as the Canaanite language closest to biblical (classical) Hebrew of which a large amount of texts are extant. Although Dahood produced a Hebrew grammar of the Psalter (with Tadeusz Penar) in light of Ugaritic

(Dahood 1970, 3:361–456), these are not identical languages. Still, Ugaritic word usage and grammatical features offer possible solutions for solving some remaining obscurities in Hebrew. Most significant have been the religious (mythological) texts, which contain terminology also used in the OT, especially the Psalms (e.g., Baal the storm god who rides a chariot across the sky, Lotan the sea monster or dragon, and El the ancient god whom Baal wants to dethrone, with the help of three other gods: Death, the Sea, and Lotan). The Canaanite words for these three are the same as the Hebrew words in the OT. The language used by Abraham in Canaan (ca. nineteenth century B.C.) would have been similar to Ugaritic but more similar to other contemporary Canaanite dialects.

Yet, Hebrew poetry was not limited to the Psalter. Biblical psalms span both OT and NT, from Moses and Miriam (Exod. 15; fifteenth century B.C.) to Mary's Magnificat in Luke 1:46–55 (ca. 6 B.C.), followed soon after by Zechariah's poetic prophecy (Luke 1:68–79). Hebrew poetry or possible remnants of complete psalms may be found from (Mosaic?) Genesis 1:2b to the apostle John (Rev. 20; first to second century A.D.). Thus, the psalms as a literary form or as psalmic poetic expressions are not confined to the book of Psalms but are located throughout Scripture.

Biblical Chronology of Various Psalms in Scripture			
Traditional Author	**Psalm/Poetic Verse Content**	**Location**	**ca. Period**
Moses	storm at Creation (parallelism)	Genesis 1:2b	15th cent. B.C.*
*Genesis 1 could rather have originated among postexilic Levites for a Sabbath lesson			
Moses/Miriam	Song (שִׁירָה) of the Sea (יָם)	Exodus 15	1446 B.C.
Moses	Psalm 90	OT Psalms	1420 B.C.
Deborah	Deborah's Song ((שִׁיר	Judges 5	1300 B.C.

Biblical Chronology of Various Psalms in Scripture			
Traditional Author	**Psalm/Poetic Verse Content**	**Location**	**ca. Period**
Hannah	Hannah's Prayer (פלל)	1 Samuel 2	1100 B.C.
David	73–76 psalms	OT Psalter	1000 B.C.
Solomon	Psalms 72 and 127	OT Psalter	900 B.C.
Jonah	Jonah's prayer (פלל)	Jonah 2	780 B.C.
Hezekiah	Psalms 120–134	OT Psalter	700 B.C.
Jeremiah	Psalm 137	OT Psalter	600 B.C.
Ezra	Psalm 119	OT Psalter	450 B.C.
Mary	Luke 1:46–55 (Magnificat)	NT Gospel	6 B.C.
Zechariah	Luke 1:68–79 (a poem)	NT Gospel	6 B.C.
Paul	Philippians 2 (poetry)	NT Epistle	A.D. 50
John	Revelation 20 (poetry)	NT Apocalypse	A.D. 90–110

David and Goliath by Caravaggio (ca. 1600)

Furthermore, there are other Jewish collections of psalms. The Syriac OT (Peshitta) includes Psalms 152–155. Another existing collection of eighteen psalms (in Greek or Syriac) is called The Psalms of Solomon. This indicates that our Jewish and Christian Psalter was created from a larger set of psalms. Among the Qumran Hebrew manuscripts (1QH) and the Septuagint, there is an additional psalm, Psalm 151. It is included in the Greek Orthodox biblical canon, but not in Catholic or Protestant Bibles. It is ostensibly by or about David. The author is described as Israel's king, anointed by Samuel, and the one who killed Goliath. Notable differences exist between the Hebrew and Greek versions (but this is also true of some MT psalms).

The Hebrew version appears as two separate texts. Tradition has rejected this psalm as belonging to the "inspired" canon, accepting it only as part of a secondary canon. Stylistically and substantively, pre- and post-biblical psalms are very similar to those in the traditional canon.

Psalm 151A [11Q5; 1QH] (Wise 1996, 572–73; Abegg 1999, 585–86)	Cf. Psalm 151 [NETS; cf. Rahlfs's Septuagint]
A hallelujah of David, Jesse's son. [1] I was the smallest of my brothers, the youngest of my father's sons. He made me shepherd of his flock, ruler over their young. [2] My hands made a flute, my fingers a lyre. Let me give glory to the Lord, I thought to myself. [3] The mountains cannot witness to God; the hills cannot proclaim him. But the trees have cherished my words, the flocks my deeds. [4] Who can proclaim, who can announce, who can declare the Lord's deeds? God has seen everything; God has heard everything; God has listened. [5] God sent his prophet to anoint me; Samuel to make me great. My brothers went out to meet him, handsome in form and appearance: [6] Their stature tall, their hair beautiful, but the Lord God did not choose them. [7] Instead, he sent and took me from following the flock. God anointed me with holy oil; God made me leader for his people, ruler over the children of his covenant.	[1] This Psalm is autographical. Regarding Dauid and outside the number. [Rahlfs adds: "When he fought Goliad in a single combat"] I was small among my brothers and the youngest in the house of my father; I would shepherd the sheep of my father. [2] My hands made an instrument; my fingers tuned a harp. [3] And who will report to my lord The Lord himself, it is he who listens. [4] It was he who sent his messenger and took me from the sheep of my father and anointed me with the oil of his anointing. [5] My brothers were handsome and tall, and the Lord did not take delight in them. [6] I went out to meet the allophyle, and he cursed me by his idols. [7] But I, having drawn the dagger from him, I beheaded him and removed reproach from Israel's sons.

In conclusion, the individual psalms in our current OT psalter were a unique means of understanding biblical revelation via poetic personal and public praise, prayers, protestations, and pleas for mercy and judgment. Yet, similar poems and poetry existed long before the Hebrews, but only the latter provided the proclamation that their God Yahweh (יְהוָה) was the only God and the only one worthy of worship. The OT Book of Psalms provided a selection of 150 poems and songs from Israel's history to a people for whom praise and prayer and public witness were invaluable, inescapable, and indispensable.

The Septuagint

The Septuagint (LXX) is a Greek translation of the OT that was made during the third and second centuries B.C. Two legends attend to the origin of the earliest Greek translation of the Hebrew OT. One reputed legend speaks of the Septuagint as a "perfect" version. This title (meaning "70") come from the story that seventy-two translators (six from each of the twelve Hebrew tribes) created a Greek version of the Torah. Another disputed story (based on the "Letter of Aristeas") holds that the chief priest in Jerusalem, Eleazar, sent these men to Alexandria at the request of Ptolemy II (285–246 B.C.; cf. Britannica 2017, n.p.). Regardless of whatever legend may be favored, the numbering of the psalms differs between the Masoretic Hebrew Text and the Septuagint Greek Text.

MT (Masoretic Hebrew Psalms) numbering	LXX (Greek) and Vulgate (Latin) numbering	English Bible numbering
1–8	1–8	1–8
9–10	9	9–10
11–113	10–112	11–113
114–115	113	114–115
116	114–115	116
117–146	116–145	117–146
147	146–147	147
148–150	148–150	148–150

GENRE IN THE PSALMS

Considering the genre of the Psalms involves both the Psalter's title as well as the types of individual psalms. First, the Hebrew title of the book of Psalms is "Praises" (תְּהִלִּים from הלל) but translated as "Sacred Songs" (ψαλμοί in the Septuagint [LXX]). This eventually led to the Latin *Psalmi* and the English "Psalms." The Hebrew title "Praises" (תְּהִלִּים) was added later when they were assembled as a collection. The Greek title "Sacred Songs" (ψαλμοί) referred to a song accompanied by stringed instruments. From the ancient Israelite viewpoint, these "psalms" were focused on praise. Later they became sacred songs or "hymns" to modern worshipers. C. S. Lewis (1967, 2) called them "poems to be sung." Consequently, sacred musical poetry reflected the form of the psalms, but their function was worship or praise. Ironically, the word "praise" is used in the Psalter only once as a descriptive term (in the editorial superscription to Psalm 145 [תְּהִלָּה לְדָוִד; "praise for David"]). The word for "prayer" (תְּפִלָּה), on the other hand, was used five times in the superscriptions (Pss. 17, 86, 90, 102, 142). Psalms 17, 86, and 142 were related to David in the superscriptions, while Psalm 90 was associated with Moses and Psalm 102 with "an afflicted man." So, those who received the Hebrew psalm collections had different ideas about their purpose. This was because the various psalms had various purposes when initially written. Over time the OT Psalter, therefore, was used for worship, prayer, and musical praise. It was not just a prayer, praise, or hymn book. Nor was it an ancient Hebrew hymn book. It did, however, become a Christian hymn book. Each psalm originated in one of a number of different settings and for one of several different reasons.

Psalms with Superscription Categories	
Category	**Psalms**
Prayer (תְּפִלָּה)	17, 86, 90, 102, 142
Love/Wedding Song (שִׁיר יְדִידֹת)	45
Sabbath Day Song (שִׁיר לְיוֹם הַשַּׁבָּת)	92
Psalm for testimony (לְתוֹדָה מִזְמוֹר)	100
With stringed instruments (בִּנְגִינוֹת)	4, 6, 54, 55, 61, 67, 76
With wind instruments or "flutes" (אֶל־הַנְּחִילוֹת)	5

Second, the numerous psalms of the Psalter differ in form and are often grouped into types of psalms. Unfortunately, scholarship has not reached consensus on the various number and nature of these types. The word "form" (*Gattung* or *Gattungen* plural) has to do with types of psalms. These "types" are usually a matter of themes. So, when you scan commentaries you find anywhere from three to seven types named. Some cite three major themes: hymn, lament, and thanksgiving. Others cite five: praise, lament, thanksgiving, wisdom, and royal. Still others cite seven types: thanks (or praise), lament, enthronement, royal, wisdom, imprecatory, and pilgrim.[1] Each of these groups contains a number of subgroups; for example, psalms of praise or lament may be presented as individual or community worship or prayer/petition. Laments usually make selective and creative use of five to six structural elements.

Moses with the Ten Commandments
by Rembrandt (ca. 1659)

---

1   According to the *Jerusalemer Bibel-Lexikon*, there are four main categories of psalms, which are hymns or praise psalms, psalms of lamentation, psalms which express trust in God, and teaching psalms (Hennig 1990, *in toto*, n.p.).

BOOK[2]	PSALM	TYPE	FEATURE	ASSOCIATIONS
THE 150 PSALMS IN ORDER AND BY GENRE				
		INTRODUCTION TO THE OT PSALTER		
I	1	Wisdom	revelatory (God's Word); creation	Anonymous
I	2	Royal National Praise	anointed king as God's son; creation	Anonymous
		INTRODUCTORY SECTION OF THE PSALTER		
I	3	Personal Lament	many enemies; creation	Davidic
I	4	Personal Lament	creation; "my prayer" (תְּפִלָּתִי), v. 1	Davidic
I	5	Personal Lament	imprecation; creation; "I will pray" (אֶתְפַּלָּל), v. 3	Davidic
I	6	Penitential Lament	creation; "my prayer" (תְּפִלָּתִי), v. 9; with protest	Davidic
I	7	Personal Lament	imprecation	Davidic
I	8	Praise Hymn	creation; cf. Gen. 1–2	Davidic
I	9a	Praise Hymn		Davidic
I	9b	Personal Lament	9–10 = 9 in the LXX	Davidic
		THE MAIN BODY OF THE OT PSALTER		
I	10	Personal Lament	acrostic	Anonymous
I	11	Personal Lament		Davidic
I	12	Personal Lament	perhaps communal lament; imprecation	Davidic
I	13	Personal Lament		Davidic
I	14=53	Personal Lament		Davidic
I	15	Wisdom	revelatory (God's Word)	Davidic
I	16	Personal Lament		Davidic
I	17	Personal Lament	a prayer (תְּפִלָּה), v. 0	Davidic
I	18	Personal Praise	cf. Rev. 1	Davidic
I	19	Wisdom	revelatory (God's Word); creation	Davidic
I	20	Royal Praise	prayer style	Davidic
I	21	Royal Praise	prayer style	Davidic
I	22a	Personal Lament		Davidic

---

2   For a summary for each major book of the Psalter see H. W. Bateman IV and D. B. Sandy, eds., *Interpreting the Psalms for Teaching and Preaching* (St. Louis: Chalice, 2010), 46, 75, 97, 119, 149.

		THE 150 PSALMS IN ORDER AND BY GENRE		
BOOK[2]	PSALM	TYPE	FEATURE	ASSOCIATIONS
I	22b	Personal Praise		Davidic
I	23	Personal Praise	confession of trust	Davidic
I	24	Ascent Song	cf. Pss. 120–134	Davidic
I	25	Personal Lament		Davidic
I	26	Personal Lament	with protest	Davidic
I	27	Personal Lament	with protest	Davidic
I	28	Personal Lament		Davidic
I	29	Royal Praise		Davidic
I	30	Personal Praise		Davidic
I	31	Personal Praise	with penance	Davidic
I	32	Personal Praise	"let him pray" (יִתְפַּלֵּל), v. 6; with penance	Davidic
I	33	Praise Hymn	descriptive praise	Davidic
I	34	Personal Praise		Davidic
I	35	Personal Lament	"my prayer" (תְפִלָּתִי), v. 13	Davidic
I	36	Personal Praise		Davidic
I	37	Wisdom	revelatory (God's Word); acrostic with penance	Davidic
I	38	Penitential Lament		Davidic
I	39	Personal Lament	"my prayer" (תְפִלָּתִי), v. 12	Davidic
I	40a	Personal Praise	confession of trust	Davidic
I	40b	Personal Lament		Davidic
I	41	Personal Lament		Davidic
II	42	Personal Lament	"a prayer" (תְפִלָּה), v. 9	A son of Korah
II	43	Personal Lament	= 42b?	Anonymous
II	44a	Personal Praise		A son of Korah
II	44b	Personal Lament		A son of Korah
II	45	Royal Praise		A son of Korah
II	46	Personal Praise	confession of trust	A son of Korah
II	47	Royal Praise		A son of Korah
II	48	Royal Praise		A son of Korah
II	49	Wisdom	righteousness (God's way)	A son of Korah
II	50	National Praise	descriptive; with penance	Asaph

		THE 150 PSALMS IN ORDER AND BY GENRE		
BOOK[2]	**PSALM**	**TYPE**	**FEATURE**	**ASSOCIATIONS**
II	51	Penitential Lament		Davidic
II	52	Personal Lament	confession and imprecation	Davidic
II	53=14	Personal Lament		Davidic
II	54	Personal Lament	"my prayer" (תְּפִלָּתִי), v. 2	Davidic
II	55	Personal Lament	"my prayer" (תְּפִלָּתִי), v. 1	Davidic
II	56	Personal Lament		Davidic
II	57	Personal Lament		Davidic
II	58	National Lament		Davidic
II	59	Personal Lament	imprecation and protestation	Davidic
II	60	National Lament		Davidic
II	61	Personal Lament	"my prayer" (תְּפִלָּתִי), v. 1	Davidic
II	62	Personal Praise	confession of trust	Davidic
II	63	Personal Lament		Davidic
II	64	Personal Lament		Davidic
II	65	Personal Praise	confession of trust; "a prayer" (תְּפִלָּה), v. 2	Davidic
II	66	National Praise	declarative; royal ("bow to you" יִשְׁתַּחֲווּ לָךְ), v. 4 a prayer (תְּפִלָּה), v. 19 and "my prayer" (תְּפִלָּתִי), v. 20	Anonymous
II	67	National Praise	descriptive; communal prayer	Anonymous
II	68	Personal Praise	imprecation; "cloud rider" (לָרֹכֵב בָּעֲרָבוֹת), v. 4	Davidic
II	69	Personal Lament	"prayer" (תְּפִלָּה), v. 13; zeal for God's house	Davidic
II	70	Personal Lament	imprecation	Davidic
II	71a	Personal Lament		Anonymous
II	71b	Personal Praise		Anonymous
II	72	Royal Praise	"may he pray" (וְיִתְפַּלֵּל), v. 15; but see editorial note about this psalm	Solomon

THE 150 PSALMS IN ORDER AND BY GENRE

BOOK[2]	PSALM	TYPE	FEATURE	ASSOCIATIONS
Editorial note: Psalm 72:20, "the prayers" (תְּפִלּוֹת) of David are ended"; but what about Psalms 86, 109, 141, and 143? They must have not yet been composed or added to the canonical psalter when Psalm 72:20 was added to Psalm 72. N.b.: Before Psalm 72:20, Psalms 4, 6, 17, 35, 39, 54, 55, 61, 65, and 69 are Davidic per the superscriptions but are "prayers" (תְּפִלּוֹת) per the psalm per se (in addition to or apart from the superscription). After Psalm 72:20, Psalms 86, 109, 141, and 143 are Davidic per the superscriptions but are each a "prayer" (תְּפִלָּה) according to the psalm per se (in addition to or apart from the superscription). Psalm 142 is a Davidic prayer only per the superscription. "Pray" (פלל) is found only in Psalms 5, 32, 72, and 106 (never in the superscriptions). Only in Psalm 5 is it used to characterize that current psalm or prayer. But note that only the two before Psalm 72 (Pss. 5 and 32) are Davidic per the superscriptions.				
III	73	Personal Praise	confession of trust	Asaph
III	74	National Lament		Asaph
III	75	National Praise	descriptive	Asaph
III	76	National Praise	descriptive	Asaph
III	77a	Personal Lament		Asaph
III	77b	Personal Praise		Asaph
III	78	Wisdom	righteousness (God's way)	Asaph
III	79	National Lament		Asaph
III	80	National Lament	God against their "prayers" (תְּפִלּוֹת), v. 4	Asaph
III	81	National Praise	declarative	Asaph
III	82	Personal Lament		Asaph
III	83	Personal Lament		Asaph
III	84	Personal Lament	"my prayer" (תְּפִלָּתִי), v. 8	A son of Korah
III	85	National Lament		A son of Korah
III	86	Personal Lament	"a prayer" (תְּפִלָּה), v. 0	Davidic
III	87	National Praise	descriptive song of Zion	A son of Korah
III	88	Personal Lament	"my prayer" (תְּפִלָּתִי), v. 2	A son of Korah
III	89	Royal Praise	human king; with lament section	A son of Korah
IV	90	National Lament	*"prayer" (תְּפִלָּה), v. 0	Moses
IV	91	Wisdom	revelation (God's Word); chiasm	Anonymous
IV	92	Personal Praise	descriptive; song for the Sabbath	Anonymous
IV	93	Royal Praise	enthronement	Anonymous
IV	94	National Lament	confession and imprecation	Anonymous

BOOK[2]	PSALM	TYPE	FEATURE	ASSOCIATIONS
		THE 150 PSALMS IN ORDER AND BY GENRE		
IV	95	Royal Praise	theocratic; heavenly king	Anonymous
IV	96	Royal Praise	theocratic and enthronement; heavenly king	Anonymous
IV	97	Royal Praise		Anonymous
IV	98	Royal Praise		Anonymous
IV	99	Royal Praise		Anonymous
IV	100	National Praise	confession of trust	Anonymous
IV	101	Royal Praise	human king; with penance	Davidic
IV	102	Penitential Lament	"my prayer" (תְּפִלָּתִי), v. 1 cf. v. 0	An afflicted man
IV	103	Personal Praise	descriptive	Davidic
IV	104	Personal Praise	descriptive; creational	Anonymous
IV	105	National Praise	descriptive	Anonymous
IV	106	National Praise	descriptive; "their cry" (רִנָּתָם), v. 44; "he intervened" (וַיְפַלֵּל), v. 30	Anonymous
V	107	National Praise	descriptive	Anonymous
V	108a	Personal Lament	= Psalm 57:7–11	Davidic
V	108b	National Lament	= Psalm 60:5–12	
V	109	Personal Lament	I am [a man of] "prayer" (תְּפִלָּה), v. 4	Davidic
V	110	Royal Praise	human king	Davidic
V	111	Wisdom	revelatory (God's Word); acrostic	Anonymous
V	112	Wisdom	revelatory (God's Word)	Anonymous
V	113	National Praise	descriptive; "praise!" (הַלְלוּ, 113:1; 115:18)	Anonymous
V	114	Personal Praise		Anonymous
V	115	National Praise		Anonymous
V	116	Personal Lament	"praise Yah!" (הַלְלוּ־יָהּ), v. 19	Anonymous
V	117	National Praise	descriptive; "praise Yah!" (הַלְלוּ־יָהּ), v. 1	Anonymous
V	118	National Praise	descriptive; "testify about Yahweh" (הוֹדוּ לַיהוָה), v. 1	Anonymous
V	119	Wisdom	revelatory (God's Word); "I praise you" (הַלַּלְתִּיךָ), v, 175; cf. v. 7; acrostic; longest psalm	Anonymous

BOOK[2]	PSALM	TYPE	FEATURE	ASSOCIATIONS
		THE 150 PSALMS IN ORDER AND BY GENRE		
V	120–134		SONGS OF ASCENT	
V	120	Personal Lament		Anonymous
V	121	Personal Praise	descriptive	Anonymous
V	122	Personal Praise	descriptive; cf. Psalm 24	Davidic
V	123	National Lament		Anonymous
V	124	National Praise	declarative; cf. Psalm 24	Davidic
V	125	National Praise	descriptive	Anonymous
V	126	National Praise	descriptive	Anonymous
V	127	Wisdom	righteousness (God's way)	Solomon
V	128	Wisdom	righteousness (God's way)	Anonymous
V	129	National Lament	with penance	Anonymous
V	130	Penitential Lament		Anonymous
V	131	Personal Praise	confession of trust; cf. Psalm 24	Davidic
V	132	National Praise	descriptive	Anonymous
V	133	Wisdom	righteousness (God's way)	Davidic
V	134	National Praise	descriptive	Anonymous
V	135	National Praise	declarative; "praise Yah!" (הַלְלוּ־יָהּ), v. 1	Anonymous
V	136	National Praise	confession; the Great Hallel; "testify about the Lord of all lords" (הוֹדוּ לַאֲדֹנֵי הָאֲדֹנִים), v. 1	Anonymous
V	137	Penitential Lament	imprecatory	Anonymous
V	138	Personal Praise	descriptive	Davidic
V	139a	Personal Praise	confession of trust	Davidic
V	139b	Personal Lament	with an imprecation	Davidic

THE 150 PSALMS IN ORDER AND BY GENRE				
BOOK[2]	PSALM	TYPE	FEATURE	ASSOCIATIONS
THE CONCLUDING SECTION OF THE MAIN BODY OF PSALMS				
V	140	Personal Lament	with an imprecation	Davidic
V	141	Personal Lament	"my prayer" (תְּפִלָּתִי), v. 5	
V	142	Penitential Lament	*"a prayer" (תְּפִלָּה), v. 0; *with protestation of innocence*	
V	143	Penitential Lament	"my prayer" (תְּפִלָּתִי), v. 1, *with penance*	
V	144a	Personal Lament		
V	144b	Personal Praise	theocratic; human king	
V	145	National Royal Praise	heavenly king; with wisdom feature; Final Hallel; in v. 1 "I will praise your name forever . . . as praiseworthy" (וַאֲהַלְלָה שִׁמְךָ לְעוֹלָם. . . וּמְהֻלָּל)	
THE CONCLUSION TO THE OT PSALTER: Final Hallel concluded				
V	146	National [Royal] Praise	with a wisdom feature	Anonymous
V	147			Anonymous
V	148		with a theocratic allusion	Anonymous
V	149		royal; heavenly king; imprecatory feature	Anonymous
V	150		with possible didactic feature	Anonymous

* = only in the superscription, which is v. 0 (all verse numbers are for the English translation).

Unfortunately, some of the psalms in the OT psalter have a mixed character; that is, they now (after editing or redactions) exist as single psalms that originally were two. These are Psalms 9, 19, 22, 40, 44, 57, 66, 71, 77, and 89, at least. In what follows, these will be examined not only under the category or genre of their first component, but also will be mentioned again under the second format (e.g., Psalm 22 begins with a lament and ends with a praise hymn, so it is fully explained not only as a lament psalm in the commentary volume on Lament Psalms, but also is included in passing in the commentary volume on Praise Psalms).

Unlike other commentaries on the Psalms that evaluate individual psalms in their numerical order (e.g., Ross, 2011, *in toto*), the Kerux commentary evaluates the various psalms not in numerical order but according to themes as follows:

Volume 1: Wisdom Psalms
Volume 2: Lament Psalms
Volume 3: Praise Psalms

Wisdom Psalms

Wisdom Psalms (vol. 1) divide into wisdom about God's Ways (Righteousness) or God's Word (Revelation/Revelatory). The former acknowledges the benefit of godly advice for a prosperous or blessed life. The latter focus on God's will through trustworthy principles and righteous/just rules, via creation and commands (Pss. 1, 19, 119). These psalms are more properly called Torah ("Law") or Didactic Psalms. In these, God's gracious guidance is honored. All the psalms, of course, fall under the rubric of divine revelation in Scripture.

As for the wisdom theme, those who follow a righteous rather than wicked lifestyle will avoid for the most part those bad choices that lead to ruin, and therefore will typically have a better life (more successful in all ways, although not necessarily more wealthy) than those who do what is criminal or risky in spiritual or physical ways). Such psalms contain a wisdom motif, in that OT Wisdom (Proverbs, e.g.) has to do with trustworthy principles upon which a long and enjoyable life may be built. Of course, there can be exceptions, but these "prove the rule." These are truths based on and tested by experience, not absolute pronouncements as the Ten Commandments. That a dishonest person sometimes prospers does not change the fact that most of the time "crime does not pay." Wise people will order their lives around godly teachings because they offer the best opportunity for a fulfilling and prolonged life, not because they guarantee old age and riches. This is the nature of wisdom wherever it is found in the OT. This relativity is what makes Job and Ecclesiastes wrestle with the reality that the righteous can suffer and the wicked prosper. They lived in a world that wished for a black-and-white formula that would explain life simply: failure proves God's disappointment and punishment, and success proves his approval and blessing. Yet OT wisdom taught that suffering was not proof of unrighteousness, but wickedness would tend to produce a life of despair and difficulty more often than not.

It is fitting that the first psalm of the canonical Psalter is such a Wisdom song, followed by a Royal Praise Psalm extolling Yahweh as the king who rebukes and ruins all persistent rebels. Yet, God provides refuge for those who submit to the laws of his kingdom and king. Psalms 1–2 offer praise for righteous rules given by a righteous ruler (cf. Taylor, 2010, 47–62). Word or Revelatory Psalms uphold the credible character of God's revealed directives, by which, it is implied, wise people will conduct their lives.

Lament Psalms

Lament Psalms (vol. 2) are psalms described as either lamentations proper, imprecatory psalms, or penitential laments. These are psalms in which the poet cries out to God in the midst of trouble, seeking rescue from some ailment or assailant, sometimes seeking forgiveness and punishment for his enemies. They can be individual or communal. Structurally they revolve around three pronouns: I/me, you (God), and they/them. The psalmist's problem often involved all three, but one tends to be the main emphasis of a given psalm. The main idea was that I am hurting, you are not helping, and, therefore, the enemy or situation is about to gain victory and cause my defeat or death, unless you, God, act quickly. This logically led to how the psalmist presented his petition to God: heal or help me, pay attention to me and stop being otherwise preoccupied, and put an end to my agony or antagonists. These laments usually began with a short but strong appeal to God by his covenant name, Yahweh (יְהוָה). Along the way the pleas, problems, and petitions were enhanced often but not always by one or more of the following elements, and not always in the same order. The psalmist sometimes tried to convince God through some argumentation that helping or rescuing him is also to God's benefit. This is called a justification for divine intervention or a motivation clause. Having sometimes used strong language accusing God of not caring, the psalmist might add what is called a confession of trust. He wants to assure God that although he *feels* like God is distant and disinterested and that the end is near, he still really does trust in God and anticipates his help. Finally, sometimes attached to the petition or prayer section is an imprecation or a curse (like casting a spell) on the psalmist's enemies. Since he believed his enemy was also God's enemy, he was emboldened to ask God to destroy them.

Praise Psalms

Praise Psalms (vol. 3) may be divided into hymns of praise or public acknowledgement that describe God or declare that he has answered the psalmist's prayer. These may be personal/individual or national/institutional. To praise God was to honor him verbally and publicly for who he was or what he had done. However, there is no consensus on how to label each psalm precisely. For example, a theme like "creation" is not considered a genre but a theological feature contained in various types of psalms. Sometimes called "creation psalms," the following are considered under various headings like praise, lament, or enthronement: 1–6, 8, 19, 104. Some psalms resist being placed in one category because they are actually combinations of two types (e.g., a lament and a praise psalm like Psalm 22). So, the number and nature of the praise types is debated. Some approaches seem to overly reduce the types, while others manage to overly divide them, into major camps. Regardless, following current and historically persistent themes, the praise psalms of the OT will be examined in this commentary according to the following

King David Playing the Harp
by Gerard van Honthorst (ca. 1622)

categories and characterizations: Personal Hymns (descriptive or declarative and confessions of trust), National Hymns (descriptive or declarative, confessions, and pilgrim songs), Royal Psalms (enthronement and theocratic), and the groups of "Hallel" (הַלֵּל) Psalms (Egyptian, Great, and Final).

Many approaches focus on the requirement for praise and the reasons for praise. But other types of adoration are recognized due to certain thematic characteristics. These may be treated as subcategories of Lament or Praise in broad terms. For instance, a Royal Psalm can be viewed as praise of Yahweh (יְהוָה) as King. A Confession of Trust (such as Psalm 23) is also an acknowledgement of "Yahweh's" faithfulness. In fact, confessions of trust are also a feature of many laments. The Hallel Psalms as well as those exalting divine revelation (e.g., Ps. 119), so-called Torah or

Didactic Psalms, can be considered versions of praise. Praise and lament are actually linked, like two sides of a coin, in that praise often or mostly results from divine rescue from a perilous circumstance. When the psalmist says "Praise Yahweh" (יְהוָה)!," it is not a response to good fortune per se, but a summons for God's people to enter into a time of public and vocal and musical recognition of God's good and gracious attributes and actions. OT praise is never theoretical or in spite of failure, but always in response to help or healing, or for continued blessing or God's goodness. Praise is witness and testimony about God. This was only done once there was a victory to announce. Failure was a reason for prayer, success a reason for a poetic testimony.

PSALTER COLLECTION

On the one hand, historically and editorially the OT Psalter has been divided into five "books" based on a closing benediction or doxology. A Jewish tradition claims that the fivefold division was based on the Five Books of Moses (the Torah, or Pentateuch).[3]

Book 1 (Psalms 1–41)	Genesis
Book 2 (Psalms 42–72)	Exodus
Book 3 (Psalms 73–89)	Leviticus
Book 4 (Psalms 90–106)	Numbers
Book 5 (Psalms 107–150)	Deuteronomy

It is obvious that the current arrangement is not based on authorship or chronology (if we go along with the superscriptions). Many believe the Psalter was organized in its current form, more or less, around the time of Ezra. Among the manuscripts discovered in the Dead Sea caves, the earliest extant Psalms scroll dates to the first century A.D. and gives evidence of the five-book division. Each of the five divisions ends with a doxology or hymn

of praise (Pss. 41:13; 72:19; 89:52; 106:48; 145:21), each hymn ending with a statement of praise and often with a concluding remark like "Amen." However, Aquinas rejected this grouping into five books, mentioning in his "Commentary on the Psalms" that others see the Psalms grouped into perfect thirds:

> The third distinction is that the Psalms are distinguished into three groups of fifty: and this distinction takes in the threefold state of the faithful people: namely the state of penitence; and to this the first fifty are ordered, which conclude in "Have mercy on me, O God," which is the Psalm of penitence. The second concerns justice, and this consists in judgement, and concludes in Psalm 100, "Mercy, and justice." The third concludes the praise of eternal glory, and so it ends with "Let every spirit praise the Lord." (Aquinas 2012, n.p.)

On the other hand, some psalms are collected around a central figure (perhaps the author, or the person or persons in some way intrinsically related to their setting or purpose). Seventy-three of the psalms in the OT book by that name are associated with David (Pss. 3–9, 11–41, 51–65, 68–70, 86, 101, 103, 108–110, 122, 124, 131, 133, 138–145). This is a thematic not chronological arrangement, and it was another editorial development, not an undertaking done under inspiration, as was the writing of the original texts (the so-called autographs, which have been lost to history), yet what we have was copied and cared for with integrity. We do not know why or how the Psalms arrived at their current arrangement, but these editors had a purpose. The NT connected David with two others (Psalm 2 in Acts 4:25, and Psalm 95 in Hebrews 4:7). By contrast, the Septuagint associated David with more of the 150 psalms in the OT Psalter than

---

3   For a summary for each major book of the Psalter see H. W. Bateman IV and D. B. Sandy, eds., *Interpreting the Psalms for Teaching and Preaching* (St. Louis: Chalice, 2010), 46, 75, 97, 119, 149.

does the Hebrew Bible (Sheehan, 2013, *in toto*). While a translation and not authoritative as with other editorial changes, the Septuagint demands our attention as a sincere effort at making the Hebrew Scripture accessible and discernible. Twelve psalms are associated with Asaph (Pss. 50, 73–83), eleven to Korah's descendants (Pss. 42, 44–49, 84–85, 87–88), and fifteen are grouped as Songs of Ascent (temple pilgrimage; Pss. 120–134 in the MT [= Pss. 119–133 in the Greek LXX and Latin Vulgate]; also called Gradual, Degrees, Steps, or Pilgrim Songs).

THE PSALTER'S STRUCTURE

The order or structure of the 150 psalms of the OT canonical Psalter at first glance may seem to be random; but numerous attempts have been made to demonstrate that often certain psalms precede or follow others on purpose or contain intentional internal structures. There is a logic to the order at times, if not usually. The beginning and ending poems of the book of Psalms (1–2 and 145–150) also seem to be placed intentionally as a kind of introduction and conclusion. Clearly some similar types of psalms are grouped together by design, for example those connected to Korah by the superscriptions (44–49). But Psalm 42 also is assigned to Korah, while Psalm 43 is anonymous. Why this order? Was Psalm 43 originally part of Psalm 42? Did Psalm 43 at one time have a superscription mentioning Korah, which was lost in transmission? Otherwise why insert a non-Korah psalm between two related to Korah? Korah comes back with Psalms 84, 85, and 87 (with a Davidic psalm also interspersed curiously).

The Psalms about or by Korah's sons per superscriptions in the Hebrew and Greek OT							
Psalm	Directions	Wisdom מַשְׂכִּיל	Tune named	Psalm מִזְמוֹר	Song שִׁיר	Instrument named	Extra information
Book II							
42 MT **41 LXX**[4]	To the leader	מַשְׂכִּיל					
	Regarding completion	Regarding understanding					
44 MT **43 LXX**	To the leader	מַשְׂכִּיל					
	Regarding completion	Regarding understanding		A psalm			
45 MT **44 LXX**	To the leader	מַשְׂכִּיל	According to lilies				A love song
	Regarding completion	Regarding understanding			An ode		Over the beloved & over those that will be changed

---

4   The translations used are from NETS for the LXX, Greek and NRSV for MT, Hebrew.

The Psalms about or by Korah's sons per superscriptions in the Hebrew and Greek OT							
Psalm	Directions	Wisdom מַשְׂכִּל	Tune named	Psalm מִזְמוֹר	Song שִׁיר	Instrument named	Extra information
46 MT **45 LXX**	To the leader		"According to 'maidens' [?]" (עַל־עֲלָמוֹת)		A song		
	Regarding completion		Things Hidden	A psalm			
47 MT **46 LXX**	To the leader			A psalm			
	Regarding completion			A psalm			
48 MT **47 LXX**				A psalm	A song		
				A psalm	An ode		Pertaining to the second day of the week
49 MT **48 LXX**	To the leader			A psalm			
	Regarding completion			A psalm			
Book III							
84 MT **83 LXX**	To the leader			A psalm		"according to 'the [instrument of] Gath' [?]" עַל־הַגִּתִּית	
	Regarding completion			A psalm			Over wine vats
85 MT **84 LXX**	To the leader			A psalm			
	Regarding completion			A psalm			

The Psalms about or by Korah's sons per superscriptions in the Hebrew and Greek OT							
Psalm	Directions	Wisdom מַשְׂכִּל	Tune named	Psalm מִזְמוֹר	Song שִׁיר	Instrument named	Extra information
87 MT [LXX]				A psalm	A song		
--------------	----------	------------	---------	-------	-----------	----------------	
88 MT 87 LXX	To the leader	מַשְׂכִּל of Heman the Ezrahite	"According to" עַל־מָחֲלַת לְעַנּוֹת "	A psalm	A song		
	Regarding completion	Regarding understanding	"Over μαελεθ [?] in order that he be answered"	A psalm	An ode		Pertaining to Haiman the Israelite

Similarly, Davidic psalms (per superscriptions) are arranged together as Psalms 3–9, 11–41, 51–65, 68–70, 108–110, and 138–145. Asaph is mentioned in the headings to Psalms 73–83. Psalm 24 stands alone as a Song of Ascent between Davidic praise/confession (Ps. 23) and lament (Ps. 25); then the remaining ascent or pilgrim songs appear as Psalms 120–134. A series of Royal Psalms describes Psalms 95–99, but then other similar psalms (per genre or subtheme) are found as Psalms 2, 18, 20–21, 29, 45, 47–48, 72, 89, 93, 101, 110, 145, 148–149. Is there a method to this madness? Certainly, along the editorial road, leading to the final form of the book of Psalms, collections were made, but to what purpose other than a shared feature? The final form, however, failed to gather all similar psalms together, yet this also could have a purpose and not just reflect oversight. We have to keep in mind the arrangement of the various psalms into five books over time. If a later book accepted a psalm that matched (thematically) a former collection of psalms in the previous book, the editors apparently could or would not add it to the former book. This may explain the isolated ones, at least in some cases.

Consequently, the Psalter as we know it today begins with first a Wisdom and then a Royal psalm.[5] Psalm 3 is a Lament that heads a grouping of five lamentations (Pss. 3–7). To many it seems fitting that the Book of Psalms would be initiated with psalms recognizing their didactic and theocratic potential. A creation element in each is also highlighted by some commentators. Both psalms are anonymous and neither has a superscription in the Hebrew or Greek versions. As Westermann (1981, in toto) noted, the bulk of the OT Psalter is about praise or lament. The introductory nature of Psalms 1–2 is then suggested in that Psalm 3 begins a lament section, which continues until Psalm 14 (with praise interspersed

---

5   J. G. Taylor, "Psalms 1 and 2: A Gateway into the Psalter and Messianic Images of Restoration for David's Dynasty." In *Interpreting the Psalms for Teaching & Preaching*, ed. by H. W. Bateman IV and D. B. Sandy (Grand Rapids: Chalice Press, 2010), 47–63.

by Psalms 8–9; although technically, Psalm 9 mixes first a praise and then a lament portion). This main body of the Psalter (beginning with Psalm 3) could be explained as beginning with lament because (as Westermann explained) lament must precede praise in the Hebrew way of thinking in the psalms. Praise naturally follows being rescued from a lamentable or painful circumstance. An extended praise section first comes with Psalms 65–68 as Book II (Pss. 42–72) comes to a close. Book I (Pss. 1–41) ends with four Lament psalms (Pss. 38–41, although Psalm 40 is a mixture of praise followed by lament). Book II alternates Praise and Lament with nineteen Laments of thirty-four total psalms, having eleven laments in a row (Pss. 51–61) and four praises (Pss. 65–68). Book III also alternates Praise and Lament throughout, with Psalm 89 mixing a Royal and Lament part. Book IV begins with Lament (Pss. 90, 94, 102; with didactic and theocratic psalms interspersed) and ends with Praise (Pss. 103–106).

CRITICAL STUDIES OF THE PSALTER

In the past, the academic study of the OT Psalter was pioneered by a number of German scholars. Much of their work had to do with imagined oral or written sources or reconstructing the social-religious occasion in which many psalms were created and for what liturgical purposes. This was done apart from the superscriptions, which were considered unreliable. Often this research was highly speculative. One area that was less speculative is the examination of a psalm's form or genre (*Gattung* or *Gattungen* [pl.] in German). Following especially H. Gunkel's investigations, exegetically useful schools of analysis have since then focused on structural features of the OT psalms that enable the student to classify each psalm as fitting into one of several formal categories or genres. The concern has always been with reconstructing how the ancient biblical psalmists communicated their poetry and how their ancient audience received

it in terms of its literary nature, structural components, and lexical or thematic features shared by the poems of a certain type. This is relatively objective (compared to other and more subjective studies searching for literary sources [Documentary Hypothesis] or a *Sitz im Leben* [life setting]), because it is based on lexical and grammatical aspects of the text per se.

Gunkel's idea was that genre identification must "flow from the character of the material itself" (Gunkel 1998, 7). Our problem is that while the psalms were created from real life (the Romantic approach), we do not know a lot specifically about the actual circumstances (the Rationalistic approach). Herder's call to imagine the psalmists' world without imposing categories on them was absorbed by Gunkel and aided his search for the "original" historical *Sitz*, that for Gunkel included the sociological, cultural, and religious realities of the OT context (Gignilliat, 2012, 94), as best could be reconstructed. He arrived at four types of psalms: hymns, laments (corporate and individual), and individual thanksgiving (Gunkel 1998, 19; this last type being what this commentary will reclassify as praise or testimony). His moods for the psalmists were enthusiasm, adoration, reverence, praise, and exaltation (Gunkel, 1998, 47). His Psalms Introduction (Einleitung, 1933), not completed before he died, was finished and published by Begrich (Westermann, 1981, 16).

Another well-known Psalms scholar is Claus Westermann. He was drawn to the Psalms and their subject matter during his theological studies. Taking a stand with the Confessing Church against the Nazi-approved German Church during World War 2, he was a rare scholar who sought to serve the churches and not just other academics with his research. Some experiences during his five years as a soldier influenced his theology. In a Russian prison camp, he said he learned the difference between praise and lament and between praise and how we think about prayer. His experiences helped him identify with the psalmists. At times he traded bread for paper and began his "dissertation" (Limburg, 1981, 170, citing Westermann, 1977, n.p.). Perhaps best known for his work on Genesis, his most influential research for English-speaking evangelical scholarship has been the publication of (1981).

THE PSALTER'S THEOLOGICAL THEMES

While numerous theological themes are evident in the 150 psalms, the following are some selected doctrinal themes in the Psalter (cf. Kraus, 1992, *in toto*).

God: His Names, Descriptions, and Character

God's Names: Often, we encounter comments about God's many names. While many are metaphorical description, God is often referred to as "Lord." But technically God has only one personal name in the OT, Yahweh (יְהוָה) (being an approximate reconstruction by scholarly consensus to date) and not Jehovah. "Jehovah" (יְהֹוָה; a one-time popular version of Yahweh [יְהוָה]) is an artificial name and one that is impossible according to Hebrew grammar rules. Ignorance of Hebrew led someone to make both a vowel and a consonant out of one Hebrew letter (the *waw* [ו] or *vav*—depending on the Hebrew pronunciation system being used—which can also be a vowel [*o*], but not both at the same time). Hebrew syllables can only be consonant-vowel, open (CV) or consonant-vowel-consonant, closed (CVC). Hebrew *yod* (י) or *y* became interchangeable in the West with *j* when it later received a *y* pronunciation in some languages. Note it has an *h* sound in Spanish. The letter *j* does not have the *y* sound in English as in German. So, Yahweh (יְהוָה) not "Jehovah" (יְהֹוָה) is technically the one and only name for God.

In the ANE, the gods had many names or designations. In one text, Marduk has fifty names. "God" or "Elohim" (אֱלֹהִים; but Hebrew does not use uppercase letters) is what he *is* (a divine being), whereas his name Yahweh tells us *who* he is. Other titles (like "*El Shaddai*" [אֵל שַׁדַּי], "*El Elyon*" [אֵל עֶלְיוֹן], or "Most High God" or the "Lord Will Provide," etc.) are just that, and not names per se (although in the course of Hebrew history some of these were used as God's name in a certain location or time period before Yahweh [יְהוָה] was established). "Adonai" (אֲדֹנָי) is simply the word "lord, master" ("Lord" when used for God), not to be confused with Lord (a symbol representing Yahweh [יְהוָה]). The command not to misuse God's name has in mind exactly the name Yahweh [יְהוָה]. The OT God has one personal "Name" and many characteristic descriptions. "Jehovah" is an impossible word because it is based on the vocalization of "YHWH" in the OT, which is done in a manner to prohibit pronunciation or spelling.

God's Name

The decision in antiquity to hide the original spelling of God's name left us with the consonants (יהוה), which suggests the verb "to be" (/היה הוה), resulting in an inability to know precisely what his name signified. In modern times, some came up with the impossible name "Jehovah (*j* substituted for Hebrew *y* [י]). As it stands vocalized in the Hebrew Bible, God's name cannot be pronounced or spelled properly by the Hebrew rules of syllabification. When God told Moses whom to say sent him to Pharaoh, he revealed himself as "I am/will be." A verb with a prefixed pronoun can indicate future or present tense. So, the name in that case apparently signifies God's self-existence and eternal nature, and his complete separation as immaterial and as creator from all that is material and creation itself. He is in no way compromised or corrupted by the created world, as are the gods of the nations. The Psalms reflect the passions of the psalmists in the midst of great joys and sorrows, in an ANE context.

Readers of English Bibles frequently encounter the term "Lord." Why uppercase (often with small capitals)? This is to alert the reader that the Hebrew word behind this translation is not the usual word for "Lord" (אֲדֹנָי) but God's personal name Yahweh (יהוה). In the Hebrew Bible, God's name is vocalized in a manner that makes it unpronounceable. The correct rules for vocalization were not followed in order that the informed reader would not say the name but substitute "Lord" (אֲדֹנָי) or "the Name" (הַשֵּׁם), lest the divine name be spoken in vain. Translators chose to substitute "Lord" whenever God's name appeared in the OT. This began as early as the Septuagint, which substituted the Greek word for "Lord" (κύριος). Since God told Moses to inform Pharaoh that "I Am" sent Moses to him (Exod. 3:10–14), a popular view is that the name indicates God's eternal and unchanging nature or his self-existence ("I am what I will be," or "I am" [meaning, "uncreated"]). If God is Creator, then all else is created and subject to him. This would seem to be the most essential aspect of what it means to be the one, true God. The decision in antiquity to hide the pronunciation of God's name from history was unfortunate because the name was supposed to be used, just not abused. This is equivalent to refusing to eat in order to avoid obesity. The Psalms especially call on believers to praise this Name (in relation to what it tells us about God). But, sadly, we cannot praise what we do not understand.

Metaphorical Descriptions of God. The Psalter employs at least eight metaphors to describe God: conqueror, fortress, horn, judge, king, redeemer, shepherd, and shield.

Conqueror of chaos. This was not related to a singular word or phrase, but in the Psalter Yahweh [יהוה] was sometimes described as the one who truly was master over or "conqueror, controller" of powers in creation that threaten peace, security, and stability (which the other nations defined as gods; see Historical Setting, pp. 36–41; e.g., the sea monster, Leviathan). He also at times defended Israel and defeated these enemy nations (cf., e.g., Pss. 93–99 with Gen. 1:1–2).

Fortress (מְצוּדָה or מִשְׂגָּב or מָעוֹז in the Psalms). In the Psalter, these terms for "fortress" were used in conjunction with others like "rock" (18:2, 31; 19:14; 28:1; 31:2; 42:9; 62:2; 71:3; 78:35; 89:26; 92:15; 94:22; 95:1; 144:1) or "strength" (Pss. 18:2; 28:8; 31:2–3; 46:7, 11; 48:3; 59:9, 16–17; 62:2, 6; 71:3; 91:2; 94:22; 144:2). As such God was also a "deliverer" (מְפַלְטִי; "my deliverer"), "refuge" (מַחְסֶה), and a "shield" (מָגֵן; see below), meaning "protector." In the ANE, a king would be called a fortress for his people. The metaphor "the rock" (הַסֶּלַע or הַצּוּר; interchangeable) also would suggest protection as well as a sound foundation, something solid and steadfast, or used for shade or a place to hide (behind it in a cleft). See Psalms 9:9; 18:2; 27:1; 28:8; 31:2–3; 37:39; 43:2; 46:7, 11; 48:3; 52:7; 59:9, 16–17; 62:2, 6–8; 71:3; 91:2; 94:22; 144:2

Horn (קֶרֶן). Only once in the Psalms (18:2 [3 in MT]) was Yahweh (יהוה) described as "the horn of my salvation" (קֶרֶן־יִשְׁעִי). Animal horns symbolized power in the ANE, and in the case of kings, projections from a crown or a radiance from a king's head suggested divine power or glory (called the *melammu* in Mesopotamia). See Psalms 18:2; 81:3; 89:17, 24; 92:10; 98:6; 112:9; 132:17; 148:14.

Judge (שׁפט or דין). More than a dozen times in the Psalms a noun or verb derived from one or the other of two Hebrew roots describe Yahweh (יהוה) as the righteous renderer of verdicts on individuals, groups, or nations. His judgments are always just, equitable, and timely. See Psalms 7:8, 11; 9:8; 50:4, 6; 51:4; 58:1; 72:2; 75:2; 76:9; 82:8; 94:2; 96:10, 13; 98:9; 110:6.

King (מֶלֶךְ). Frequently in the OT Psalter, Yahweh (יְהוָה) was heralded as king. He rules over his people and the world through human kings in biblical and ANE thought. At the same time, it has to be remembered that monarchy was not God's but Israel's choice. Yahweh (יְהוָה) wanted to be the only king, but his people demanded to be "like the nations" (1 Sam. 8:5), so he let them have what they wanted with all its liabilities (as defined in 1 Sam. 8:10–18) and assets (what few there were). See Psalms 2:6; 5:2; 10:16; 18:50; 20:9; 21:1, 7; 24:7–10; 29:10; 33:16; 44:4; 45:1, 11, 14–15; 47:2, 6–7; 48:2; 63:11; 68:24; 72:1; 74:12; 84:3; 89:18; 95:3; 98:6; 99:4; 105:20; 135:11; 136:19–20; 145:1; 149:2.

Redeemer (גָּאַל or פדה). In Israelite society, this person who redeemed was a close relative who helped reverse bad fortunes of family members (גָּאַל; see Ruth 4:1–12). "Buy back" (פדה; e.g., Num. 18:16) is frequent in the OT, but this word can also be used for "free someone from the punishment deserved" (see Ps. 130). For readers of the book of Psalms, it must be understood that this word never had the sense of the English term in Christian theology (i.e., forgiven or "saved" from eternal punishment for sins). The psalmists asked for "salvation" or "redemption" (better is "deliverance") in the sense of rescue from defeat, death, or disease. The NIV translates Psalm 130:8 as "He ['Yahweh' (יְהוָה)] himself will redeem [פדה] Israel from all their sins," but in context the psalmist was referring to the nation not suffering destruction for disobedience if it "hopes in 'Yahweh' [יְהוָה], whose love is faithful" (130:7). The same verb is used of Canaanite and Mesopotamian gods, but still the OT presented Yahweh (יְהוָה) as one who forgave moral debts owed and could choose to extend life by rescuing a petitioner from imminent harm. See Psalms

25:22; 26:11; 31:5; 44:26; 49:7, 15; 69:18; 119:134, 154; 130:8.

Shepherd (I רעה). Three times Yahweh (יְהוָה) was named the Shepherd of Israel or of an Israelite in the OT Psalter (Pss. 23:1; 28:9; 80:1). This was a widespread image for ANE kings or gods, highlighting their role as providers and protectors. Yahweh (יְהוָה) provides all essential needs in Psalm 23:1. In Psalm 28:9, he protects ("saves" [יָשַׁע], the root for Joshua) and preserves Israel.

Shield (I מָגֵן or [a few times in Psalms] II צִנָּה). The principal term used refers to a small, rounded shield used in close combat. Again, this image was used in the nations around Israel for their gods. And, again, Yahweh (יְהוָה) is pictured as a protector of his people, especially against enemy onslaught. See Psalms 3:3; 5:12; 7:10; 18:2, 30, 35; 28:7; 33:20; 35:2; 59:11; 84:9, 11; 89:18; 91:4; 115:9–11; 119:114; 144:2. See Walton 2000, 514–15, and Keel 1978, *in toto*, for the ANE background of these images).

God's Character. Often the psalmists referred to God as "good" (טוֹב). No English word truly captures the essence of this Hebrew term "good" (טוֹב). "Good" is maybe the best word we have to use in translation, but the problem is that our current usage of "good" is far from what the ancient Israelites understood when they heard that God was "good" (טוֹב). This is because we speak of many different things being "good" in many different ways: good food, a good time, a good man, good grades, good health, good grief, etc. To us, something being "good" is not extraordinary but just OK or satisfactory. God's goodness was, however, something extraordinary and excellent. The gods of the ANE were great or powerful (a god by definition), but they were not necessarily or ever good in a perfect or ideal moral or behavioral sense. Yahweh (יְהוָה)

by contrast was good because of his qualities of remembrance, forgiveness, loyal love, compassion, mercy, and faithfulness (which is often a better translation of the word often rendered "truthful," אֱמֶת). He was the polar opposite of all that is bad or wrong.[6] When Jesus said, "Only God is good" (Luke 18:19), he meant this in the sense that God was truly and fully the opposite of all that is corrupted, not that nothing and no one is "good" in the basic way we use this term in English today. No human teacher, as the ruler viewed Jesus, is so good (Luke 18:18). In other words, God is good in that he is never evil, wrong, or bad. This Hebrew word, however, can also be used of earthly and mundane things, which can be "good" in a satisfactory but not eternal or absolute way (e.g., creation in Gen. 1; marital union in Gen. 2:18; fortune in Gen. 30:11; grain in Gen. 41:24; years in Gen. 41:35; land in Deut. 4:21–22; fighters in Josh. 10:2; a report in 1 Sam. 2:24, etc.).

Creation

This theme of creation is found in Psalms 8:3; 24:2; 104:1–35. The OT often communicated the cosmology of the ANE. Since what was said was directed to the ancient Israelites, concepts with which they were familiar had to be used (the OT was *to* them but *for* us). Although the Psalms are divine revelation, this does not require that these texts speak in modern terms to its audience, which would have been nonsense to them; therefore, premodern scientific understandings are not errors, because the intention was not to reveal more than was known cosmologically (and cosmology was not the issue beyond its use for illustrative purposes). These texts do not pretend to teach the reader anything scientific (beyond the science of that age). The lessons to be learned are theological. Yahweh (הְוִהָי) is creator and sustainer of the universe.

Worship

The theme of worship may conjure a connection with the tabernacle or temple worship. But most Hebrews saw the temple only a few times if ever, apart from the most pious who had the proximity and prosperity to travel to Jerusalem. The synagogue did not exist in OT times. Perhaps this in part explains why the Hebrews were tempted to visit the Canaanite religious "high places." Sabbath observance was connected only to temple activities. The temple should not be thought of as a cathedral, where large numbers of believers gathered for a communal worship service (although some group events took place there, like certain annual festivals). It was God's house, where he lived, according to Israelite theology. The priests maintained its purity so Yahweh (הְוִהָי) could stay in residence. This is why biblical words for worship and service overlap. Often David or another psalmist promised to go to the "temple" and give witness to the people about God's help and his deliverance. In such cases the so-called temple is a circumlocution for God's house (tabernacle) since the actual Solomonic temple and its ministry was not in operation yet; although before and after the temple was constructed, there could have been congregational events (like sacrifices and singing) in the environs. In some way corporate prayers, laments, praises, worship, sacrifices, and festivals occurred but exactly how remains obscure. Words that get translated "worship" in the Psalms principally are derived from roots meaning "bow down" (הוח) and "serve" (דבע). The temple housed the "ark" (box) containing the covenant (stone tablets), and this ark of the covenant had "cherubim" (םיבֻרְכּ) on top symbolizing God's seated presence.

---

6   The "tree of the knowledge of good and 'evil,'" is better defined as the Right and Wrong Knowledge Tree; since the Hebrew word usually rendered as "evil" [עַר] basically means "bad," and is used in the OT interchangeably with, and categorically as, words for wickedness, sinfulness, and unlawfulness.

"Cherubim" (כְּרֻבִים) in OT and Psalms

The כְּרוּב or כְּרֻבִים are mentioned only two times in the Psalms (Pss. 18:10; 80:21). In Psalm 18:9–10 (10–11 MT), the psalmist's prayer presents God descending in dark clouds from the heavens and mounted "upon a cherub [עַל־כְּרוּב]." Cognate usage in the ANE referred to an intercessory priest or a tutelary spirit, often depicted by a sculpted and mythical gatekeeper (cf. HALOT, s.v. I כְּרוּב, 497). "Cherubim" and "Seraphim" should not be confused with "messengers" (ἄγγελος) in the New Testament. "Cherubim" appeared as a guardian in the story of the garden in Eden (Gen. 3:24) and in relation to the Tyrian king (Ezek. 28:14, 16). In the ANE, a statue of a "cherub" was placed outside entrances to important buildings (so it is likely that the king of Tyre was a "cherub" in this sense historically and his statue guarded the entrance into a royal garden palace with Eden-like beauty). A "cherub" (כְּרוּב) of hammered gold was placed at each end of the lid for the ark (box) containing the covenant (stone tablets), facing each other but looking down at the lid, with wings spread upward and covering the lid (Exod. 25:18–20). Solomon's temple sanctuary held a pair of these statues made from olive wood and overlaid with gold, each about 15 feet high and with wings 15 feet from tip to tip, placed in the innermost room (1 Kings 6:23–28).

Salvation

When the psalmists cried out for salvation, they were seeking rescue from an enemy (human or health-related). The concept of "salvation by grace apart from works of righteousness" found in the NT (see, e.g., Rom. 3:21–28; Gal. 2:16; Eph. 2:8–9; Phil. 3:8–11). seems to run afoul of much that was said in the OT. In OT wisdom, especially in the Psalms (especially those with a wisdom motif included), we read how the righteous prosper but the wicked-perish. The covenant that God made with Israel promised blessings for obedience but cursing for disobedience. God declared that if Israel turned to idols, it would be defeated by and dispersed among the nations. It must be kept in mind that the Hebrews had, and therefore the OT has, it seems, nothing like our views today regarding life after death and future judgment leading to heaven and hell. Outdated versions like the KJV mistakenly translate "sheol" (שְׁאוֹל) as "hell," when it actually just means "grave" (this is clear when the poetic parallel lines are considered, along with the fact that righteous people went to "sheol" [שְׁאוֹל; the realm of death] when they died). So, the Hebrews believed that rewards and punishments were experienced during life not after death. A successful person was thought to be the recipient of God's blessings as a reward for right living, and failure or misery was viewed as the (natural) consequence of transgressing God's righteous and life-giving laws. Israel would receive the "Land" for serving Yahweh (יְהוָה) but would lose it if the nation turned from Yahweh (יְהוָה) to serve other gods. Gain or loss in connection with pleasing the gods was a widespread belief in the ANE.

Evil

The so-called problem of evil is a modern and not an OT fascination. Old Testament authors used several words or expressions for "disobedience to God's laws" interchangeably (see Ps. 5). This means that even when "evil" (רַע or רָעָה) was used, readers need not make any more out of it than the word "sin" or "wickedness." All lawbreakers were evildoers. The word usually translated "evil" in the OT had no particular or unique association with demonic or devilish activity, as is a frequent association today. In the OT all that was contrary to God's will and ways was bad or wicked or evil. The main term translated "evil" simply means something "bad" or "wrong" as opposed to "good" or "right." The tree with the forbidden fruit in the garden located in Eden in Genesis should be called the "right/wrong knowledge tree" (meaning moral knowledge). If a hendiadys,[7] this would mean "omniscience tree." Remember, they wanted to "be like God." Many are troubled (mentally or emotionally or theologically) over how a morally perfect God could create evil (when defined as the devil or horrible acts like the Holocaust). Old Testament thinkers like Job and Ecclesiastes wrestle with why righteous people suffer and wicked people prosper. But the OT authors had no struggle with our modern "problem of [the source or cause of] evil." Creatures were given a free will to chose to obey or disobey God's laws, and when they choose to disobey, this was "bad" (רַע) and resulted in bad and very bad attitudes and actions. The initial state of life before humans rebelled was "very good" (טוֹב מְאֹד; Gen. 1:31). God was considered only the cause of an allowance for human freedom to "break bad," and humanity has excelled in rebellion (the devil's influence notwithstanding, even though the OT does not recognize such a being, at least in any direct manner other than the tempter "snake" in Gen. 3; and the "accuser" or "adversary" or "satan" [שָׂטָן] in 1 Chron. 21:1, Job 1–2, and Zech. 3:1). Consequently, "evil" should be (per English dictionaries and current usage) reserved for only what is demonic/devilish or despicable in human behavior.

Afterlife ("Sheol" [שְׁאוֹל])

Throughout the OT and the Psalms, the concept of "the afterlife" did not mean what we mean today when we speak of "the afterlife" or "eternity" (eternal joy or suffering in a heaven or a hell).[8] The Hebrew word שְׁאוֹל was sadly mistranslated in the past as "hell," when it only meant "the realm of death" or the "grave" (this is clear when the poetic parallels using this term, like "pit/hole, are studied and in their immediate textual contexts). Some of

Israel's neighbors had a fairly elaborate system of belief about the "world beyond the grave," especially in Egypt (the netherworld). But the OT does not give (even if lost texts do) a Hebrew theology of this existence other than vague ideas like "going to be with ancestors." Sometimes OT authors inferred the idea of a "spirit" (רוּחַ) that left the body after death (Ps. 146:4 and Eccl. 3:21). The modern world has the tradition of a "soul" apart from the body, but the NT only speaks of resurrected bodies not bodiless beings, and the "soul" (*nephesh* [נֶפֶשׁ]) in the OT is never without a body, which is interesting since the "soul" theology in the church has mainly looked to OT texts for support. When the psalmist said things like "I lift up my soul" (Ps. 25:1) or "my soul will rejoice" (Ps. 35:9), this "soul" was his integrated being, his emotions along with his physical being. At times this *nephesh* was interchangeable with the person or the pronoun "I" (see Ps. 119:20, where "my soul is consumed" means "I am consumed"; even God has a "soul" in Ps. 11:5). Dead Israelites (per OT theology), even the righteous ones, entered "Sheol" (שְׁאוֹל), but what happened after that is vague. When psalmists prayed for being kept out of "Sheol" (שְׁאוֹל), they meant for God to keep them alive on earth (i.e., not die). When Psalm 11:6 says the wicked will suffer fiery coals and burning sulfur, the context was not about the afterlife, only God's judgment on those who were violent and are judged on earth (11:5b). The righteous will "see his face" because they were preserved from this earthly judgment and can still visit the temple (see Ps. 63:3). Being "redeemed from 'Sheol' [שְׁאוֹל]" in Psalm 49:15 meant being healed and preserved from death. Parallel statements are found in Mesopotamian literature (Walton 2000, 512,

---

7   A hendiadys is a figure of speech that communicates a single idea with two words connected by "and."

8   J. M. Rochford, "Did the Ancient Jews Believe in Life after Death?," in *Evidence Unseen: Exposing the Myth of Blind Faith*, http://www.evidenceunseen.com/bible-difficulties-2/ot-difficulties/psalms-song-of-songs/did-the-ancient-jews-believe-in-life-after-death, accessed July 9, 2020.

527). The KJV mistranslates "sheol" (לֹאשׁ) as "hell" (see Marlowe 2002 and 2016, *in toto*). It referred always to the realm of death but says nothing about a given person's destiny in the grave world. Also, the larger phrase "my soul" [יִשְׁפֵּן] in "sheol" [לֹאשׁ] suffers from the popular problem of misunderstanding this word for "soul" as a disembodied spirit; whereas it spoke of an embodied set of feelings or emotions or psychology (see "Soul" in the OT and Psalms, p. 77).

Hades and Sheol in the OT

The NETS's "Hades" is a transliteration (not a translation) of the Greek (LXX) equivalent (ᾄδης) for the Hebrew word for "grave" or "realm of death" (as is the NRSV's, NASB's, and JPS's "Sheol" for שְׁאוֹל). The KJV has "lowest hell," an eisegetical theological interpretation, which has since been corrected to a more contextual exegetical rendering "grave" (cf. the NIV, e.g.). Whereas the KJV has "hell" in the OT more than thirty times, the NIV and other modern versions never or almost never render שְׁאוֹל as "hell," since every occurrence has to do with the grave or death, and never with issues of the eternal state of a person (see Marlowe, 2016, 171–92; 2002, 5–24). The problem with "Hades" or "Sheol" or "Underworld" in a number of versions is that these renderings

suggest an Israelite perspective on death and the afterlife that is equivalent or near equivalent to that of other ANE nations like Egypt. While many Hebrews in practice were influenced by the beliefs of neighboring nations, the OT does not teach a detailed afterlife scenario that parallels other and more elaborate ANE conceptions of the Underworld. In the OT, all who die (righteous or wicked) enter the grave or afterlife or realm of death (i.e., שְׁאוֹל, "Sheol").

Messiah

When you read the Bible, you will notice that the Psalms are quoted throughout the NT. There are sixty-nine uses of forty-one psalms in twelve NT books. Many of these psalms are often referred to as Messianic Psalms, but the title is a misnomer. The Hebrew noun "messiah" (מָשִׁיחַ), is an Anglicized rendering translated "anointed one" (the verbal root from which this noun is taken means "to anoint" [מָשַׁח]). In reality, the psalmists of the so-called Messianic Psalms used "anointed one" only once (Ps. 2). In addition, only one so-called Messianic Prophecy in the OT ever incorporated the noun or verb "anoint[ed one]" (Dan. 9:25–26). All the other OT passages that are regarded as anticipating a coming one use expressions like "[a coming] one / king / shepherd / ruler," etc.

MESSIANIC USE OF PSALMS IN THE NT			
PSALMS USED BY NT REGARDING JESUS		NT USAGE SEEING PARALLELS WITH JESUS	OT THEME SEEN AS TYPICAL OF JESUS
2	2:7	Matt. 3:17; 17:5	An Israelite psalmist announced his new king's (his lord's) position as YHWH's (the Lord's) anointed (מְשִׁיחוֹ) and his son.
		Mark 1:11; 9:7	
		Luke 3:22; 9:35	
		Acts 13:33	
		Heb. 1:5; 5:5	

MESSIANIC USE OF PSALMS IN THE NT				
PSALMS USED BY NT REGARDING JESUS		**NT USAGE SEEING PARALLELS WITH JESUS**		**OT THEME SEEN AS TYPICAL OF JESUS**
	2:9	Rev.	2:27	Victory over enemy nations, whose loyalty was expected, was promised to the new king of Israel.
8	8:2	Matt.	21:16	Yahweh had strengthened even young children to silence all foes.
	8:4–5	Heb.	2:6–9	Yahweh had cared for humans and honored them with a status a little lower than the "gods" (מֵאֱלֹהִים; or other heavenly beings).
	8:6	1 Cor.	15:27–28	Everything was made subject to humanity.
		Eph.	1:22	
16	16:8–11	Acts	2:25–32; 13:35–37	The psalmist (ostensibly David) was confident that Yahweh would not allow him to be killed but continue to serve him.
22	22:1	Matt.	27:46	"David" was in such danger and near death that he felt God had forsaken him.
		Mark	15:34	
	22:7–8	Matt.	27:29, 41–44	"David's" enemies ridiculed him for believing that Yahweh would rescue him.
		Mark	15:18, 29–32	
		Luke	23:35–39	
	22:18	Matt.	27:35	Clothes "David" had left behind in a cave were gambled over by the soldiers chasing him in the wilderness.
		Mark	15:24	
		Luke	23:34	
		John	19:24	
	22:22	Heb.	2:12	"David" vowed to testify about Yahweh's deliverance.
31	31:5	Luke	23:46	"David" trusted Yahweh with whether he lived or died.
34	34:20	John	19:31–36	"David" believed that Yahweh would protect him from breaking a bone because he was righteous.
35	35:19	John	15:25	"David" claimed his enemy hated him for no credible reason.
40	40:6–8	John	6:38	"David" recognized Yahweh's preference not for sacrifices but for righteousness, for zeal to follow God's will and laws.

MESSIANIC USE OF PSALMS IN THE NT			
PSALMS USED BY NT REGARDING JESUS		**NT USAGE SEEING PARALLELS WITH JESUS**	**OT THEME SEEN AS TYPICAL OF JESUS**
		Heb. 10:5–9	
41	41:9	John 13:18	"David" felt forgotten by Yahweh and oppressed by an enemy who was likely a former friend.
45	45:6–7	Heb. 1:8–9	The psalmist (perhaps one of Korah's daughters) sang about her love, the king, whom she honored as one whom God had anointed (מָשַׁח) to spread divine justice and hate wicked injustice.
68	68:18	Eph. 4:7–11	Yahweh was exalted for taking many captives up into his mountaintop sanctuary (vv. 16, 18a) after scattering foreign kings (v. 14) and then plundering them for gifts in order to dwell there.
69	69:4	John 15:25	Cf. Psalm 35. "David" claimed his enemy hated him for no credible reason.
	69:9	John 2:14–22	"David's" zeal for Yahweh's house was so strong that it set him apart from others, and David was personally affected when God was insulted (cf. vv. 8–10).
	69:21	John 19:29	"David's" enemies tried to poison his food and substituted wine (or vinegar) when he needed water for grave thirst.
	69:25	Acts 1:20	"David" asked for divine vengeance on his enemies, that they be driven from their homes (exterminated?; cf. vv. 22–28).
78	78:2	Matt. 13:34–35	Asaph tells the people he would teach with parables and keep alive the forgotten past for the next generation.
102	102:25–27	Heb. 1:10–12	An afflicted man exalted his God for his unchanging and unending nature.
110	110:1	Matt. 22:41–45	"David" announced Yahweh's intention to humble the new Israelite king's (David's son's) enemies.
		Mark 12:35–37	
		Luke 20:41–44	
	110:4	Heb. 5:6; 7:11–22	The Israelite king was also a priest of the Melchizedek order.
118	118:22–23	Matt. 21:42–44	The psalmist praised Yahweh for making him a "cornerstone" despite being rejected by others.
		Mark 12:10	

MESSIANIC USE OF PSALMS IN THE NT				
PSALMS USED BY NT REGARDING JESUS	NT USAGE SEEING PARALLELS WITH JESUS		OT THEME SEEN AS TYPICAL OF JESUS	
	Luke	20:17–19		
	Acts	4:10–11		
	1 Peter	2:7–8		
118:26a	Matt.	21:9	The psalmist asked for deliverance for Israel from one who was favored by Yahweh's Name (reputation) and vowed to praise Yahweh in his temple (vv. 25–26).	
	Mark	11:9		
	Luke	19:38		
	John	12:13		
16 total psalms	10 books	55 references	25 different themes	
	4 Gospels	Acts	5 Epistles	

Messianic theology, however, grew prior to NT times (Bateman, 2012, 211–330). When NT authors cited the OT and applied it to Jesus, they were following current hermeneutical practices with which the Jews were familiar (based on their post-OT writings and teachings), so that the Jews could identify with and relate to the Christological arguments. This explains why many Jews were converted, but many also chose not to believe as has always been the case with Jews and all other nations to whom the gospel has been proclaimed.

So, if historically the king in Psalm 2 was David (for the psalmist), then he is a type of the future Son of God and Messiah (transliterated Hebrew for "anointed one"), Jesus the Christ (transliterated Greek for "anointed one") in retrospect for Christian readers. We have only two OT texts using "anointed one" that can be applied to Jesus. So, to talk literally about OT Messianic prophecy is an overstatement and anachronistic. Messianic theology developed more fully during the centuries

between the close of the OT and the beginning of the NT. The authors of the NT books were in dialogue with the intertestamental Jewish theology about Messiah more than the OT. Since they used many OT texts to demonstrate how the OT anticipates, typifies, foreshadows, or forecasts the life and ministry of the Messiah as fulfilled in the person of Jesus of Nazareth, the NT authors therefore proclaimed Jesus (who is) the Christ. Rather than an "anointed one," the OT looks mostly for a coming Seed, Prophet, Priest, King / Ruler / Shepherd / Prince, and/or a Servant (see, e.g., Gen. 3:15; 49;10; Deut. 18:18; 1 Sam. 2:35; Jer. 23:5; Isa. 1:1; 11:10; 52:13; Hag. 2:23; Zech. 3:8; see Marlowe, 2015, *in toto*; also Marlowe 2009, *in toto*, regarding Isa. 53:9).

Typology

"Type" (τύπος) in OT prophecy was derived from the Greek word signifying an "impression" or "likeness" (Goppelt, 1977, 8:246). It occurs in the LXX in reference to the model upon which the tabernacle was based (Exod. 25:40). If something in the OT operates as a "type" of something or someone in the future, then it "points to" or "prefigures" or "anticipates" it or the person. NT writers speak of Jesus having "fulfilled" (πληρόω) a previous event, meaning he "completed" it in some manner. This is not meant as we use the term "predicted" but has more to do with a divinely ordained historical parallel (in terms of first-century thinking and employment of a Jewish hermeneutic to get the attention of the Jewish community). A type has been described as "a historical event or person in the Old Testament that serves as a prophetic pattern or example of a New Testament event or person" (Duvall and Hayes, 2005, 195) or "a biblical event, person or institution which serves as an example or pattern for other events, persons or institutions" (Baker 1976, 153). The author of Hebrews in the NT saw Melchizedek (Heb. 6:20) and the tabernacle (Heb. 9–10) as types of Christ (John 3:14–15; 1 Cor. 5:7).

The parallels between the OT texts and NT events in Jesus's life are remarkable and uncanny, as well as amazing if not miraculous (which they are). These many close parallels did not happen by coincidence. One that is amazing, and found in the Psalms (while keeping in mind that prophecy is not usually prediction), is how a psalmist, likely David, described his deteriorating physical condition, while on the run and hiding in the wilderness, in ways that parallel Jesus's crucifixion (Ps. 22; although the NIV's "pierced" in 22:16[17] is hopeful more than exegetical and not what the Hebrew text says, yet the LXX does have "they dug out" [ὤρυξαν] his hands and feet). What is remarkable is that this ancient fugitive experienced and recorded events that could be read in retrospect and so closely picture Jesus's punishment and execution by the Romans (i.e. and e.g., his emaciated physical condition, words of ridicule, and the soldiers gambling for his clothing). On the cross, Jesus purposefully quoted the opening words

of this psalm as an indication that it should be interpreted as an ancient Israelite mirror of his situation and evidence of his messiahship to the first-century Jews. The author of the psalm clearly did not craft these words as a prediction (as we use the word today), but nevertheless the uncanny connection stands. Accepted hermeneutical practices of that time likely included such typological or midrashic readings or perhaps an expected corporate solidarity between Israel and whoever would be the Messiah. This is why the NT says certain events "fulfilled" (πληρόω) an OT text, since this Greek word has to do with something being "made full" or completed.

Anthropological Themes

Hating or Loving Enemies. Some psalmists (typically David) often viewed an enemy's attack or hatred as equivalent to opposing God, since they viewed themselves as God's anointed agents. Anyone who hated the Hebrew God was automatically the psalmist's enemy (Ps. 139:21). At times, a psalmist lamented over the great number of his enemies and the severity of their hatred towards him (Pss. 25:19; 38:19a; 69:14). Often the psalmist claimed his enemies had no real justification for their hatred or superiority (Pss. 35:19; 38:19b; 69:4). The enemy at times was from within Israel (Ps. 105:24–25). Death was often a feared consequence if the enemy was victorious (Ps. 7:5). Another fear was that the enemy would gloat over the psalmist's defeat, which was viewed as bad press for God (Ps. 13:4; 74:10). Waiting too long for God's help created emotional distress (Pss. 13:2; 42:9; 43:2; 143:3–4). Dealing with an enemy was always through personal or divine revenge (Pss. 9:6; 129:5; 74:18; 89:20–23; cf. 44:16). Loving an enemy was not considered. This is likely because the OT law had focused on loving fellow countrymen. Leviticus 19:18a had prohibited revenge only against other Hebrews. In the parallel line in verse 18b, the "neighbor" to be treated as self is a restatement of this fellow Hebrew. God had to help because these enemies were usually too strong for the psalmist to conquer (Pss. 18:17; 60:11; 64:1; 74:3; 106:10; 108:12). Success over an enemy was viewed as a sign of God's pleasure (Ps. 41:11). Sometimes failure against an enemy was blamed on God (Ps. 44:10).

Imprecations ("Curses") in the Psalms. An imprecation is a curse or an invocation of something bad to happen to an opponent. Cursing in the OT is not the use of "bad words" but akin to a plea for condemnation or misfortune (where God is the agent of doom). No OT psalm is fully an imprecation, but some lament psalms contain an imprecatory statement within the section where the psalmist asks God to remove his problem, which at times involves requesting that God destroy his enemy. The most famous and longest OT imprecation is that found in Psalm 137. Readers of the OT are sometimes troubled by the existence of such a lack of compassion since Jesus taught love for enemies. The question arises if this is a contradiction in the Bible between the OT and NT. That this is not the case can be explained in that both Testaments emphasize loving others as well as leaving vengeance to God (Lev. 19:18a; Rom. 12:19), albeit that the OT commands loving neighbors (Lev. 19:18b) not enemies (which is consistent with Israel needing to fight enemy nations; see Luke 6:27–35). When the psalmists call on God to judge their enemies, they view these people also as God's enemies and look to God for help rather than taking the law into their own hands. It is true that at times in the OT Hebrew warriors are an instrument for God's justice and judgment on those opposing God's purposes. The transnational church was not commissioned to wage war, while national Israel was used for military purposes in the ANE, when Canaan was a prized territory and nations generally ascribed the highest honor to the God whose army was victorious in battle (see Hating or Loving Enemies, p. 75). Some suggest that this makes God inconsistent with his commands; but the answer is not as simple as saying that God can do what he wants and cannot be blamed, no matter how horrible or hypocritical, because God by definition is perfect. At times in the OT, to hate people is to not choose them for a special purpose in favor of another (who is "loved"; e.g., God loved Jacob but hated Esau [Mal. 1:2–3], where these terms are not about an emotion but about having or not having a covenant with the named individual). However, in this psalm these words do convey God's sentiments, so why can he "hate" people without doing wrong? The difference is that his hatred is of what these people are doing that is immoral, so-called righteous anger. We hate sinfully because we often hate the sinner instead of, or in addition to, the sin. As morally righteous or perfect, God cannot tolerate or prefer what is immoral or imperfect (but cf. Prov. 6 above). The OT also thinks in terms of imperfect but right-living people (e.g., Noah) in contrast to those Israelites or Gentiles who are imperfect but lawbreakers or wicked. The fact that all people sin (i.e., disobey God) is accepted, but also accepted is the distinction that people in the ancient world are divided between those who are wise and fools (especially in the wisdom books like Proverbs). Yet these are not absolute categories. The distinction is between those who have lifestyles built on consistently and purposefully adhering to wise and godly regulations and those who take risks and ignore these moral and ethical laws usually to their harm and regret.

"Soul" ("nephesh" נֶפֶשׁ) in the OT and Psalms. The word "nephesh" (נֶפֶשׁ) should seldom if ever be translated "soul" in modern and contemporary versions, as is typically done. This is because the way we use "soul" currently does not correspond to its use in the OT (see commentary on Pss. 6 and 9; see also Ps. 31 in vol. 3, *Praise Psalms*, and Pss. 42, and 63 in vol. 2, *Lament Psalms* (both forthcoming); also see Gen. 2:7, where נֶפֶשׁ is translated as a "living being," and 1 Kings 19:4, where it means "life"). This word should not be confused with the later concepts of an "eternal/immortal soul" (which is a concept that is problematic anyway since the NT speaks of a resurrected body, not just an incorporeal being, consistent with the OT concept that keeps the life force connected to a body; but this is not the case in some Egyptian and Mesopotamian documents, yet cf. 1 Sam. 28:13). In a related Semitic language to Hebrew (Akkadian), the cognate term *"napashu . . .* refers to the neck or throat and by extension to breath" (Walton, 2000, 537). Usually "nephesh" (נֶפֶשׁ) is used in the OT in reference to a living person or to one's emotional state as a person, and often can be left untranslated without changing the meaning of a statement or can be substituted with the pronoun "I" or "me." The parallel poetic line usually clarifies how this word is being used in a verse in a psalm.

PRACTICAL THEOLOGY

The book of Psalms in the Hebrew Bible (Christian OT) is sublime and strategic. It remains what most Bible readers usually say is their favorite book in the Old Testament if not in the whole Bible. It was one of Luther's favorites. This is because most people can relate to its honest expressions of excitement over the Lord's favor to them at times contrasted to their exasperation over life's unfairness and disfavor at other times. The psalms add a feature to OT faith that would otherwise be missing. While much OT literature is prophetic (God speaking to Hebrew people or prophets directly or indirectly), or proverbial (godly guidelines spoken by wise sages to fellow Hebrews), the musical poetry of the Hebrew psalter offers a platform in which the reader encounters and experiences the unfiltered prayers and praises of hopeful or hurting Hebrew commoners or kings. When we read an OT psalm, we read the poetic personal confessions and celebrations of people who are broken or blessed. They often have a "no holds barred" approach to God, using language some have found offensive or at least quizzical, but which in reality is a refreshing honesty about their pleasure or pain in regard to their victories or defeats in light of God's understood omniscience and omnipotence and promises to save his people and reward righteous living. Consequently, a number of psalms include a wisdom theme. Westermann generalized psalms as laudatory or laments (Westermann 1987, *in toto*). This is because life is typically composed of good and bad, holy or hard, times since while God is good, life often is not. The OT Psalter is strategic because it affirms our emotional life and frees us to be honest with God about our feelings.

A number of the editorial superscriptions mention, even require, the use of certain instruments or melodies. Luther famously said that music is second only to theology, "next to the Word of God, music deserves the highest praise" (quoted in Westermeyer 1998, 142–43). In a letter to the Catholic chief conductor and court composer for the Duke of Bavaria, Luther wrote: "Indeed I plainly judge, and do not hesitate to affirm, that except for theology here is no art that could be put on the same level with music, since except for theology [music] alone produces what otherwise only theology can do, namely, a calm and joyful disposition" (quoted in Leaver 1989, 265, cited by Leroux 2007, 94, n. 41). In his commentary on the OT psalms, Luther emphasized their Christology and patterns for prayer. He categorized the various psalms as prayers and thanksgivings that are prophetic, didactic, and therapeutic; and he connected them to the Ten Commandments and the Lord's Prayer (Luther 2007, *in toto*).

Do the Psalms Call Us to Be Perfect? In Psalm 26, God is expected to vindicate a blameless follower who has been falsely accused of dishonesty and destruction. But how can anyone sinful from birth claim to be blameless? This is because the word "blameless" does not mean "sinless," but rather not guilty of a specific false accusation. A man like Noah (Gen. 6:9b) was "righteous" (צַדִּיק) and "blameless" (תָּמִים) in comparison to others in his generation because, despite his sins, "Noah walked with God." David, in this psalm, claims innocence in regard to consorting with and going along with the corrupt deeds of violent criminals or those unfaithful to God or unbelievers. Instead, he delights in declaring God's nature as one who helps those who trust him and seek to obey his laws. The psalmist believes he can claim rescue based on his proven pattern of doing right as evidence of his unflagging trust in God.

Giving Thanks: "todah" (תּוֹדָה) and "hodu" (הוֹדוּ; from the root II-ידה) in the Psalms. The expression "Give thanks!" is frequent in English versions of the OT psalms. But the appropriateness of this translation for the OT contexts (social or linguistic and literary) is debatable. The first clue is that this verb is often in synonymous parallel with concepts of praise (e.g., Pss. 35:18; 75:1; 100:4; 105:1; 106:47; see commentary on Ps. 6:5 below). A second issue is the consideration that saying "thank you" as an act of gratitude, apart from an accompanying action of public witness to that person's nature, is apparently a modern, Western rather than ancient, Eastern custom. A third argument is that only Psalm 100 has a superscription that identifies the psalm thematically as a "psalm for

giving thanks" or better "for testimony" (מִזְמוֹר לְתוֹדָה). But its content is exclusively about exhortation to sing, shout, acknowledge, and make known God's goodness as a faithful Creator. In the psalms, gratitude is not so much an attitude as an act of testimony; e.g., Psalm 105:1, "Confess! [or 'Testify!'] about Yahweh [יְהוָה]. Cry out! concerning his name [reputation]. Make known! among the nations what he has done"; and Psalm 95:2, "Let's come before him 'with testimony' [בְּתוֹדָה] and let's shout about him [NIV has 'extol him'] with songs"; and perhaps also Psalm 75:1 (75:2 MT), "We confess [הוֹדִינוּ] about you, O God, we profess [הוֹדִינוּ]; crying out your name [reputation]; and telling about your wonderful deeds." HALOT has two homographic roots for ידה (I. to shout; throw and II. to praise; confess [perhaps with thanksgiving]). תּוֹדָה is a noun based on the root ידה. I (C. Marlowe) reached this understanding through contextual exegesis before I ever read Westermann's well-known book on the Psalms, which supports these conclusions (Westermann 1965, 1987, 25–30). Often this verb or noun is used in parallel with a word for praise (e.g., Ps. 100:4, "Enter his gates with תּוֹדָה and his courts with תְּהִלָּה"). The NIV and others inconsistently translate תּוֹדָה with "thanksgiving." But the parallelism in all such poetic lines in the OT demonstrates that "thanksgiving" is a misleading modern, English notion. In the ancient, Hebraic conception, this appreciation is gratefulness demonstrated by public acknowledgement or confession or profession of God's goodness and/or greatness and grace.

The "Workers of Iniquity" in the Psalms. The expression "workers of iniquity" (some form of כָּל־פֹּעֲלֵי אָוֶן) occurs seven times in the OT Psalter (MT 5:6 [5 EB]; 6:9 [8 EB]; 14:4; 92:8 [7 EB], 10 [9 EB]; 94:4; and 101:8). They are described as boastful (5:5a; 94:2–4), hated and shunned by God (5:5), as those who "eat" others like bread (14:4), as wicked (92:7a; 101:8a) and widespread, yet doomed for destruction (92:7), as "Yahweh's" (יְהוָה) enemies, who will be disunified and destroyed (92:9) and "cut off" (slain) in "Yahweh's" (יְהוָה) territory (101:8). In Psalm 41, David (ostensibly) complains about someone he trusted, with whom he thought he shared peace and did share meals, who was in the end dishonest and slanderous and tried to step on him. For a related discussion, see Miller 2012, 423–30.

FINAL CHALLENGES

We lack a good understanding of how biblical words and expressions and idioms were used apart from what we find only in the OT. We have no extant, ancient grammar of biblical Hebrew. The verbal system is still debated. The OT lexicon is open to many questions. There are rare words hard to translate. The OT exegete has to rely a lot on context (the immediate text as well as all that is known for sure about the historical, cultural, and literary contexts). Another challenge is that we lack complete knowledge about the date and setting of many psalms and OT chapters, and even when we can get an approximate idea of these, our knowledge about the language and life of that time is limited or nonexistent.

Frequently the reader will encounter the comment that the Hebrew text in a certain place is unclear. This is important not just for academic but practical reasons. When preaching from a passage in the Bible, it is necessary to know when a proposed interpretation or translation is questionable, and especially when a word or phrase is very difficult to understand. This information is useful to teachers/preachers because it alerts them to places in the text where dogmatic explanations or applications are unwarranted. Preachers especially need to know when exegesis allows them to (or not to) pound the pulpit. This is also a major reason that pastors and Bible teachers need to have at least a working knowledge of OT Hebrew and NT Greek. One does not have to be a scholar to be an effective and accurate Bible expositor, but being completely ignorant of the biblical languages puts the student at the mercy of only second- and third-hand commentary. And when the languages are used and explained in commentary, critical analysis is impossible. Translations make educated guesses when texts are unclear, which means that these texts seem perfectly clear in the versions; however, that can mislead the reader into thinking the Hebrew or Greek text in all cases is straightforward.

FOR FURTHER READING

For a study of the beginning and ending of the OT Psalms, see Gillingham 2012, 383–94, and Miller 1993, 83–92.

To read more about psalms from Qumran see Abegg 1999, 505–89; Evans 2010, 182–265; and Wise 1996, 257–531.

For worship at Qumran, see Schiffman 2000, 991–96; Schiffman 2010, 219–364; Martinez 1994, 419–31; and Martinez 1997, 806–837, regarding:

4Q400	4QShirShabb[a]	Songs of the Sabbath Sacrifice[a]
4Q401	4QShirShabb[b]	Songs of the Sabbath Sacrifice[b]
4Q402	4QShirShabb[c]	Songs of the Sabbath Sacrifice[c]
4Q403	4QShirShabb[d]	Songs of the Sabbath Sacrifice[d]
4Q404	4QShirShabb[e]	Songs of the Sabbath Sacrifice[e]
4Q405	4QShirShabb[f]	Songs of the Sabbath Sacrifice[f]
4Q406	4QShirShabb[g]	Songs of the Sabbath Sacrifice[g]
4Q407	4QShirShabb[h]	Songs of the Sabbath Sacrifice[h]

For wisdom literature comparing non-Jewish with Jewish sources, see Arnold 2002, 175–204; Lambert 1996, *in toto*; Noth 1955, *in toto*; *ANET*, 495–601; Sparks 2005, 56–83; Walton 1989, 135–97; Matthews 1991, 179–234; and Toorn 2018, n.p.

INTRODUCTION TO THE WISDOM PSALMS

OVERVIEW

Author: Numerous authors

Provenance: Judah, Israel, Babylon

Readers: Ancient Jewish communities

Date: Preexile (Davidic) to exile

Historical Setting: Israelite monarchy through postexilic period

Occasion for Writing: Personal and/or public praise or lament

Genre: Poems set to music

Theological Emphasis: The right way to live or the nature of God's verbal revelation

---

AUTHORSHIP OF THE WISDOM PSALMS

While fourteen Wisdom Psalms (1, 15, 19, 37, 49, 73, 78, 91, 111, 112, 119, 127, 128, and 133) do not indicate authorship, seven of them (15, 19, 37, 49, 73, 78, 133) have editorial superscriptions, which attach the respective psalm in some manner to David (15, 19, 37) or Korah's sons (49) or Asaph (73, 78). The superscriptions to many OT psalms (added by Jewish scribes) should be considered with great respect, but since they were not part of the original text, they do not partake of its authority and inspiration. The preposition *lamed* (ל) is typically prefixed to these names and is often translated by traditional versions as "of" meaning "by"; but the LXX used a dative τῷ, which the NETS renders "pertaining to." Authorship is, therefore, not confirmed by this, but these persons are related to the respective psalms in some manner by the credible tradition in the superscriptions. Even if the person named was not the author per se, whoever was the editor intended the psalm to be read in light of that person's life.

These people may or may not have been the authors of the psalms bearing their name, but a scribal editor had some reason to pass down the tradition about their relationship with these psalms. So, regardless of who wrote them or when, their content was reliably related to the person named in the superscription. Understanding these psalms, in these scribes' opinion, ought to be enhanced by reading them in light of what is known about the persons named. This means, for example, that if David is named and especially if an episode in his life is mentioned, whether he wrote the psalm or not, the actual psalmist or editor had David's situation in mind as he wrote.

PLACE OF WRITING

A few times in the OT Psalter the superscriptions mention a place or region, but never in terms of where the author was at when he wrote the psalm. The contents are sometimes interpreted as reflecting the author's location in Judah or Israel or exile, but these (and especially cities) are not specified in relation to the psalm's creation. None of these Revelatory Psalms (1, 19, 37, 49, 73, 78, or 119) mention any locational setting in the superscriptions. Israel is mentioned in Psalm 73:1, 78:5 and 78:21; Ephraim in Psalm 78:9, 67, Egypt and Zoan in Psalm 78:12, 43, and the desert of Sinai in Psalm 78:17, 40; Shiloh in Psalm 78:60; and Mount Zion in Psalm 78:68. But none of these are named as the psalmist's location when writing. Psalm 78 looks back to places of God's past interactions with the Hebrews.

DATE OF WRITING

When a psalm was written may not be the same as when the events it describes occurred. Jonah 2, for example, was not composed inside a fish. However, when a psalm can be connected to specific events that can be dated, the composition of the psalm, it is safe to assume, took place relatively soon thereafter. Only David, Korah's sons, and Asaph are mentioned in these seven Revelatory Psalms (1, 19, 37, 49, 73, 78, 119). If we take them as the authors, then David is placed at ca. 1000 B.C. Several different men named Asaph are mentioned in the OT, the psalmist being either the singer of David's Levites (1 Chron. 6:39) or the one who dedicated Solomon's temple (2 Chron. 5:12), dating him from 1000 to 930 B.C. Korah's descendant who is associated with Psalm 49 could be also the one or ones connected to Psalms 42, 44–49, 84, 85, 87, and 88, which suggests the preexile period due to similarities with other psalms.

OCCASION FOR WRITING

Some of the superscriptions in the OT Psalter offer information about the circumstances that prompted the psalm. Again, as with possible authorship, these data reflect a reliable source but were not included when these psalms were originally composed under inspiration. At the same time, nothing disproves the connection between a given psalm and its respective setting as explained in its superscription. None of the superscriptions of these seven Revelatory Psalms (1, 19, 37, 49, 73, 78, or 119) mentions any occasion for the psalm other than musical directions in Psalms 19 and 49. The author of Psalm 1 needed to remind the Hebrews that following God's ways would avoid divine judgment. Psalm 19 reminds them that God's laws cannot be improved upon and are completely reliable. Psalm 37 warns them not to be envious of those who break God's laws yet still (at least in the short run) succeed. Eventually, as always in the past, they will be destroyed by their unwise choices, and God's people will be delivered from destruction. Psalm 49 encourages the Israelites not to be anxious at a time when lawbreakers dominate because they will soon perish and by contrast those who trust in God will rule. Psalm 73 also pictures a time when the faithful are tempted to despair and be bitter over the success of criminals; yet the people are comforted with the knowledge that the wicked and wealthy rulers will be swept away suddenly without warning. Psalm 78 reflects on the Hebrews' past patterns of rebellion in spite of God's provisions or punishments. Even when they were disloyal, he forgave them and did not completely abolish them. Eventually he blessed them with David as a shepherd-king and established his presence on Mount Zion. Psalm 119 tirelessly expounds the benefits of obedience to God's laws, specifically that the psalmist expects to be rewarded with rescue from death at the hands of his enemies for his loyalty. Specific people, places, and periods are hard to prove. See above table, "Occasions for Psalms in the Superscriptions."

ORIGINAL READERS

The intended and immediate audience for these psalms is the ancient Hebrew nation in preexilic or exilic times.

HISTORICAL SETTING

Wisdom was valued throughout the ancient world. It emphasized practical skill at living so as to avoid dangers that would cut life short and to do what would enhance a long and healthy existence. Wisdom is truth about the ways to best navigate life, often learned by experience. While the OT includes documents containing wise instructions from people who experienced verbal revelation from God, much of the advice reconfirms what also was learned from the classroom of life. God revealed these texts not as information that could not otherwise be known, but as guidance to which he especially wanted the Hebrews to pay attention for successful living. Consequently, we find some of the truths expressed in OT wisdom also already perceived by sages in other ANE lands, like Egypt and Mesopotamia. This does not diminish the nature of the OT as divine revelation; rather, it only shows that the OT also includes experiential wisdom or indirect revelation. This is similar to saying all truth is God's truth. The Hebrews were influenced by their neighbors' extant wisdom writings and wise teachers, but borrowed terminology is not borrowed theology. Much wisdom truth has to do with realities that can be learned from experience and does not require a direct, verbal "thus says the Lord" moment. Yet what is in the OT is God's affirmation of which wisdom truths are most important. Just like physical laws govern the physical universe, God's laws govern the moral universe. That means that certain aspects of life are discernable by any human. An Egyptian or Mesopotamian or Hebrew could observe how certain consequences are not always but are usually associated with certain choices or behaviors. A wise person in any of these cultures would advise for or against certain lifestyle choices because the odds are they would lead to life or death, success or failure (e.g., for honesty or against theft or sexual promiscuity). As a result, we find some parallel wisdom in the OT that appears also in other ANE wisdom texts; but in general the OT wisdom is more elevated ethically and morally, and naturally includes unique wisdom related to the "fear of Yahweh [יהוה]" not found elsewhere. Some of the best-known examples are the similarity between Proverbs and the Egyptian "Instructions of Amen-em-ope" and Assyrian "Teachings of Ahiqar" (cf., e.g., Matthews 1991, 190–98). The latter has a number of parallels with verses in the OT Psalms. The extant documents likely are not originals but are based on earlier sources.

Proverbs (Hebrew; cf. NIV)		Amen-em-ope (Egyptian; 1200–1000 B.C.)	
15:17	Better only vegetables than meat with family conflict	6:9	Better one loaf with happiness than wealth with sorrow
17:5	Mocking the poor is also contempt for [God]	25:24	Do not make fun of the handicapped
22:17–18	Keep [what I teach] in your heart	1:3	Lock my words in your heart
22:20–21	I wrote thirty sayings	Ch. 30	Study these thirty sections
22:22	Do not exploit the poor	2:2	Do not steal from the poor
22:25	Do not befriend a hothead	9:13	Do not embrace fools
22:28; cf. 23:10	Do not move an ancient boundary stone	6:7	Do not covet another's land

Proverbs (Hebrew; cf. NIV)		Amen-em-ope (Egyptian; 1200–1000 B.C.)	
23:4	Do not ruin yourself seeking riches	Ch. 7; lines 13–14	Work only for necessities
25:21–22	Feed your enemy and God will reward you	2:5	Feed fools until they are full . . . and ashamed

Proverbs (Hebrew; cf. NIV)		Ahiqar (Assyrian; eighth century B.C.)	
6:1–5	Do what is necessary to free yourself from a debt quickly	9: lines 130–34	Pay back a loan as soon as possible
13:24; cf. 19:18	If you spare the rod, you hate your child	6: line 81	Spare the rod, spoil the child
20:20	Those who curse parents will be snuffed out like a light	9: line 137	The gods curse those who do not honor their parents
26:2	A misspoken word never rests, like a sparrow	7; line 98	A word is a bird, it flies away and never returns
27:3	A fool's anger is heavier than stone or sand	8; line 111	Nothing (even a load of sand or salt) is heavier than debt

In the OT especially, wisdom is not about intellectual but moral ability. The opposite of the wise person is the fool, who is not stupid or ignorant but spiritually and ethically deficient. Hebrew wisdom is found not only in the so-called Wisdom Books (Job, Proverbs, Ecclesiastes) but also in the Psalter and among the Prophets. A wisdom text is often identified by the contrast being made between the righteous or wise and the wicked or foolish person. A wise person does what is right or just and generally is rewarded with a successful or "blessed" life in terms of longevity and satisfaction. According to Psalm 14:1 (= 53:1), a fool is one who decides to live apart from God's revelation and reality.

LITERARY GENRE

"Wisdom" is not really a genre for a psalm but a theme that occurs in a number of psalms that fit other well-defined literary genres such as Praise or Lament. Other psalms sometimes included in a Wisdom classification actually belong to another major genre, such as Praise or Lament. Such psalms contain a sermonic (wicked versus righteous) or didactic (revelatory word) element, but in terms of structure or form (*Gattung*) belong to another classification. The mere presence of a wisdom verse or pericope does not make a psalm "wisdom" as to its overall purpose or design, e.g., Psalms 11, 27 (lament), and 34, 36, 105–106 (praise). Wisdom, as a broad category, in the OT is often applied to Job, Proverbs, Ecclesiastes, and sometimes to Song of Songs, the latter because it also is called the Song of Solomon. Wisdom truth has to do with experience-based more than prophetic-based information about the right ways to live.

We could say that the Psalms help us know how to feel about God while other books teach us how to think about God (Allen 1980, 41–48). The psalms that have a wisdom component combine this horizontal, experiential truth with the nature of a psalm as response literature. The term "Revelatory" is applied to a certain collection of psalms (not because they alone are revelation, which is another term applicable to all Scripture, but) because they involve divine communication (by whatever means) that is related to God's laws, wisdom, and teachings. In the Wisdom Psalms, there is a wisdom characteristic in which the righteous and the wicked are contrasted. Some psalms called Torah or didactic do not contain this wisdom feature. What they do have is some manner of focus on God's laws or instructions or revealed will, through general creation or specific communication. Yet all psalms fall into the category of "human to heaven" communication, through which God also reveals himself, with subcategories of the right way or Torah (God's revelatory spoken Word).

THREE MODES OF REVELATION IN THE OLD TESTAMENT

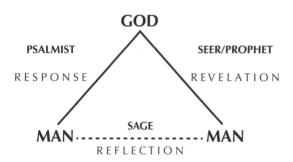

THEOLOGICAL EMPHASES OF THE WISDOM PSALMS

No psalmist thought about creating doctrine when he wrote; however, "Yahweh" (יְהוָה) was and is understood as unchanging. Unlike the Canaanite deities, Yahweh (יְהוָה) offered the security of knowing that he is not whimsical or subject to a coup d'état. His relationship with his people is based on goodness and loyal love. His wrath is only for sustained rebellion, and he never tricks or teases people for entertainment. His rule is everlasting.

Therefore, unlike the Canaanites, the Hebrews did not have to worry if their God would be ruling tomorrow, if his reign might be overturned by a competitor god, leaving the worshipper on the wrong side (the losing side) of the conflict and the god who is in charge. What this means for the modern reader and believer is that whatever is propositional about God's nature is still the case. But God's promises to Israel and certain Israelites are not necessarily the same for the institutional church and some individual Christians. How one reads many texts in the Psalms depends on presupposed theological commitments. Some believe, going in, that whatever is true for Israel is true in some way, even if spiritual rather than literal, for the church. Others have been taught that God's dealings with Israel were restricted to its history, and that not every Scripture transfers directly or indirectly to Christians. The doctrinal emphasis here will be on what is transferable to modern readers, who live in different historical contexts, about this Hebrew God who is also the NT God and Father of Jesus the Christ, the unique Son of God.

Doctrinal
Theologically, the "way of wisdom" psalms present God as having graciously intervened in human life by providing clear commands for his people (Ps. 1). The faithful will receive what has been promised (Ps. 37). God saves those who trust in his precepts and provisions (Ps. 49). But he does not guarantee a trouble- or tragedy-free life to those who are law keepers and can allow lawbreakers to prosper for a season (Ps. 73). Yahweh (יְהוָה) is a rock of safety and a redeemer of those who trust in him, yet his anger can burn toward those who rebel (Ps. 78).

The "words of wisdom" psalms present God as having revealed himself generally in nature and specifically through verbal communication (Ps. 19). His promises and pronouncements are trustworthy and lead to life (Ps. 119).

Practical

Practically the "way of wisdom" psalms base a successful and stable life on following God's laws. Wisdom is the determination to trust and obey God (Ps. 1). Repentance is the road to renewed life, but prosperity is also dependent on the generosity of good and godly people (Ps. 37). Being good does not purchase freedom from pain, problems, or poverty. Wealth is not proof of God's approval (Ps. 49). Suffering is not an excuse to stop trusting God or striving for justice (Ps. 73). Those who forget God's past acts are more likely to falter in their faith (Ps. 78).

Practically, the "word of wisdom" psalms honor God's verbal revelation as the basis for right belief and behavior (Ps. 19). The purity and power of God's verbal communication is praised as a means to restore and revive those who conscientiously and consistently follow divine precepts (Ps. 119). This should not be construed as spiritual or eternal salvation from the guilt of sin earned by good works or obedience in contrast to NT teachings. The context of the psalmist is that of earthly deliverance from sin's temporal consequences, especially when a faithful follower of Yahweh (יהוה) is victimized or persecuted by enemies of God and his servant. God is expected to be faithful to his spoken promises (words) to protect his people.

WISDOM PROMISES

Consistent with the nature of ancient and biblical wisdom, such "promises" are not intended as absolute guarantees but as reliable principles, where the exceptions prove the rule. Those who break laws (are criminals and) typically pay a price that ruins their lives, and the fact that a few "get away with murder" is not a good reason to "tempt fate" and live dangerously. A wise person, therefore, is law-abiding. God is described as overseeing these consequences because he is the source of the moral laws that govern life. Our suffering is usually a natural consequence of bad choices in a world set up to operate properly and productively when the Creator's ethics are followed. Note how at the same time, wisdom books like Job and Ecclesiastes struggle with the seeming contradictions (to such "promises") that wicked people (lawbreakers) sometimes "live long and prosper," while righteous people (law keepers) sometimes die young and experience defeat. Israel as a nation was guaranteed spiritual and material success if obedient, while Israelites could expect but not demand a fruitful and full life when focused on and following Yahweh's decrees (Ps. 1:6a), in spite of advice to the contrary from lawbreakers, whose experience so far might suggest that crime does pay. Eventually it does not (Ps. 1:6b).

OUTLINE OF THE WISDOM PSALMS

WISDOM PSALMS ABOUT GOD'S WAYS / RIGHTEOUSNESS

- Right and Wrong Ways to Live Contrasted (Ps. 1)
- Hallmarks of a Holy Lifestyle (Ps. 15)
- How to Live with Lawbreakers (Ps. 37)
- Do Not Be Fearful When the Wicked Prosper (Ps. 49)
- Do Not Be Envious When the Wicked Prosper (Ps. 73)
- Why It Is Wise to Remain Faithful to God (Ps. 78)
- The Fruitful Benefits of Relying on God (Psalm of Ascents) (Ps. 127)
- The Future Benefits of Reverencing God (Psalm of Ascents) (Ps. 128)
- The Wisdom of Faithful Family Fellowship (Psalm of Ascents) (Ps. 133)
- Right and Wrong Ways to Live Contrasted (145, especially v. 20; cf. Ps. 1:5–6)

WISDOM PSALMS ABOUT GOD'S WORD/REVELATION

- Creational and Verbal Revelation Contrasted (Ps. 19)
- Wisdom of Relying on God's Promise (Ps. 91)
- Wisdom Comes by Prioritizing Divine Revelation (Ps. 111)
- Obeying God's Revelation Leads to Wisdom and Well-Being (Ps. 112)
- What It Means to Love God's Laws (Ps. 119)

FOR FURTHER READING

Chisholm Jr., R. B. (2010). "Interpreting the Psalms: Basic Methods." In *Interpreting the Psalms for Teaching and Preaching*, 16–29. Edited by H. W. Bateman IV and D. B. Sandy. St. Louis: Chalice.

Dockery, D. S. (2010). "The Psalms and Their Influence on Christian Worship." In *Interpreting the Psalms for Teaching and Preaching*, 233–40. Edited by H. W. Bateman IV and D. B. Sandy. St. Louis: Chalice.

Kaiser Jr., W. C. (1993). *The Journey Isn't Over: The Pilgrim Psalms for Life's Challenges and Joys*. Grand Rapids: Baker.

Ralston, T. J. (2010). "Preaching the Psalms: Sermonic Forms." In *Interpreting the Psalms for Teaching and Preaching*, 30–44. Edited by H. W. Bateman IV and D. B. Sandy. St. Louis: Chalice.

Stedman, R. C. (1973). *Psalms of Faith: A Life-Related Study from Selected Psalms*. Ventura, CA: Regal.

Swindoll, C. R. (2012). *Living the Psalms: Encouragement for the Daily Grind*. Brentwood, TN: Worthy.

Taylor, M. A. (2010). "The Psalms Outside the Pulpit: Applications of the Psalms by Women of the Nineteenth Century." In *Interpreting the Psalms for Teaching and Preaching*, 16–29. Edited by H. W. Bateman IV and D. B. Sandy. St. Louis: Chalice.

WISDOM PSALMS ABOUT GOD'S WAYS / RIGHTEOUSNESS

This first section of Wisdom Psalms focuses on a righteous lifestyle as opposed to an unrighteous or wicked lifestyle. These are Psalms 1, 15, 37, 49, 73, 78, 127, 128, and 133. A frequent theme of the wisdom genre is the contrast between people who do what is right and those who do what is wrong, between law-keepers and lawbreakers. Wisdom is not about mental but moral skill. The wise person succeeds at navigating life's pains, problems, and perplexities. The unwise or foolish person, by contrast, may be highly intelligent but fails at life due to frequent immoral or unethical or dangerous decisions. Wisdom Psalms have some of the same themes found in wisdom books like Job, Proverbs, and Ecclesiastes. Some psalms more fully, and others only partially, contain wisdom statements or purposes, but all these psalms include some recognition of a wisdom principle that is relevant to the overall message. Some of these psalms may be classified as another type of psalm in other commentaries. For example, Psalm 145:20 parallels Psalm 1:5–6 but is discussed later in the Praise Psalm volume. It is mentioned here not as a Wisdom Psalm but as a psalm that contains a wisdom element.

This major section of Wisdom Psalms about God's Word contains nine preaching units:

1. Right and Wrong Ways to Live Contrasted (Ps. 1)
2. Hallmarks of a Holy Lifestyle (Ps. 15)
3. How to Live with Lawbreakers (Ps. 37)
4. Do Not Be Fearful When the Wicked Prosper (Ps. 49)
5. Do Not Be Envious When the Wicked Prosper (Ps. 73)
6. Why It Is Wise to Remain Faithful to God (Ps. 78)
7. The Fruitful Benefits of Relying on God (Psalm of Ascents) (Ps. 127)
8. The Future Benefits of Reverencing God (Psalm of Ascents) (Ps. 128)
9. The Wisdom of Faithful Family Fellowship (Psalm of Ascents) (Ps. 133)

cf. Right and Wrong Ways to Live Contrasted (Ps. 145; cf. 1:5–6; Psalm 145 has a wisdom element parallel to Psalm 1:5–6 but is categorized and covered in vol. 3, *Praise Psalms*, of this commentary).

PSALM 1

EXEGETICAL IDEA

Israelites who loved and lived by Yahweh's laws would succeed in life, but those who despised and disobeyed his ways would vanish, having a vain existence.

THEOLOGICAL FOCUS

Success in any endeavor requires fascination and familiarization with God's desired way of living, while corruption and condemnation characterize those who ridicule righteousness.

PREACHING IDEA

Successful living involves loving God's Word and understanding the implications of failing to do so.

PREACHING POINTERS

Unlike the nations surrounding Israel, worshipping and praising Yahweh was more than merely appeasing a pantheon of gods with animal sacrifices. The ancient Israelite understood that praising Yahweh involved more than the lips, and living well involved more than good intentions. The wisdom motif of Psalm 1 contrasted the lifestyle of an Israelite who did right with one who did wrong, according to the religious rules established by God through his prophets like Moses. The secret of this wisdom was delighting in the law of God, recognizing the folly of rejecting God's law, and knowing that God would judge our attitudes and actions in light of his law.

For Christ-followers today, this timeless truth remains virtually unchanged. While many in the world today value experience over truth (and some would even deny the existence of truth at all), this first psalm, then and now, reminds us of the importance of knowing God's Word. Psalm 1 uses vivid imagery from nature and farming to portray the stark contrast between the lives of the righteous and the wicked. This contrast will be noted by people as they see how one is to avoid the unrighteous (v. 1) and in how the Lord watches over the righteous (v. 6). This is an important contrast to make when the lines of right and wrong are being blurred or eliminated altogether.

RIGHT AND WRONG WAYS TO LIVE CONTRASTED

LITERARY STRUCTURE AND THEMES

The psalmist communicated to his fellow Hebrews that God's blessings (fruitfulness in all areas of life) awaited those who maintain a commitment to the commandments of Yahweh in the face of social pressure to be cynical and sinful. He began with the positive and productive rewards of being righteous (obedient to God's ways; vv. 1–3). The psalmist highlighted the privileges and power of having access to verbal revelation from God. Human words and human ideas about God's words can be fallible, but communication from God can only be true and trustworthy. A wise and righteous person will treasure divine revelation by spending time in reflection and repetition. The psalmist then moved to speak of the regrets of an unwise and wicked person (a sinner) will avoid God's advice and admonitions. Each will reap, respectively, positive and productive or negative and destructive consequences (vv. 4–6). The psalmist spoke of sinners and wicked people as a distinct category from those who are righteous and love God's laws. Words like "evil," "wicked," and "sinful" are used interchangeably in the Old Testament (note v. 5). They all have to do with living in opposition to God's revealed will and ways. Here, the disobedient person is antithetical to the person who treasures and trusts Yahweh's verbal revelation of regulations for right behavior and related blessings or rewards. To summarize, the key themes are (1) the delight of devotion to divine directives; (2) the misfortunes of following those who are faithless and foolish; and (3) God's special care for those who do what is right.

- *The Rewards of Lawful Living (1:1–3)*
- *The Regrets of Unlawful Living (1:4–6)*

EXPOSITION (1:1–6)

The nations surrounding Israel appeased a pantheon of gods by sacrifice. The Moabites even practiced child sacrifice, which some Israelites copied (1 Kings 11:7; Jer. 32:35). Abraham prepared to sacrifice his son, but God stopped him since the command to do so was only a test of his faith. A Babylonian cylinder seal depicts a child being sacrificed (Singer 1906, n.p.). The psalmist contrasted the lifestyle of an Israelite who did right with one who did wrong according to the religious rules established by God through his prophets like Moses and reinforced by subsequent prophets like Isaiah and Jeremiah. Psalm 1 has no known setting, date, or author. A late composition is suggested by its choice to be the opening salvo of the Psalter at the time the present arrangement of psalms was decided, perhaps when ordered into Five Books. That an anonymous wisdom poem was chosen to kick-start this collection has led some to view it (often along with Ps. 2) as an introduction to the Psalter proper. The *IVP New Bible Commentary* considers it a song about faith and commitment to a distinct lifestyle and God's revelation (Motyer 1994, n.p.; see also Taylor 2010, 47–62). Israelites who loved and lived by Yahweh's laws would succeed in life, but those who despised and disobeyed his ways would vanish, having a vain existence.

The Rewards of Lawful Living (1:1–3)

The fortunate results of obedience to God's commands were revealed.

1:1. The psalmist's traditional "Blessed is the

man" (אָשְׁרֵי הָאִישׁ) indirectly included women; but in his social context, he was probably thinking primarily or only of males. However, modern Christian application does not require a conclusion that the text "teaches" an exclusive male spiritual and theological leadership in reading the OT Law. The modern translation "Happy" (for אַשְׁרֵי; e.g., in the NRSV and JPS) is not consistent with the immediate literary context. For the psalmist, the fruit of delighting in God's revelation was not about being emotionally happy but spiritually competent and content (in terms of doing what was right because of knowing what was right). An alternative is "Fortunate [or 'Favored'] is the one who refuses to follow" (Ps. 26:4–5). Most versions have "who does not walk," but actually the text says, "has not/never walked" (לֹא הָלַךְ), with the strong negative participle.

1:2. The rendering "meditate" (יֶהְגֶּה; derived from I-הגה) is misleading due to its current usage in English, which does not square with the psalmist's point. The psalmist delighted in, or prioritized, God's law(s) that led to mental rehearsal and reflection. "He will meditate" (יֶהְגֶּה; usual translation) can mean moan, mutter, or speak/proclaim depending on context (HALOT, s.v. "I הגה," 237; Ps. 119:23; Marlowe 2007, 3–18). The psalmist spoke of the person who would meditate "upon" (ב, "in" or "on") God's law (בְּתוֹרָתוֹ; "upon his law").

Meditation in the Psalms

Meditation, even in evangelical circles, is often thought of in a manner not too far removed from what is practiced in Eastern religions, whereby practitioners empty their minds and enter a subjective realm of waiting on insight from the Spirit or spiritual world. A study of the Hebrew words most often translated as "meditation" or "meditate," demonstrates that biblical meditation is nothing of the sort, especially as contextually considered in the book of Psalms. Meditation in the Psalms is objectively based on verbal, divine revelation; and, therefore, comes closer to what we would call revelatory reflection. In short, "meditate" is a misleading translation in light of its current English usage. It is not literally "chewing the cud" (as a popular word picture has it); but illustratively, that procedure may be used to picture an aspect of meditation as portrayed in the Psalms. Anything but silent and subjective, "meditation" is the understanding and utterance of what a revelation from God teaches: the recital, rehearsal, or repetition of what is revealed as God's law (Marlowe, 2007, 3–18).

The lack of multiple and personal copies of texts resulted in people remembering what they had heard read to them by repeating it daily and throughout the day, which likely involved voicing it privately in a low tone or murmur. An Israelite would not have memorized a translation (as we do today). His description "day and night" was a meristic figure of speech that indicated totality (i.e., throughout the day or regularly or daily). The psalmist was not speaking about daily devotions based on a Torah passage. Before OT texts were recorded, God's laws were communicated orally by prophets like Moses and delighting in them had to do with memorization through personal or instructional rehearsal. After texts were recorded, they were costly (in time and money) to reproduce so they were rare and only possessed by the religious leaders. This ancient Israelite psalmist was focused on the importance of the practical need to remember to obey divine instructions as the foundation of a life God will favor (i.e., the fruitfulness he mentions next).

1:3. The reward of knowing and doing what was lawful (right), according to the psalmist, was illustrated by a thirsty, healthy, and productive plant. The streams of water were symbolic of the source of godly knowledge (the LORD's "law" [תּוֹרַת, v. 2] in this case), the regular "drinking" of which ensured life, growth, and good results.

The use of the word "prosper" in many English versions should not mislead the reader into an interpretation focused on some guarantee of material wealth for all who are devoted to God and his directives. Ancient Hebrews included material and spiritual success (often corporately but sometimes as here individually) in the concept of God's blessings, in line with God's promises of temporal national, martial, societal, and theological success and influence among the nations, predicated on obedience and especially on rejecting all foreign gods (idolatry; cf., e.g., Deut. 4:23–28). Words like "spiritual" in this kind of reflection on an ancient Hebrew text had to do with the OT concept of "righteousness," which was essentially right living or law keeping.

This psalm continues with a description of and warning about the negative, empty and destructive consequences of being unrighteous or wicked (disobedient to God's ways) in 1:4–6.

The Regrets of Unlawful Living (1:4–6)
The unfortunate outcomes of ignoring God's commands were revealed.

1:4. By contrast, "blessing" eluded those Israelites who listened to the advice of ungodly people (1:1), and who did not spend time thinking about God's directives (1:2). Who were the ungodly to whom the Israelites listened? They could have been foreigners or fellow, unholy Hebrews. Therefore, they were not like a fruitful (transplanted) tree nourished by a constant source of life-giving "water" (1:3; divine refreshments). Instead, they were unstable and unusable, like the dried up and discarded parts of a crop being blown by the wind (1:4).

1:5. As a result, they were not allowed to stand and influence the righteous (those who want to be obedient) when they gathered for discussion and decision-making ("judgments"; בְּמִשְׁפָּט). The ancient Greek translation of the OT was equivalent of "in the council" where the NIV, for example, has "in the assembly"

(בַּעֲדַת). Wise people did not make decisions "upon the advice of" (בַּעֲצַת) wicked people (1:1b). To rise "in judgment" (1:5a) was restated as "[rise] in the congregation of the righteous" (1:5b) and must never happen: "he must not arise" (לֹא־יָקֻמוּ; imperf. with strong negation, cf. Ten Commandments). In the Baal Cycle, one of El's sons stood up and opposed Baal in the divine assembly, which supported that Psalm 1 (in ANE terms) referred to a judicial assembly to determine justice.

1:6. The psalmist concluded with the encouragement that the LORD (יהוה) "knows" or "acknowledges" ("watches over" in the NIV) the value of righteous or obedient choices (1:6a; since they coincide with his laws); but rebellious conduct is vain and worthless (1:6b; "it will perish"; תֹּאבֵד). The text speaks of a singular "way" (דֶּרֶךְ) of a group ("the righteous ones" or "the wicked ones"). So, the point is not the destiny of an individual who is good or bad, but the general perspective that God governs and guides the consequences of respect for, or rebellion against, of loving or loathing, his laws. These "ways" of those who do right or those who act wickedly are the moral and ethical laws or regulations established by "Yahweh." Positive and productive consequences are naturally generated by right behavior (divine directives) and negative and destructive ones by wrong behavior (disobedience of those directives). In context, this is about temporal and earthly success or failure, a long and/or fruitful versus a short and/or fruitless life. In this verse the KJV renders "wicked ones" (רְשָׁעִים) as "the ungodly."

THEOLOGICAL FOCUS
The exegetical idea (Israelites who loved and lived by Yahweh's laws would succeed in life, but those who despised and disobeyed his ways would vanish, having a vain existence) leads to this theological focus: Success in any endeavor requires fascination and familiarization with God's desired way of living, while corruption

and condemnation characterize those who ridicule righteousness.

The theological thrust of Psalm 1 is about two ways of life. A successful and stable life requires fascination and familiarization with God's verbal revelation, while corruption and condemnation characterize those Israelites, who ridicule obedience. Those who compiled the OT Psalter decided to begin its first "book" (Pss. 1–41), of five books, with a wisdom poem. This is because, like the Wisdom Books (Job, Proverbs, Ecclesiastes), the Psalms emphasize the reality of two ways of life, godly or ungodly, with the respective consequences of life or death. This psalm addresses God always personally as Yahweh, "The Eternal One," never more distantly as "Elohim" (אֱלֹהִים), "[the greatest] God." Perhaps this underlines the close connection between obedience and fellowship. The wisdom motif of the "two ways" draws us back to the first humans, who were challenged with the choice of obedience and "life" (immortality) or disobedience and "death" (mortality). They were commanded not to eat the fruit from the "Right and Wrong [Moral] Knowledge Tree," or another way to explain it is as a literary merism using opposites for totality, therefore "The Omniscient Knowledge Tree." This would explain why the temptation was irresistible. The chance to understand everything is something for which we all long. Life would make sense. Either way Adam and Eve had two paths before them, obedience or disobedience. Biblical wisdom is the skill to make the right choice, to make the decision that enhances rather than erases life.

PREACHING AND TEACHING STRATEGIES

Exegetical and Theological Synthesis

The psalmist, functioning like a sage, provided insight into how one is to live a blessed life. He or she was to avoid walking with the wicked, standing with sinners, and sitting with scoffers

Adam and Eve by C. J. Behem (ca. 1642)

(v. 1). Rather than spending time with this unholy trifecta, one was to invest time in the law of the Lord (or the Bible) in order to live spiritually productive lives that have lasting value (unlike chaff that blows away) (vv. 2–4). Spiritually productive lives help to build spiritually productive communities that have the blessing of the Lord and avoids the spiritually unproductive and perishing ways of the wicked (vv. 5–6).

Sage

A sage is a wise person who seems to function or is recognized in some official or semiofficial capacity in the ANE to provide wise counsel (2 Sam. 15:31–37; Jer. 18:18; Ezek. 7:26). The position is not as clearly defined as that of king or priest, and there is little known about their education or specific function.

Preaching Idea

Successful living involves loving God's Word

and understanding the implications of failing to do so.

Contemporary Connections

What does it mean?

What does it mean that successful living involves loving God's Word and understanding the implications of failing to do so? A professor at the seminary I (Charles) attended used to remind his students that no Christian sets out to be a spiritual failure. And he was not simply speaking of Christians serving in vocational Christian ministry. As Christ-followers, we yearn to live lives pleasing to God and to have the sense of his blessing upon our lives. So why do we often fall frustratingly and miserably short?

The psalmist does not provide all the answers in Psalm 1, but he does point a way forward that is stunning in its simplicity yet profound in its implications.

The first key to avoiding failure and living lives of spiritual blessedness is to choose not to ally one's self with those who will lead one away from the will of God (e.g., the wicked, sinners, and scoffers). The psalmist is not advocating a form of monasticism but simply reminding his hearers that one who wants to live a spiritually meaningful life cannot do so if they take their cues from those whose values are diametrically opposed to God's. Companions like these hinder spiritual growth. Paul reminds us that "a little leaven leavens the whole lump" (1 Cor. 5:6).

Second, spiritually fruitful lives are nurtured by delighting and soaking in God's Word. In our day and age, this has become easier to achieve but paradoxically harder to do. The proliferation of print and especially digital Bibles and Bible study resources mean that access is no longer a problem for most. But, this ease of access leads many to avoid memorizing that which they can look up in seconds on their device, and meditation is hindered by the numerous distractions afforded by the digital age. Those who desire to live spiritually meaningful lives must realize that it takes real time and effort to move from a digital app to life-transforming application. Meditation may be a lost art, but it is not an extinct one. Lives nurtured in God's Word will be like fruitful trees in an otherwise barren wasteland occupied by the wicked.

Third, those who seek to live spiritually successful lives recognize that such lives are enabled by the Lord. It is the Lord who acts on behalf of the righteous and rejects the ways of the wicked. Ultimately, delighting and meditating in God's Word should not be merely another of the prolific self-help strategies that permeates our culture. It is a means, not an end.

Is it true?

Is it true that successful living is characterized by loving God's Word and understanding the implications of failing to do so? Charles Spurgeon noted that "a Bible that's falling apart usually belongs to someone who isn't." God's Word has served as the foundation and impetus for people of faith, motivating them to pursue numerous social reforms that have made the world a better place.

On the flipside, one can see numerous tragic examples of those whose lives have been devastated by walking in the counsel of the wicked, standing in the way of sinners, and sitting in the seat of scoffers. I have personally witnessed this while ministering in a maximum-security prison. And how many times have we witnessed news reports about a famous celebrity who has lived a godless life of material success and then accidently dies as a result of the excesses of that lifestyle or ends his or her own life out of sheer hopelessness or despair that such a lifestyle brings?

Now what?

So, if it is true that successful living involves loving God's Word and understanding the implications of failing to do so, then what should we do?

First, define what God means by "successful living." Success can mean a number of different things to different people. For some, success relates to achieving a particular status or goal that the person deems desirable. Others view success as relative to others, that is, success means that we have done better/more than person X. For still others, success simply means not failing. But what we mean in this commentary by successful living is a life that reflects the moral, philosophical, and theological perfections of God. This is reflected in a life that is blessed by God. Reread Psalm 1 and write down at least three criteria from the psalm for a successful life.

Second, cultivate a love for God's Word. The psalmist writes of delighting *in* and meditating *on* the law of God. The former speaks of an inner encouragement, the sense of spiritual competency and contentment; while the latter speaks of inner nourishment as one consumes and considers God's law specifically, and God's Word generally. Commit to memorizing one Bible verse a week. That would mean at least fifty-two verses in one year.

Third, consider the tragic implications of failing to live a spiritually successful life. It is not simply about what is not gained but about all that is lost. Lost is the opportunity to live a spiritually fruitful life. Lost is the opportunity to be a good and godly influence on others. And lost is the blessing of God himself. Commit yourself today not to be a spiritual failure. I (Charles) used to have a note taped to my desk that read, "Lord, help me to study your Word not so I would be an intellectual giant but so that I would not remain a spiritual midget."

Creativity in Presentation

The preacher or teacher could begin by talking about the slang term "automagically." Although the term "automagically" (or "auto-magic") has been around for decades, it has become popular once again to describe the intuitive magical nature of many of our digital devices. One can simply tap in the first few letters of a name or word and the rest "automagically" appears. After introducing the term, point out that some Christians think that spiritual growth occurs "automagically." But Scriptures like Psalm 1 teach that there really is no "auto" or "magic" involved. Spiritual growth requires commitment and discipline.

For a thought-provoking video, Christopher W. Bailey has written and directed a short four-minute video titled *Psalm 1* (2012). The IMDb site contains the following description: "A short film meditation on Psalm 1. A woman alone in a city follows a mysterious young girl through a magical doorway and embarks on an unexpected journey." Search the internet (e.g., Vimeo) to see if you can find a video of it. The connection to Psalm 1 is a bit ambiguous, but that might be helpful in stimulating a conversation about the psalm.[1]

Contemporary Christian artist Kim Hill's eponymously titled debut album (1988) has a song entitled "Psalm 1" that tracks fairly closely to the words of the psalm.

Use a healthy potted tree and chaff to illustrate Psalm 1:3–4. For chaff, one might purchase a small straw bale available in many arts and crafts stores. These small bales usually have chaff among the straw. One could also contact a wheat farmer. Blowing chaff might make for a messy but effective visual. The point that you want to emphasize here

---

1   If your preaching will be audio and/or video recorded, you may need to purchase a site license to show movie clips, film shorts, or use similar copyrighted audio and/or visual material. In this case, for example, you might simply locate the film on Vimeo and contact the film director through Vimeo or his website at https://www.cbaileyfilm.com. For further guidance, see "6 Things Your Church May Be Doing Illegally," Lifeway Research, September 13, 2018, https://lifewayresearch.com/2018/09/13/6-things-your-church-may-be-doing-illegally.

is that successful living involves loving God's Word and understanding the implications of failing to do so. This simple but profound truth can be summarized into three points.

- To live successfully, love God's Word (1:1–3).

- To live unsuccessfully, reject God's Word (1:4–5).

- There is a difference, according to God's Word (1:6).

DISCUSSION QUESTIONS

1. Explain why it is significant that the book of Psalms begins with a wisdom psalm.

2. How do you define success in life? How does God define a successful life?

3. What does it mean to delight in the law of God?

4. How does one meditate on God's Word?

5. Does obedience to God always lead to prosperity? Why or why not?

6. Does disobedience to God always lead to poverty? Why or why not?

7. How do or can we show love or hatred for God's verbal revelation?

PSALM 15

EXEGETICAL IDEA
The psalmist saw that the person who stood confidently in God's presence was one whose life was characterized by honesty.

THEOLOGICAL FOCUS
People who can approach God with confidence are those who live lives characterized by personal integrity.

PREACHING IDEA
Enjoying access to God is tied to doing right before God and people.

PREACHING POINTERS
The specific circumstances behind Psalm 15 are uncertain. The superscription and content provide little to go on other than its association with David and that he was concerned about personal integrity.

For many today, David's opening question ("Lord, who may dwell in your tent?") seems antiquated, maybe even irrelevant. But this question is not what is out of touch here, but rather the idea that one can approach a holy God in a careless and thoughtless way. Psalm 15 reminds us that enjoying access to God is a privilege, not a right. As a privilege it is not tied to social or economic status, gender, age, or ethnicity, but it is a privilege, nonetheless. Psalm 15 is not a call to ritual, or even doctrinal formalism. It is, however, a call to personal integrity exercised before God and with people.

HALLMARKS OF A HOLY LIFESTYLE

LITERARY STRUCTURE AND THEMES

After the superscription, the psalmist opened his psalm with a question about the qualifications for approaching God (v. 1). He then answered his own question (vv. 2–5). The person qualified for approaching God is someone whose lifestyle was consistently blameless and upright and spoke the truth (v. 2). Their speech was not slanderous, nor did they mistreat or make fun of a person in close community (v. 3). They were people of integrity who despised those who rejected honesty but honored those who revere God's laws and kept a promise at all costs (v. 4). If such people had the means, they lent money to a community member at zero interest, and they could not be bribed to hurt an innocent party (v. 5a). The psalmist concluded his psalm with a declaration about such people: they stood confidently before God (v. 5b).

This very short psalm likely was a poem or song that reflected a wisdom theme and depicted a wise person as opposed to a foolish or wicked person. While the word "fool" did not appear, wickedness was foolishness. The fool was morally not intellectually inept. The psalmist's theme of Psalm 15 addressed people with integrity and their ability to approach God.

- ***The Psalmist's Question (15:1)***
- ***The Psalmist's Answer (15:2–5a)***
- ***The Psalmist's Conclusion (15:5b)***

EXPOSITION

In the editorial superscription, "A מִזְמוֹר about King David" in Psalm 14 (which most date postexilic), "David" was presented as one concerned about wicked people who did not seek God and who devoured good people like bread (perhaps by slander at least in part). In Psalm 16,

the psalmist presented David, who sought safety and vowed not to speak about the blood of those who followed false gods. Perhaps Psalm 15 was purposefully placed between these two psalms as an interlude in which David reflected on the wickedness of slander. The title that identified Psalm 15 as Davidic seems to correlate with Psalm 24, "which is generally thought to have been written for the translation [movement] of the Ark to the tent which David had prepared for it in Zion (1 Sam. vi. 17)" (Kirkpatrick, 1939, 69). As to genre, although debated, some call Psalm 15 an Entrance Liturgy in light of a comparable Egyptian inscription about requirements for temple admission or audience with God (Anderson, [1981] 1995a, 135–36, citing Kraus, 1960, 111; Ringgren, 1963, 120). Regardless, the psalmist saw that the person who stood confidently in God's presence was one whose life was characterized by honesty.

The Psalmist's Question (15:1)

He considered what qualifies someone to serve God.

15:1. The psalmist asked and answered his own question: "Who is qualified to stand in God's presence, in his holy place such as the Tent of Meeting or Tabernacle?" (15:1). The phrase "in your tent" parallels "on your holy hill."

> **Tent of Meeting or Tabernacle**
> The juxtaposition of "tent" (אֹהֶל) and "holy hill" (הַר קָדְשֶׁךָ) in Psalm 15:1 on the surface is confusing because the "tent" suggests the tabernacle while the "hill" suggests Mount Zion and the temple. Perhaps the psalmist was writing from a time when he could look back at, and refer to, each

as a synthetic type of parallel ("A, and also B"; cf. Kugel 1981, *in toto*). If not, then he would have had in view a hill with the tabernacle. In this case the "hill" is part of an idiom for a "holy place." In Psalm 27:5, the NIV translates this "tent" as "tabernacle." However, in 1 Chronicles 15:1, David built a "tent" for the box ("ark") containing the covenant documents in David's City. This city is thought to be on a hill just outside the old city walls of Jerusalem, and part of Mount Moriah. Mount Zion is essentially the site of the Jebusite town David conquered (2 Sam. 5:6–9). The tabernacle (or "meeting tent"; אֹהֶל מוֹעֵד) was a portable tent used by the Hebrews and viewed as God's dwelling place. There was a courtyard outside the tent and then a "holy place" and "most holy place" inside. Within these, the Levitical priests carried out various functions and sacrifices.

The Psalmist's Answer (15:2–5a)

He determined that the qualifications were lawfulness, honesty, guarded speech, reliability, and lack of greed.

15:2. While some commentators suggest that Yahweh spoke here, it's the psalmist who answered his own question. The one who could dwell with God had to have a lifestyle (lit., "walk") characterized by doing what is right and telling the truth. The verb for "walk" (הוֹלֵךְ) is a participle and can stress habitual behavior.

15:3. While the verb (רָגַל) could mean "to go on foot" or "to spy," the psalmist meant something concerning the tongue. The Syriac version has "he does not deceive with his tongue" (see BHS text critical note). The NIV renders it "has no slander" and the NETS (= LXX) has "did not beguile" (the Greek word [ἐδόλωσεν] means "to distort; deceive"). Literally, the psalmist spoke of "spying/wandering with the tongue," and the parallel line (15:3b) applies this to a friend or neighbor. So what is described is the dissemination of some sort of misinformation about someone in close community. Modern

versions often use "slander." The KJV has "backbiteth." The end of 15:3 speaks of one who does not raise "reproach" (חֶרְפָּה) against a neighbor. This Hebrew noun (here a direct object) has to do with a shameful taunt. The idea is that of making fun of or ridiculing someone for no good reason, tearing someone down just to build up oneself by contrast.

15:4. The psalmist spoke of a "vile person" (נִמְאָס; NIV, KJV) or "the wicked" (NETS, NRSV), which described people who were the opposite of the one "fearing Yahweh." "Vile" (מאס) has to do with refusal or rejection and describes the "one who is rejected" (נִמְאָס; pass.). But was he or she rejected by God or by the community? The Syriac speaks of a detestable person. Perhaps this person was one who fled from, so did not fear/follow, Yahweh. The righteous person honored those who feared God and kept their vows even to the point of personal "harm" (לְהָרַע; the root רעע is "to do bad" or "wrong." Here the form indicates "cause harm"). This righteous person was someone who never went back on their promise. The NETS captures the sense of meaning the best: "he who swears to his fellow and does not renege." He refused to break a vow under any circumstance.

15:5. Finally, the psalmist spoke of "usury" (בְּנֶשֶׁךְ; NIV, KJV). Yet the idea of "usury" was more of requiring "interest on a loan" (cf. NET, ESV, NASB, NRSV, NLT). Nevertheless, it's unclear whether it described "any interest" or only "excessive interest." When we use the word "usury" today, it typically suggests the latter (resulting from Calvin's application to his times). If such an OT text condemns loaning money for any interest, then "usury" is an inaccurate translation for a modern audience. When the KJV was being read in the seventeenth century, "usury" may have had a different usage in English than today. Regardless, the data suggest that in OT times, charging any interest to a fellow Hebrew was forbidden (e.g., Exod. 22:25;

Lev. 25:36–37; Deut. 23:19–20; as is still true in the Arabic or Islamic world today among Muslims). In this case the proper translation would be "who does not lend his money at interest."

The Psalmist's Conclusion (15:5b)

He concluded that an honest person is forever unshakable (i.e., able to stand with confidence before God).

THEOLOGICAL FOCUS

The exegetical idea (the psalmist saw that the person who stood confidently in God's presence was one whose life was characterized by honesty) leads to this theological focus: People who can approach God with confidence are those who live lives characterized by personal integrity.

The theological focus of this psalm underscores God's concern with how we use words, especially about others in our community. Righteousness is rooted in honesty and integrity. This psalm has close connections with James's warnings about the misuse of the tongue in his NT book. The person to be despised, who is the opposite of those who fear God (v. 4), is likely the one just described or implicated (vv. 2–3) as untruthful, a slanderer and gossip, who uses words as weapons. Such a person is also likely greedy and would never give monetary help without thinking first of personal benefit from the profit margin (v. 5a). He would even verbally harm an innocent person for a payoff (v. 5b). God will not tolerate such people in his presence (15:5b). The use of words and wealth is a litmus test for a righteous person.

PREACHING AND TEACHING STRATEGIES

Exegetical and Theological Synthesis

Psalm 15 begins with a question that is not intended to solicit answers (What does 2 + 2 equal?) or to ponder the imponderables (What is life?). It is a question to elicit reflection and self-examination. Namely, who is able to enjoy access to God (here represented by the tabernacle ["your tent"])? David (or the LORD) answers the question through a list of criteria that are likely representative rather than exhaustive. One who wants to enjoy access to God lives blamelessly and upright (15:2a), speaks the truth and does not slander (15:2b–3a), does not mistreat others (15:3b–c), distinguishes between the vile and righteous (v. 4a–b), keeps his word (v. 4c), and acts in financial integrity (v. 5a–b). In sum, as Donald Williams notes, this psalm "covers our walk, our works, and our words" (Williams, 1986, 119). And we could add another *w*, namely, our wealth. The one who lives rightly before God is able to enjoy steadfast access to God.

As Christians we do not have a physical tabernacle/temple as Israel did. Rather, our bodies are the temple of the Holy Spirit (1 Cor. 6:19), and we are called to be royal priests (1 Pet. 2:9) who offer ourselves to God as living sacrifices (Rom. 12:1). Yet, the idea of enjoying God's presence as more of a privilege rather than a right is still true today. For example, in the Sermon on the Mount, Jesus teaches that interpersonal reconciliation is a prerequisite to offering one's gift at the altar (Matt. 5:23–24). Similarly, Paul calls Christ followers to "lift up holy hands" (1 Tim. 2:8), and James likewise to come to God with clean hands and pure hearts (Jas. 4:8).

Preaching Idea

Enjoying access to God is tied to doing right before God and people.

Contemporary Connections

What does it mean?

What does it mean that enjoying access to God is directly correlated to doing right before God and people?

Two thoughts merit further explanation here. First, we need to try and understand how tabernacle worship might have looked for Israel in David's day (assuming Davidic authorship of the psalm). Unfortunately, there is not much that can be said about specifics other than to reflect on what the Torah had recorded concerning the tabernacle and its activities. If the psalm reflects the time of the first temple built by Solomon one could state a bit more. But what does seem fairly clear is that sacred space tended to be egalitarian and not restricted to a particular age, gender, or social status. However, it was also segregated with increasingly restricted access the closer one approached the place of God's presence (the Holy of Holies; Wilson talks in terms of "concentric circles"; see Wilson, 2002, 301–302). And it was also a place of specific protocol. How one approached the tabernacle (and later the temple) was regulated. All these concepts help to inform Psalm 15. The way to God was open, but it was not wide open.

Second, we need to see the vital connection between religion and ethics. In the ancient Near East, one's relationship to God had much more to do with devotion than ethics. But in Torah, devotion and ethics are strongly intertwined. The Ten Commandments are frequently divided into the first four relating to one's vertical relationship to God and the last six to the horizontal relationship involving one another. Later, the prophet Micah asked the question, "What does the LORD require of you?" And then he answered it with the horizontal "to do justice, and to love kindness" followed by the vertical "to walk humbly with your God" (Mic. 6:8).

Is it true?

Is it true that enjoying access to God is directly correlated to doing right before God and people? The answer seems obvious when we consider that access can be restricted in other areas of life. For example, getting security clearance from the United States government is not an easy task. Applicants have to undergo a thorough evaluation to determine if they are loyal to the U.S. government and are free from influence by foreign individuals, are honest, trustworthy, morally upright, mentally and psychologically sound, and have avoided criminal activity. If the government has standards for those who seek access, why should we be surprised that God has standards?

But some might argue that the idea of linking access to God with one's actions is fine in the Old Testament, but it seems out of place in the New Testament. It does not seem to fit our conceptions of God or a "come as you are" theology so prevalent today. One might ask, "Where is the grace in all that?" But let us begin with some distinctions. For one thing, we are not talking about a works-based salvation that requires you to do right before you get right with God. This psalm is addressing people of faith, not making people of faith. Nor is this passage about some form of puritanical legalism.

Rather, Psalm 15 recognizes the interrelationship between the vertical dimension between God and people and the horizontal dimension between people. Our relationship to God affects how we treat others, and how we treat others affects our relationship to God. This truth carries over from the Old Testament into the New Testament. This can be seen in Jesus's so-called "Great Commandment": "'Love the Lord your God with all your heart and with all your soul and with all your mind.' This is the first and greatest commandment. And the second is like it: 'Love your neighbor as yourself.' All the Law and the Prophets hang on these two commandments" (Matt. 22:37–40 NIV). But note that Jesus is quoting from the Old Testament here, namely, Deuteronomy 6:5 and Leviticus 19:18. This idea of love for God and love for others is portrayed in absolute terms in texts like 1 John 4:7–12. So, it is still true today that the ability to enjoy access to God is tied to doing right before God (vertical) and people (horizontal).

Now what?

If the ability to enjoy access to God is tied to doing right before God and people, then what should we do?

First, determine that you really want to enjoy access to God. Such an application might seem absurd, but more than a few are quite comfortable in their humdrum spiritual lives. Drawing near to God will challenge a person to the core of their being. After all, we call them spiritual disciplines and not spiritual "easies." But those who have been in God's presence know that there is no better place to be this side of eternity.

Second, develop a hunger for true righteousness. How does one do this? Perhaps the place to begin is to think about how one gets physically hungry. Physical hunger comes from an absence of food. So maybe before we develop a hunger for righteousness, we have to stop "eating" that which is not righteousness. Then when we are no longer sated by the things of this world we will seek to be filled with God's food.

Third, devote oneself to ethical living. Do people right. In the 1990s there was a movement using the acronym WWJD (What would Jesus do?). This movement resulted in a whole cottage industry of Christian kitsch and was theologically problematic. But its heart was in the right place. It recognized the vital role of Christian ethics in interpersonal relationships. This is not a call to wear Christian wristbands but a call to doing right to others as a way of drawing near to God.

Creativity in Presentation

One could introduce the message by noting that there are numerous exclusive clubs or resorts in the world usually reserved for the rich and famous. The qualifications and requirements might differ, but they all have them.

So, if that is the case with human institutions, why should we be surprised that a holy God has some requirements for those who seek to access to him?

One could also begin by referring to offering envelopes that some churches still use. These envelopes have checkboxes to check off such as being present, bringing your offering, attending Sunday school, having your Bible, etc. These envelopes allow you to grade yourself and some churches even keep records. While this might be helpful, what if we put God's checklist from Psalm 15, especially verses 2–5, on the envelopes? Now our envelopes would have things like walked blamelessly, spoke the truth, did not slander, was a good neighbor, etc. Now that might get really interesting!

Clearnote Songbook has a song simply entitled "Psalm 15: Your Holy Hill" that would be suitable either before or after the message. Lead sheets and PowerPoint are available to help facilitate the performance.[1]

Whether you choose one of these suggestions or use one of your own, you will want to reinforce the idea that enjoying access to God is tied to doing right before God and people.

- "Who enjoys access to God" is a question worth asking (15:1).

- How one enjoys access to God is an answer worth hearing (15:2–5a).

- What we have with access to God is a promise worth believing (15:5b).

---

1   Jody Killingsworth and Jake Mentzel, "Psalm 15 | Your Holy Hill (MSAL)," Clearnote Songbook, 2017, http://clearnotesongbook.com/song/psalm-15-your-holy-hill-msal. Killingsworth notes that "nearly all of our songs are licensed under the following terms: Creative Commons license BY-NC-SA graphic. This means . . . you do not need a CCLI membership in order to use our songs. You may copy, distribute, and perform our works for free." Jody Killingsworth, "Why Clearnote Songbook . . .," Clearnote Songbook (blog), November 16, 2012, http://clearnotesongbook.com/blog/2012/11/why-clearnote-songbook.

DISCUSSION QUESTIONS

1. How would such a poem/song function in the community?

2. What societal conditions might have led to such a composition?

3. How does such wrongdoing keep one from remaining before God?

4. According to Psalm 15:2, what responsibilities do people have before God?

5. What does "will not be shaken" mean for a person who obeys verses 2–5?

PSALM 37

EXEGETICAL IDEA
The psalmist taught his readers not to worry that unlawful people had health and wealth, not to be discouraged, and not to turn to violence as an answer, but to keep trusting God because God's enemies would be defeated.

THEOLOGICAL FOCUS
God rewards those who delight in him and are dedicated to his ways, but God scoffs at and will thwart those who reject his ways.

PREACHING IDEA
Dwelling on those who do wrong can keep you from doing what is right and trusting God.

PREACHING POINTERS
The superscription of Psalm 37 is sparse on details, but many of the moral deficiencies alluded to seem to be ingrained in most societies, and Israel was no different. Later prophets such as Amos and Habakkuk would frequently condemn Israel and Judah for such sins. The psalmist faced wrongdoing head-on by encouraging his audience not to let evildoers get under their skin. Two basic reasons were given for not dwelling on the wicked. First, the success of the evildoer is temporal, and they would ultimately be judged (vv. 2, 9a, 10, 13, 15, 17, 20, 22a, 38). Second, the righteous would ultimately be delivered and blessed (vv. 6, 7, 11, 18, 22, 24, 28, 29, 33, 34, 39, 40). So, much of the rest of the psalm addresses righteous living.

Today is no different. The success of those who have cut moral and ethical corners to get where they are bothers us. More often than not, "Nice guys finish last." This often carries over into the spiritual realm. Most of us probably know of someone who was faithful in their walk with the Lord but who then was stricken with some unimaginable disease, while another person living a life of debauchery continues as a paragon of good health.

HOW TO LIVE WITH LAWBREAKERS

LITERARY STRUCTURE AND THEMES

The superscription for Psalm 37 is the same as that used for Psalm 35, "regarding David" (לְדָוִד). On the one hand, the structure, takes the form of a Hebrew acrostic, using twenty-one letters of the Hebrew alphabet, in order (however one letter, ע, is missing; cf. 37:28b in BHS) to begin each of the mostly four-line stanzas, of which each is more or less an independent unit, which some commentators describe as proverbial. On the other hand, the psalm may be divided into two major sections, the second having three subpoints. The psalmist began with counsel about how the faithful can deal with the confusion caused when sinners prosper (vv. 1–11). He continued by describing the foolishness and fate of lawbreakers in three exemplary sections (vv. 12–20, 21–31, 32–40). The major theme that runs throughout the psalm is that the material success of sinners or unbelievers masks the reality of their ultimate spiritual failure and its consequences.

- ***The Problem of the Wicked Prospering (37:1–11)***
- ***The Foolishness and Fate of the Wicked (37:12–40)***
  - *The Wicked Plot (37:12–20)*
  - *The Wicked Deception (37:21–31)*
  - *The Wicked Pursuit (37:32–40)*

EXPOSITION

People who disobeyed God's Law appear throughout the Old Testament. This even includes spiritual heroes like Moses (who committed murder and needed anger management), and David (who committed adultery and had the woman's husband killed). The first humans, Adam and Eve, set the stage for all others by directly disobeying a clear divine command because they questioned its reasonableness. Jacob, who became Israel (meaning "strives with God") was pathologically deceptive. The contrast made in the Old Testament was not between those who sin and do not sin, but between those who strive for godliness and those who habitually ignore and rebel against God's directives. Psalm 37 was consciously crafted soon after Psalm 36. Having talked in Psalm 36 about the deficiencies and sure defeat of the wicked, Psalm 37 tells the faithful not to be worried about the wicked, for they will diminish in influence and disappear. So, the psalmist focused on the rewards of obedience that far outweigh the threats of lawbreakers. Again, due to its contrast of the righteous and wicked, this psalm has been positioned as a wisdom psalm by some previous scholars, such as Mowinckel, and more specifically as "non-cultic" (Mowinckel, 1992, II:111). Consequently, the psalmist taught his readers not to worry that unlawful people had health and wealth, not to be discouraged, and not to turn to violence as an answer, but to keep trusting God because God's enemies would be defeated.

The Problem of the Wicked Prospering (37:1–11)

The psalmist advised law-keepers how to handle frustration over lawbreakers who prosper.

37:1. The righteous were advised they should not (אַל) get angry or jealous when lawbreakers prospered (see v. 7b). Some versions speak of the lawbreakers as "evildoers" (KJV) but, as mentioned before, "evil" may be too strong for current usage. The word often rendered "evil men" (מְרֵעִים; NIV) is restated in the parallel line of this verse as "workers of iniquity" (KJV) or "those who do wrong" (NIV). The wrongdoing is more inclusive than the more narrow or devilish kind of crimes "evil" may suggest. The Hebrew word translated "evil doers" (> מְרֵעִים רעע) is a participle, suggesting characteristic or frequent moral foolishness. It did not have the same meaning for these ancient Hebrews as the English word "evil" does today.

37:2. The gains of disobedient people in Israel would soon fade away just like grass, which was green only for a season. This was because God would prove his followers right and these wicked people wrong, a point the psalmist will restate in verse 6.

37:3. Instead, the psalmist's readers were to "trust" (בְּטַח) God and keep doing good even if it sometimes seemed like cheaters prospered. Trust and obedience were the way to ensure and maintain an abundant existence in the land (37:3).

This second poetic line is obscure. Literally it reads, "Dwell land! And shepherd faithfulness!" The Greek OT translated this something like "encamp in the land, and you will be tended by its wealth" (NETS; cf. LXX). The KJV sees these words as resultative, "so shalt thou dwell in the land, and verily thou shalt be fed." The JPS has "abide in the land and remain loyal." The NIV paraphrases "dwell in the land and enjoy safe pasture." The root word for "to shepherd" (or "to feed," הער) may have been chosen because it provides assonance with "wrongdoers" (עער; v. 1), although at the same time an opposite meaning (i.e., instead of doing wrong, focus on being faithful so as to ensure being fed; v. 3b).

37:4. Those who delighted in Yahweh would have their prayers answered. But the psalmist again used an imperative, calling the reader to "Take delight in God!" And then God would give them their "heart-felt petitions" (מִשְׁאֲלֹת).

37:5. The Jewish people were to hand over their plans to God. The imperative "commit" (גּוֹל) is based on the verb "to roll away" (גָּלַל) that has various renderings: "reveal" (ἀποκάλυψον; LXX), "disclose" (NETS), "commit" (NIV), and "Leave all to the LORD" (JPS). Regardless of the translation, the point is that God will reward their faithfulness. "Trust! [same verb as before] upon him and he, he will act." This emphasized that Yahweh was the one who would answer prayers and enact what the psalmist stated next.

37:6. God would exonerate his people who have been falsely accused and mistreated with injustice by those who disobey God. They will be justified in the clear light of day. Justice will eventually roll down like thunderous waters. "Your righteousness" (צִדְקֶךָ; NIV, KJV) is better understood as "vindication" (NETS, JPS, NRSV; cf. LXX). This is because the parallel line has "and your justice" (וּמִשְׁפָּטֶךָ). In the context of oppression by wicked people, the promise is that God will bring about a right judgment (not that right behavior would be made known, although "being in the right" would be).

37:7. But this would not necessarily come about overnight. So, stay calm (דֹּם; "Be silent!"), be still or silent before Yahweh, and wait on him to act (37:7a). The KJV has "Rest . . . wait patiently"; but the NETS (cf. LXX) says "Submit . . . and appreciate." The verb for "be silent" is *dom* (דֹּם) and in English we sometimes use "dumb" for speechless (as in "deaf and dumb"). This can be a memory device for Hebrew students. The word for "Wait [patiently]!" (וְהִתְחוֹלֵל) is from a root meaning otherwise "writhe, travail" (I חִיל). This term and its reflexive form were perhaps chosen to underline the likely feelings of discomfort and anguish while they waited for God to act in his, rather than their, time. As the psalm began, the poet now repeated (because it is so hard to obey) the need for God's people not to get angry or agitated (same word as in verse 1) when they observe ("wicked"—understood but not in the text) people "continuing to prosper" (מַצְלִיחַ; ptc.) along the way as they "keep making/inventing" (עֹשֶׂה; ptc.) "[ungodly—understood but not in the text] plans/schemes" (מְזִמּוֹת).

37:8. Consequently, the psalmist ordered his readers to quit being angry and abandon wrath. He commanded them to "stop" (הֶרֶף). The reason was because they might lose control and "perhaps do something bad" (אַךְ־לְהָרֵעַ).

37:9. The people of Israel needed to understand that all who "keep doing bad things" (מְרֵעִים; ptc.; including them) would "be cut off [יִכָּרֵתוּן]," which may mean killed (37:9a). But on the other hand, all who "maintain hope" (וְקֹוֵי; ptc.) toward Yahweh would inherit the land (37:9b) as promised. This is similar (and a background) to Jesus's words about the "meek inheriting the earth" ("earth" probably should be "land" contextually). They would experience the promised prosperity eventually, if patient and obedient. The "meek" were the gentle, those who refrained from violence as a solution (resorting to anger or revenge because God is taking too long to act and the "bad guys" seem to be winning; Zeph. 3:12; cf. Matt. 5:5). This was moral strength, although the lawbreakers would see it as weakness.

37:10. The psalmist continued (וְעוֹד; "And yet") his thoughts about the wicked. Before long the wicked in the land would be displaced. This statement is reminiscent of Deuteronomy and the prophets of doom like Amos (4:1–5:17) in northern Israel and Habakkuk (1:1–11) in southern Judah about invasions from foreign nations.

37:11. The psalmist described these newcomers as "gentle persons" (at least this is how the LXX translates עֲנָוִים), who would inherit the land and establish peace or wholeness (37:10–11). These people are in contrast to "the wicked," who are violent and seeking to harm them in this context (see vv. 12–14). They are restated as "those who do right" in 37:12 and as the "poor and needy" in 37:14. They were described as "blameless" in 37:18. So, the idea seems to be that those who rely on God to deal with their enemies and do not turn to personal vengeance will be rewarded and create a more peaceful society. This conforms to the summation of OT law found in Leviticus 19:18 and reinstated by Jesus (Matt. 22:37–40) and Paul (Rom. 13:8–10): "Do not seek revenge or bear a grudge against anyone among your people, but love your neighbor as yourself" (Lev. 19:18a NIV).

The Foolishness and Fate of the Wicked (37:12–40)

Wicked people were described as deserving divine wrath because they are proactively against the righteous, even seeking to kill them.

Verses 12, 21, and 32, each begin with a participle describing the "wicked" (רָשָׁע) in different ways.

The Wicked Plot (vv. 12–20)

Lawbreakers were viewed as constantly scheming in anger against law-keepers.

37:12. In the meantime, the wicked continually plot (זֹמֵם; ptc.) against the righteous "and keep gnashing [וְחֹרֵק; ptc.] their teeth" at them. To "gnash teeth" was an idiom for "anger" based on that emotion being conveyed by clinched jaws or grinding teeth. One wonders why, since they are the ones who prosper in spite of their sin.

37:13. By way of an implied contrast, the psalmist identified Yahweh as laughing at them (37:13a; Pss. 2:1–4; 59:8) because "he has seen [רָאָה]" that their "day" (= time of defeat) will arrive [Ps. 37:13b; יָבֹא]. God already was aware of their fate. Some commentators (e.g., Open Theists) wonder if God's foreknowledge makes an event inevitable, in that the action is preordained in such a manner that God is ultimately responsible and the people involved actually lack responsibility because they are only doing what God has designated. If a text says that God knows what will happen, then he in effect makes it happen. However, God, if omniscient, can logically know what someone will freely choose to do without divine coercion being required. Otherwise, God would be guilty of all that happens in the future, good or bad, or he must be defined as less than all-knowing (i.e., open to surprises as Open Theology claims). A text in a psalm, however, as this one should not be enlisted as a dogmatic defense of theology proper or used philosophically, since it mainly reflected the psalmist's confidence that God would judge his enemies. A psalm is not a theological treatise; rather, it is an emotion-laden expression of poetic or musical praise, complaint, prayer, penitence, and/or prudence.

37:14. These wicked people deserve punishment because (37:14) they "have opened [פָּתְחוּ]" (= have pulled out) their swords and "have walked [וְדָרְכוּ]" (= have bent back) bows with arrows in order (1) to knock down (לְהַפִּיל) the disadvantaged or "poor [עָנִי] and needy [וְאֶבְיוֹן]," and (2) to slaughter those whose "way" (lifestyle) is upright. The blended meaning of the parallelism is that the wicked use their weapons to kill the righteous who lack the means to defend themselves. At least that is the intention.

37:15. But the psalmist had certain hope that God would intervene and protect so that the enemy runs himself through with his own sword and his bow breaks.

37:16. The psalmist then spoke of behaviors. He used the word "good" (טוֹב) in a comparative sense of "better." He contended that right behavior was superior to having a lot of material possessions and doing wrong. There is an imbalance here in that the psalmist contrasted the material paucity of the righteous with the abundance of many wicked people. The parallelism would suggest "many righteous" were implied in the first line.

But why were the righteous necessarily impoverished and not the wicked? Why were right and riches juxtaposed? Would not the best be to have both goodness and gold? And were not some poor people also greedy and immoral? Why did the psalmist equate wealth and wickedness (Prov. 28:6)? The reason is because in the ancient world most rich people attained their wealth through criminal and corrupt means. Wealth was in the hands of a small percentage of powerful people. Most people were "poor" by comparison and had no way to become rich. In the ancient setting, unless wealth was inherited it was often gained through cheating or abusing others). Culturally, the ancient audience equated rich people with criminal behavior, as many OT texts demonstrate (Marlowe, 2009, 68–81). For example, Proverbs 18:23, Isaiah 53:9, and Micah 6:12.

37:17. The psalmist then explained why it was better to be good and poor rather than bad and rich: because "the arms" (= power) of those who do wrong will be broken while Yahweh will keep supporting (ptc.; וְסוֹמֵךְ) the ones who do right.

37:18. The LXX says that the Lord knows "the ways" (rather than the MT's "days") of the "blameless" (תְּמִימִם; again, note a plural form but often translated as a collective singular; v. 18a). This Hebrew word does not indicate "sinless" as it is often applied to people who were guilty of sins but also were considered righteous as well (such a Noah, Gen. 6:9b; and Job in Job 1:1, 8; 2:3; note that the author of Psalm 26 claimed that he had led this kind of life [vv. 1, 11]). God commanded Abram to be blameless (Gen. 17:1). The ruler of Tyre was blameless (from the time he was "created" or crowned as king) until he committed wickedness in how he traded with other nations (Ezek. 28:5, 15–16, 18).

Ruler of Tyre

The ruler of Tyre cannot be contextually interpreted properly as a sinless angel who rebelled and was no longer blameless, who became Satan (Block 1998, 28–120; contra, McCune, 2008, 1:376–80; cf. Green 1981, 36–39; and Cooper 1994, 264–70). However, such approaches tend to be not exegetical as much as spiritual. The same person is in view throughout the chapter, and he is first judged and then lamented in the same pattern as the city of Tyre previously (Ezek. 26, judgment; then Ezek. 27, lamentation; also, the same is true of Egypt and its pharaoh in Ezekiel 9–32). The author intended and his audience heard these words only in terms of human kingdoms and kings. Nothing about the nature of the language or literature suggests double meanings were involved. When Ezekiel says that this ruler was a "cherub," he meant that the king had sphinx statues (i.e., with his head on a winged bull or lion body, as is well known from archaeology) that guarded the entrance into the temple garden, which had Eden-like beauty (Ezek. 28:13–14; the prophet uses Eden metaphorically [Ezek. 31:16–18; 36:35]). When the historical and cultural contexts are applied to the exegesis of this passage, all the words fit with the actual circumstances of such a king. And most do not fit with Satan at all (e.g., covered in precious stones, which this king was in terms of his bejeweled robe and canopy and statues).

"The LORD is concerned for the needs of the blameless" (JPS). Whether Yahweh knows ways or days, Psalm 37:18b adds that their possessions will exist perpetually. "Forever" (for לְעוֹלָם) is standard, but this rendering has metaphysical or philosophical overtones that likely do not conform to how the ancient audience understood this concept. The poet was telling his audience that the rewards of righteousness last until death. No data show that he used this word in relation to an unending afterlife.

37:19. Building on verse 18, the psalmist expanded on the rewards of the righteous. They (the blameless) will not be ashamed in bad times, that is, for example, they would have plenty during a famine. Naturally, Elijah and the widow of Zarephath of Sidon, who once she ran out of food was provided food throughout a famine and clearly exemplifies the psalmist's point of view (1 Kings 17:7–16; but note how God used foreign nations to preserve the Hebrews during famine in Genesis 12 and 26; and how Joseph was providentially placed in Egypt to prepare for a famine in Genesis 41).

37:20. The psalmist reasoned ("for"; כִּי) that unlike the righteous, the wicked will not survive the famine. They will perish. This verse expands 37:18b.

A	B	[C]	D
The-Lord's enemies		[will be]	like-the-precious-things-(flowers)-of the-pastures
[A-B]		C	D
[The Lord's enemies]		will-disappear	like-smoke

The psalmist's point was that the wicked had no substance, so they would vanish like weak-rooted plants or like smoke. Both of these lack stability, and the plant also lacks sustenance.

The Wicked Deception (vv. 21–31)

Next, the consequences of being generous (righteous) or not being generous (wicked) were contrasted.

37:21. With an implied verbal contrast (וְלֹא; "but") the psalmist identified a contrastive pattern of behavior between the wicked and the righteous. A wicked person (רָשָׁע) was "always borrowing" (ptc.; לֹוֶה) but will "never complete" (וְלֹא יְשַׁלֵּם). While not "wicked" is singular, the psalmist did not signify a specific person, only something characteristic of many wicked people. By contrast, "a righteous person [צַדִּיק]"—meaning upright people in general—was one who was "habitually giving and being generous" (חוֹנֵן וְנוֹתֵן; customary ptc.). The expectation of "habitually giving and being generous" was in keeping with God's expectation to care for the poor and widow (Deut. 14:28–15:5). The psalmist indicated characteristic behavior of giving generously.

37:22. The psalmist reasoned (כִּי; "for") that "those who are being blessed [ptc.; מְבֹרָכָיו] will possess the land." He then contrasted those who were blessed with "those who are being cursed" (ptc.; מְקֻלָּלָיו), who will be "cut off [יִכָּרֵתוּ]." For the psalmist, to be "cut off" meant execution if not excommunication (Gen. 9:11; Lev. 7:25–27; 17:4–14; 19:8, 27; 20:3–18).

"Bless" and "Curse"

"Bless" and "curse" are vague terms. What is indicated is being favored as opposed to being disadvantaged or dispossessed. In both cases the action is expressed by a participle, indicating ongoing or perpetual behavior. God keeps helping or hurting as long as we keep doing the same. Those who are being blessed are the righteous, and those being cursed are the wicked of the previous verse. They are responded to by God in accordance with their greed or generosity. While salvation is not earned by good works, some blessings are, and great loss is deserved by

---

disobedience to God's will; at least OT people thought this way. In the historical context, this may have to do with those who are allowed or not allowed to enter or stay in the Promised Land of Canaan. Or it could be using "land" metaphorically of material blessings for those who are good and generous. So in short, do unto others as you would want them to do to you, which sums up the OT (Matt. 7:12).

37:23. This verse is difficult Hebrew. Literally it reads, "From Yahweh [מֵיְהוָה] steps of a warrior, they have been established; and his way, He will delight." The NETS (based on the LXX) has, "A person's steps are directed by the Lord, and his way by will." The NRSV says, "Our steps are made firm by the LORD, when he delights in our way"; and the NIV has, "The Lord makes firm the steps of the one who delights in him." The point seems to be that when one lives in a manner that pleases God, then his pathway is protected.

The God of Judaism and Islam

Note how the Muslim personal name for God (Allah) and one of the Hebrew words for God (אֱלֹהַ) compare. The same or similar words in Semitic languages use the same or interchangeable consonants. Muslims believe they follow the true God, the God of Abraham, but also believe their Scriptures (the Qur'an) correct the OT in many ways. So, the Israelites and their earliest relatives who moved eastward (cf. Ishmael) had the same God to begin with; but over time very different theologies developed so that the interpreted God is very different between Muslims, Jews, and Christians. If there is only one, true God, then all these religions are aiming at the same God, but their doctrines (mainly christology and soteriology) are drastically different (cf. Hos. 4:5–6).

37:24. This protection is what we see in verse 24: "Although he may [start] fall[ing] he will not fall headlong, because "Yahweh" [יְהוָה] is supporting him [ptc.] with his hand." The poet observed that righteousness is rewarded. Wickedness is punished. This was and is a wisdom principle. But like the observant and thoughtful author of Ecclesiastes, Qoheleth, we may wonder why we see bad people prosper and good people suffer so often.

37:25. In light of confidence in God's care for the righteous, the psalmist next observed that he has, in all his years, from youth to old age, never seen a righteous person abandoned or his children having to beg.

37:26. The psalmist recognized that the righteous ("they"), on a daily basis, were constantly showing favor and lending to others (ptc.; 37:26a). The word for "lend" is the same verbal root as "borrow" (לוה II; cf. 37:21). Consequently, their children were favored ("blessed"; 37:26b) by God, which is why they were never beggars. As with wisdom "promises," such a text does not intend to say that righteous people are never without sufficient friends or food. But it was exceptional. Life does not work as a formula: do x and always get y. If the purpose was to proclaim the impossibility of righteous people going hungry, then the problem arises of a conflict with experience.

37:27. Since law-keepers were so blessed, the psalmist implored his audience, if needed, to turn from doing wrong to doing right so they can also "dwell in the land" (literally or figuratively) perpetually ("forever"; לְעוֹלָם), that is, all their days.

37:28. This perpetual state was the result because God steadfastly loves (ptc.; אֹהֵב) justice (מִשְׁפָּט) and never will forsake (see 37:25a) those who are godly (37:28a). The major disjunctive accent (the upside-down V-shaped accent [˄] under the word) was placed by the scribes two words farther (לְעוֹלָם נִשְׁמָרוּ) than the logical break. In the second part of the verse,

the point was made that those who are "godly" (חֲסִידָיו) "will experience uninterrupted watch care" (לְעוֹלָם נִשְׁמָרוּ), while the descendants of the "wicked" (those who are steadfastly disobedient) will be "cut off," meaning that the rebellion of the parents will affect the children and both would miss out on God's oversight (the NIV has "protection" while the NETS [cf. LXX] has "be destroyed").

37:29. This verse perhaps completed a three-part parallelism in combination with verse 28. Verse 29 literally is, "Those who live right will possess the land // and they will dwell until above." The versions take this expression as an idiom for "forever"; but the ancients did not think of "endless time" as we do. So, the sense is that of staying in the land and not ever being uprooted. The Septuagint has a longer statement about the wicked: "But the lawless shall be chased away, and the offspring of the impious shall be destroyed" (v. 28 NETS).

37:30. The psalmist continued his description of righteous people in their manner of speech (פִּי "mouth"; vv. 30–31). They "muttered" (NIV, "utter") wisdom, and they spoke [proclaimed] justice" (v. 30). The text literally says their mouths mutter and their tongues speak. The word translated "[m]utter" (יֶהְגֶּה) is often translated "meditate" (cf., e.g., Douay and the lexica), but this is a problematic meaning for contemporary readers, since it carries the lexical baggage of transcendental meditation techniques. No data show that ancient Hebrews meditated as we use the term today (see Marlowe 2007, 3–18). The word has to do with reading out loud in some contexts, but the parallelism here indicates that the word was being used in the sense of speaking: "they speak wise words" (NET; cf. KJV) or "utters wisdom" (NIV; cf. ESV, NASB). In other words, those who live right are characterized by wise and just communication.

The Wicked Pursuit (vv. 32–40)

Finally, the psalmist described God's protection of his saints and destructive fate of the sinners who wanted to kill those who do what is right.

37:31. This also meant that "God's law is 'on their hearts' [i.e., of utmost importance to them], [and] they never 'slip their steps' [i.e., they never step away from it]." Of course, this presents the ideal in terms of what they desire, even if they cannot perform it perfectly, or what is possible with God's empowerment, theoretically. Psalm 37:31b in the MT does not start with a conjunction ("and" or ו in Hebrew), but it is represented in one Hebrew manuscript plus the Greek and Syriac versions. This could be haplography with the ו at the end of verse 31b. If not, then an option is to start verse 31b with "and [therefore]."

37:32. Then the observation was made that lawless people "watch for" (i.e., hide in waiting in order to ambush) the righteous, seeking (without hesitation; due to the ptc.) their death. This word for "watching" is not the same as the previous one for "watching over" or "keeping/preserving" (וְשָׁמְרוּ) in verse 28. Here the צוֹפֶה ("those who watch/wait"; nom. ptc.) was used for the "wicked" (רָשָׁע; singular) in the sense of a collective or group. The use was adjectival in the sense of wicked [people], which the NETS translates as "the sinner." The text literally has "his death," but this is for agreement with the masc. sg. form of "for a righteous one [לַצַּדִּיק]." The intention was to describe not a specific person but whichever one of the righteous group that might at some point be traveling alone, and therefore vulnerable to bandits, who will not only rob but also kill him.

37:33. The poet used a chiastic A-B-C-C'-B'-A' pattern.

A Yahweh

    B not—he-will-abandon-him

        C in-his-hand
        C´ in-his-judgment

    B´ and-not . . . he-will-condemn-him

[A´ Yahweh]

The Greek OT version takes the approach that God will not abandon the good person to a fate determined by the hands of bad people and will not let a righteous person be found guilty if brought to trial by the wicked (see NETS). This seems to be the correct sentiment however translated. The verb chosen for "condemn" has the same root letters as the noun or adjective "wicked" or "guilty person" (רשׁע). Here it means "declare guilty." The same root for "abandon [עזב]" was used here as in verse 25 (where God has never been seen forsaking the righteous). The current verse may explain that 37:25 has in view God's support when the righteous are threatened with injustice (since it cannot be true experientially that a good person absolutely never had been left wondering why God was not helping or been impoverished). Often in the psalms we find the godly petitioner in anguish because he feels abandoned by God or is suffering near death. The NIV says that God will not "leave them [the righteous] in the power of wicked [people]" (clarifications added; v. 33a).

37:34. In light of such an anxious situation, when the wicked seem to have the upper hand legally, this next verse added the exhortation to "Wait! [קַוֵּה] for Yahweh [יְהוָה]." The idea was to turn toward him and trust him even when you feel ignored. This word can also mean "hope." This was followed by another command, "Keep!" God's "ways" (directives or regulations). The word for "keep" is the same as used in verse 28b, where godly people are "protected" (NIV[84]) by God. Those who do stay on God's path will be exalted (over the wicked) by possessing the land, at which time they will witness the wicked being "cut off" (again probably implying "from the land," but could also have suggested their destruction).

37:35. At this point the psalmist confessed that he had seen a wicked person, even a very violent one (עָרִיץ), "exposing himself [מִתְעָרֶה; ptc.]" (i.e., boasting) like a prosperous (lit., "green") native-born citizen (אֶזְרָח). The words here are difficult. The NETS translates the verse, "I saw an impious one being highly lifted up and being raised up like the cedars of Lebanon." However, the NETS is translated from Septuagint manuscripts, which may reflect a different text tradition than the MT. The JPS reads "I saw a wicked man, powerful, well-rooted like a robust native tree." Regardless, the main idea was that the psalmist had witnessed a bad person prospering.

37:36. But all of a sudden, this wicked person was gone and could not be found, although the psalmist sought him. The JPS has "Suddenly he vanished and was gone; I sought him, but he was not to be found." The wicked and the rich also can lose their lives or wealth overnight. The expression "he crossed over and behold was not" (וַיַּעֲבֹר וְהִנֵּה אֵינֶנּוּ) is similar to the text in Genesis 5:24, "then he [Enoch] was no more [וְאֵינֶנּוּ] because God took him." This may show that in both cases the wording only meant the person died. Yet the wicked person may not have died, just left, crossing over to another but unknown location. Alternatively, "he was no more" may be an ancient idiom for dying. This wicked person had an unimpressive future until he did die (but see Hebrews 11:5, which may be a theological interpretation).

37:37. But speaking of a future, the psalmist continued, if you "watch" (again שָׁמַר) or "pay attention" (רָאָה) to a blameless and upright person of peace, by contrast, he does have a (significant) future, whether rich or poor.

37:38. On the other hand, wicked transgressors ("of the law" added by the Greek OT; cf. NETS) will be destroyed together and "cut off" ("from the land" could be implied, but a better counterpart to being "destroyed" in the parallelism would be "cut off" in terms of being killed or dying from their deadly life choices).

37:39. In contrast to the lawbreakers, God was a strong deliverer of the righteous from times of trouble. Without such help available the wicked were and are doomed to divine defeat.

37:40. The psalmist alluded to history past, that Yahweh "has helped them [וַיַּעְזְרֵם]" and "has enabled them to escape [וַיְפַלְּטֵם]" from wicked people, and "so he has saved them [וְיוֹשִׁיעֵם]" because "they have taken refuge [חָסוּ]" in him. The author may have had the exodus principally in mind. If David was the author, then he was likely reflecting on the times he had escaped capture or death when pursued by Saul or other enemies.

THEOLOGICAL FOCUS

The exegetical idea (the psalmist taught his readers not to worry that unlawful people had health and wealth, not to be discouraged, and not to turn to violence as an answer, but to keep trusting God because God's enemies would be defeated) leads to this theological focus: God rewards those who delight in him and are dedicated to his ways, but God scoffs at and will thwart those who reject his ways.

The theological focus is twofold. First, those who delight in and are dedicated to God are rewarded (vv. 3–6, 11, 18–19, 22–29, 31b, 33, 34b, 37b, 39–40). Second, those who reject God and his ways are punished (vv. 2, 9–10, 13, 15, 17, 20, 22b, 28b, 35–36, 38.

Against Gunkel's view of Psalm 37 as "faith in retribution," Kraus argues for the theme of God's interventions in human affairs (Kraus 1993, 408). He will remove the wicked who threaten the stability and safety of the righteous in the land. Those who delight in God's ways and wisdom will possess what was promised. Notably the righteous are the "gentle," not violent men. These "meek" will inherit the land and bring peace. Though the wicked enemies of God succeed for a season, they will come to an end. Yet while there is time, those who turn from wickedness can also live in the land. Good people have not been seen as beggars because the righteous are generous in actions and godly in attitude. "Poor in spirit" could be taken several ways. In this instance, "spirit" seems to be used in its sense of "attitude" or "passion" rather than spirituality or the Spirit.

PREACHING AND TEACHING STRATEGIES

Exegetical and Theological Synthesis
The psalm begins with an admonition not to be concerned with evildoers. The concerns apparently take two forms. One concern relates to the seeming prosperity of the wicked (vv. 1–2, 7, 10, 35). A second concern is the mistreatment of the righteous at the hands of the wicked (vv. 12, 14–15, 21, 32, 35, 40).

In response to these concerns, the psalmist encourages his audience in two ways. First, the righteous need to remember that the success of the evildoer is fleeting, and they will ultimately be judged (vv. 2, 9a, 10, 13, 15, 17, 20, 22a, 38). Judgment delayed is not judgment denied. Second, the righteous can take comfort in the fact that they will ultimately be delivered, vindicated, and blessed (vv. 6, 7, 11, 18, 22, 24, 28, 29, 33, 34, 39, 40). At the heart of both of these responses is a sovereign, omnipotent, and just God.

Since God will judge the wicked and deliver, vindicate, and bless the righteous, the psalmist challenges his hearers to live in righteousness before this very God (vv. 3, 4, 5, 7, 8, 27, 34, 37).

Preaching Idea
Dwelling on those who do wrong can keep you from doing what is right and trusting God.

Contemporary Connections

What does it mean?
What does it mean that dwelling on those who do wrong can keep you from doing what is right and trusting God? More specifically, what does the psalmist mean that we should not be concerned about what the ungodly do? The psalmist is not stating that one should absolutely ignore the wicked as if they did not exist. Nor is he advocating taking a "head in the sand" approach to deny the pain and harm that the wicked cause or that we should not pursue righteousness and justice. What the psalmist is advocating is having a theistic perspective regarding those who do evil. That is, we do not ignore or deny evil but rather we trust that God will ultimately deal with it. Our primary strategy for dealing with the evil around us is not to make the wrong world right but to live right in a wrong world.

Is it true?
Is it true that dwelling on those who do wrong can keep you from doing what is right and trusting God? Practical experience would say yes. For instance, there is the driver who while criticizing another for failing to use a turn signal is speeding twenty miles an hour over the speed limit. Or consider the husband who carefully records every one of his wife's shortcomings and yet never seems to take the time to address his own faults. What about the Christian who bemoans the rampant sexual immorality in the culture but chooses to ignore his or her problem with pornography? In all these examples, dwelling on the sins of others has led to a failure to address their own.

Still, one might question whether the response to evil above is too passive. Admittedly, there is something emotionally satisfying about the dictum, "Don't get mad, get even."

Or consider the oft-quoted but variously attributed warning, "The only thing necessary for the triumph of evil is that good men should do nothing." Is taking the moral high road equivalent to waving a white flag of surrender to evil and wickedness?

The Lord Jesus apparently did not think so. In the Sermon on the Mount, our Lord speaks of turning the other cheek, going the extra mile, and loving one's enemies (Matt. 5:38–45). In a similar way, the apostle challenges Christ-followers not to repay evil for evil, to forgo revenge, and to overcome evil with good (Rom. 12:17–21). It is worth noting that Paul's admonition is undergirded by the OT (Deut. 32:35; Prov. 25:21–22). What is implicit in Jesus's sermon and explicit in Paul's admonition is that one leaves ultimate vindication and justice in God's hands.

In sum, Psalm 37 is not an exercise in passivity or indifference to evil. Rather it is an exercise in maintaining the tension between divine sovereignty (leaving ultimate judgment and vindication to God) and human responsibility (living righteously in an unrighteous world).

Now what?

Do not let the ungodly get under your skin. We have little control over much of what we face in life, but we have a great deal of control on what we choose to dwell on. Although Martin Luther was speaking specifically of temptations, his counsel is still appropriate here: "We cannot prevent the birds from flying over our heads, [but] there is no need that we should let them nest in our hair."

Cultivate a heavenly perspective on evil. A top-down view sees the prosperity of the wicked as temporal and judgment as eternal. Remember that though the wheels of divine justice may grind exceedingly slow, they grind exceedingly fine (different versions of this saying have been oft repeated and variously attributed).

Let God be God and let the godly live godly. Leave vengeance in God's hands (Deut. 32:35;

Rom. 12:19) and choose to turn the other cheek, go the extra mile, and love your enemies (Matt. 5:38–45).

Creativity in Presentation

You might open the sermon or lesson by pointing out that one of the most controversial movies in 2007 was *No Country for Old Men* (directed by Ethan Coen and Joel Coen). The R-rated film is violent and bloody and lacks a clear resolution where good triumphs over evil. Even more than a decade later, people are debating the moral ambiguity that pervades the movie and its ending, which implies that the villain seemingly wins. This is unsettling in movies and in life.

One could also open the sermon by noting the enduring popularity of Psalm 37:4, though many quote or apply that verse out of context. One could illustrate this point by playing a clip from *The Late Show* with Stephen Colbert where talk show host Oprah Winfrey talks about Psalm 37:4 as her favorite verse. Search the internet for this video (the episode aired October 15, 2015) or a comparable video. Songs that could be considered are "Psalm 37 (Delight Yourself in the Lord)" by the Psalms Project or Jason Silver's song entitled, "Delight in the Lord," drawn from Psalm 37:1–26. For a hip-hop treatment of the psalm, one could use Shai Linne's "Psalm 37."

Remember to highlight the idea that dwelling on those who do wrong can keep one from doing what is right and trusting God. The following three points help to underscore this.

- Dwelling on those who do wrong pulls the focus off of our own life (37:1–11).

- Dwelling on those who do wrong places the focus on someone else (37:12–34).

- Dwelling on those who do wrong puts the focus on the material rather than spiritual (37:35–40).

DISCUSSION QUESTIONS

1. In what way(s) does God give those who take great pleasure in him their greatest desires (Ps. 37:4)?

2. Has Psalm 37:9–11 ever happened? When did or will it happen? Literally or spiritually? How is it that the psalmist *never* saw righteous people forsaken or begging?

3. What does it mean in Psalm 37:17 that Yahweh upholds the righteous?

4. Does Psalm 37:25 guarantee that righteous people will never starve? Why or why not?

5. Are righteous people always wise (Ps. 37:30)? Why or why not? If the latter, how is this verse true?

6. Are the words of this psalm mitigated by the reality that believers and those who behave rightly are often not the most powerful and prosperous people? Defend your answer.

7. Is it always better to be godly and poor rather than ungodly and rich? Why or why not?

8. Why does God laugh at his wicked enemies?

PSALM 49

EXEGETICAL IDEA
People are mortal and, like animals, must die. Not even the wealthiest is exempt or can bribe God to grant freedom from the grave, where the godly do find life.

THEOLOGICAL FOCUS
The psalmist summoned people from every economic level to remember that those who are oppressive, prideful, and prosperous should not be envied, for even the rich cannot purchase extended life.

PREACHING IDEA
The universality of death means that one must live wisely knowing that God, not wealth, delivers from the grave.

PREACHING POINTERS
The ascription of the psalm is to "the sons of Korah," of which little is certain, and the generalities of the contents make any attempt to identify a specific occasion for the song tenuous at best. But apparently, some in ancient Israel (as do many today) equated wealth with life and believed that the possession of the former somehow ensured the latter. But this was and is a fatal error. In fact, studies have been undertaken to determine whether one's wealth or the amount spent on health care has any effect on life expectancy. Research suggests that modest increases in life expectancy can be gained when there are greater financial resources available. But there are no studies that show that death can be defeated.

It is this reality of death that Psalm 49 addresses. Since death is universal and wealth cannot prevent it, what is one to do? Many Bible interpreters have recognized that Psalm 49 is a wisdom psalm. As such one would expect that there would be a heavy dose on righteous behaviors. So, one is a bit surprised to see that the psalm does not so much tell one how to live but how not to live (e.g., trusting in wealth, pride). The answer is not *what* but rather *who*, namely, the God who ransoms souls from "sheol" (שְׁאוֹל; v. 15). Ultimately, this will point the way forward to Christ who is the answer to the great enemy: death.

DO NOT BE FEARFUL WHEN THE WICKED PROSPER

LITERARY STRUCTURE AND THEMES

In this psalm, the poet called people from every situation in society to listen to his proverbial riddle (vv. 1–4). He asked rhetorically why he should fear when powerful (lit., "wealthy") people oppress him (vv. 5–6). Those who trust in riches or themselves (rather than God) also will die as the poor, and the wise as the foolish (vv. 7–14). Ultimately, he would have victory over death. Therefore, he should not envy his powerful and prosperous enemies, who leave all their possessions behind when they enter the grave. Wealth cannot promise wisdom or a long life. Even when a rich person has a long life, he may still lack true understanding. Wealth in itself is not impressive (vv. 15–20).

- ***The Poet's Purpose (49:1–4 [HB 2–5])***
- ***The Riddle of Riches (49:5–20 [HB 6–21])***
  - *Wealth Cannot Stop Death (49:5–13 [HB 6–14])*
  - *Right Living Will Prolong Life (49:14–15 [HB 15–16])*
  - *Trusting in Wealth Is Foolish (49:16–20 [HB 17–21])*

EXPOSITION

The superscription (49:1 in MT) is the same as that of Psalm 47. Psalm 49 provides wisdom regarding wealth, so its form-critical category is that of a Wisdom Poem/Psalm, although some suggest a more specific nuance of a didactic or instructional psalm, because it deals with how to solve a practical problem (Kraus 1993, 480, citing von Rad 1972, 48–50, where Psalms 73 and 139 are noted as other examples). Even a cursory reading immediately raises parallels in the reader's mind with

advice on riches found in other OT wisdom books (Ecclesiastes and Proverbs). Typical of OT wisdom texts, those who do right (49:14 [HB 5]) are contrasted with those who do wrong (49:5–6 [HB 6–7]), the wise with the (morally not mentally) foolish (49:10 [HB 11]). In light of Psalm 49:5–6 [HB 6–7], the historical setting is related to a situation in which the psalmist (as in many lament psalms) is oppressed and encircled by sinful opponents. Commentators have dated the specific historical setting from the eighth to the third century B.C. The ANE practice of powerful people being buried with their possessions indicates their futile attempt, and false beliefs, that they could "take it all with them." As a result, the psalmist summoned people from every economic level to remember that those who are oppressive, prideful, and prosperous should not be envied, for even the rich cannot purchase extensions to life.

The Poet's Purpose (49:1–4 [HB 2–5])

He asserted that he would give wise advice concerning one of life's perplexities: the power of riches.

49:1. The psalmist began with a command for all people to listen to "this" (49:1a [HB 2a]; meaning his advice that follows), which is restated (49:1b [HB 2b]) as a summons for "all inhabitants of the 'world' [כָּל־יֹשְׁבֵי חָלֶד]" to pay attention ("to this," understood; the word חָלֶד in another manuscript is חֶדֶל). Both words (HALOT, s.v. חָלֶד and חֶדֶל, pp. 292, 316) can mean "world" but are related to the sense of a lifespan (longevity, duration) in the world or the land of the living (Isa. 38:11). The "people" of Psalm 49:1a [HB 2a] are those living in

Israel, who understand Hebrew, redefined as those engaged in life (work and worship) in that Hebrew world (49:1b [HB 2b]). The author had no platform or purpose, or perception, to speak to all humanity on earth (as we today conceive of the global world), only to his "world," those whom he could instruct (but which included various ethnic groups within Israel).

49:2. He also addressed "collectively [יַחַד]" the rich and poor, whom he restated as, literally, "sons of a human" and "sons of a man" (i.e., apparently, those of a low or high social status; cf. Ps. 62:9 [HB 10]; Lam. 3:33). That these expressions have this sense here is reinforced by the chiastic structure:

> A "descendants of humanity" (בְּנֵי אָדָם) (v. 2ai [HB 3ai]
> > B "descendants of man" (בְּנֵי־אִישׁ) (v. 2aii [HB 3aii]
> > B´ "the rich" (עָשִׁיר) (v. 2bi [HB 3bi]
> A´ "and the needy" (וְאֶבְיוֹן) (v. 2bii [HB 3bii]

One wonders if this distinction was not already hinted at in the previous verse.

> A "Hear!" (שִׁמְעוּ) (v. 1ai [HB 2ai])
> > B "all [common] people" (כָּל־הָעַמִּים) (v. 1ai [HB 2ai])
> A´ "Give ear!" (הַאֲזִינוּ) (v. 1bii [HB 2bii])
> > B´ "all inhabitants of the world" (כָּל־יֹשְׁבֵי חָלֶד) (v. 1bii [HB 2bii])

49:3. Regardless, the poet next stated his intention to promote "wisdom [חָכְמוֹת]" restated as "understanding [תְבוּנוֹת]." Speaking "from my heart" (לִבִּי) could imply "with passion" or "with understanding," but the latter seems redundant.

49:4. The psalmist accomplished this with a proverbial riddle set to music, accompanied by a lyre.

The Riddle of Riches (49:5–20 [HB 6–21])
In this section, the psalmist reflected on the impotence and temporary value of wealth.

Wealth Cannot Stop Death (49:5–13 [HB 6–14])
The poet observed that no measure of wealth can guarantee health and a long (especially endless) life.

49:5. The psalmist asked a rhetorical question for his Jewish readers to ponder: Why should I be afraid during times of trouble (49:5a [6a])? Contextually, he had in mind the kinds of oppressions created by wealthy people in power. Some versions speak of "evil days" (e.g., NIV, JPS), but this is archaic. The word (רָע) means "something bad; wrong" and here denotes "trouble."

The second part of this verse is unclear. The Hebrew literally is "iniquity of [?] surrounds me." The problematic term (עֲקֵבַי) is obscure since there are several roots to choose from and none makes the meaning obvious, and the versions can be confusing as well. The NETS (based on the LXX) translates these words literally (and therefore curiously) as, "The lawlessness at my heel will surround me." This is because the word in question can mean "heel" (as in Gen. 3:15), but the same word can also mean "rearguard" or "footprint" (HALOT, s.v. "עקב," pp. 872–73). Another root with the same consonants means "end" or "wages," while another means "bumpy terrain" or "deceitful." The NRSV says, "iniquity of my persecutors." The JPS has "evil of those who would supplant me." This latter is chosen by translations that have something like "wicked deceivers" (e.g., NIV).

49:6. These people were described in this next verse as people who trust in riches and boast about their wealth. So, the troublesome times of 49:5a (HB 49:6a) were situations when the psalmist might be unable to find an honest person with whom to do business, one who is not only interested in profit at any price. Yet he did not fear even this prospect of potential financial loss or ruin.

49:7. Hebrew manuscripts differ on whether the opening word (אָח) in verse 8 (HB = v. 7[EB]) should be read as "brother" or the very similarly pronounced אַךְ, meaning "Surely!" Certainty is expressed by the verbal combination of infinitive absolute followed by a finite verb of the same root (פָּדֹה יִפְדֶּה; Arnold 2003, 74–75). There is also the question if "he will redeem" (יִפְדֶּה) should be passive ("he will be redeemed"), according to the BHS editors. The JPS makes the subject of the verb "redeem" the riches of the previous verse, not a theoretical person (as NIV); and the NRSV makes the "ransom" the subject. If one goes with the manuscripts that have "and not" rather than the MT's "not" (49:7b [8b]), the question is if the ו conjunction is alternative ("or") or conjunctive ("and"). Regardless, the point of the verse as it stands, seemingly, was the observation that no one has enough money to purchase life from God.

49:8. The psalmist continued his thought from verse 7 with a (perhaps parenthetical) statement about redemption: "and the redemption of life [lit., 'lives'] is costly" (v. 8a [HB 9a]). The word used for "lives" (נֶפֶשׁ) is "soul" in the KJV, but that is archaic. We seldom if ever use "soul" for a "person" today. The idea seems to have been an extension of the claim that no amount of money can purchase extended life.

49:9. The expression "[not] he will see decay [יִרְאֶה הַשָּׁחַת]" in verse 9b [HB 10b] is very similar to that used by the author of Psalm 16:10 (probably David), who spoke of God not allowing his godly king "to see decay [לִרְאוֹת שָׁחַת]." David (a foreshadow of a promised future, divine king) expected God to deliver him from a deadly situation (which the NT applied to Jesus as the risen Messiah). The psalmist here, however, spoke of the certainty of death for everyone regardless of wealth and power. Qoheleth observed how

even wisdom cannot stop death, even a premature demise, and wondered what good then was being wise (Eccl. 2:12–16).

49:10. This psalmist then made a similar point: that wise people died just like fools and all possessions were left to others (cf. the expression used by the author of Ecclesiastes in 2:16 [יָמוּת הֶחָכָם עִם־הַכְּסִיל] with the psalmist's [חֲכָמִים יָמוּתוּ יַחַד כְּסִיל]). In Ecclesiastes 2:21, the author (= Qoheleth) grieved that "a person may labor with wisdom, knowledge and skill, and then they must leave all they own to another who has not toiled for it" (NIV). We find a wisdom theme or thread here in Psalm 49 that predated and anticipated Ecclesiastes.

Ecclesiastes

The OT book Ecclesiastes is entitled Qoheleth (קֹהֶלֶת) in the Hebrew Bible, after its author. The English title comes from the Greek OT (Ἐκκλησιαστοῦ). These words have to do with a "gathering" or "assembly." The author made it clear that he assembled many proverbs (12:9). He was neither "preacher" (KJV) nor "teacher" (NIV), as we use those terms today. The book is famous (or infamous) for its theme "all is vanity" (KJV) or "everything is meaningless" (NIV); and its pessimism (actually realism) has caused its rightful place in the OT canon to be questioned. The expression (הֲבֵל הֲבָלִים) behind these translations concretely speaks of something "vaporous" (like steam), so when used abstractly it can mean "empty." The author was observing that much or most of life on earth ("under the sun") is like a vapor experientially. It is fleeting and transitory. Life is full of pain, problems, and perplexities. Repeatedly, the author advised getting the most out of life while you can by enjoying food and fellowship and festivity, as divine gifts. He stressed not ending up with regrets in old age, and said the solution was fearing God from youth (ch. 12). In a nutshell, he warned against the paralysis of analysis. Do not let life's frustration keep you from God or what is good.

49:11. The author reminded his audience that everyone, wise or foolish (= moral or immoral), even those who have streets or buildings named after them, dies and dwells perpetually in a "tomb house [קִרְבָּם בָּתֵּימוֹ]," that is, the realm of death.

49:12. Like the author of Ecclesiastes, the psalmist noted humanity's shared fate of death with all animals, despite its grandeur of wealth that pretends to exalt it over the animal world.

49:13. This section was concluded with the observation that this certain animal-like death is humanity's destiny (lit., "their way/path"; זֶה דַרְכָּם). A term (כֶּסֶל) was used that can be read either as a word meaning "strength" or "stupidity." The NETS has "pitfall," the NIV "trust," the NRSV "foolhardy," and the KJV "folly" (Vulgate, *insipientiae*). The consensus of scholarship appears to favor the sense of "foolish" (which does play off the foolish [כְּסִיל] in verse 10 [HB 11]). Yet the parallel line (v. 13b [14b]) appears to support the notion of confidence or trust (although the Hebrew words are difficult). It may be that the word (כֶּסֶל) speaks of the "confidence" or certainty of this human destiny of death.

The NIV's "those who trust in themselves" is likely not what is implied. What was meant by the first half of the verse should be clarified by the second half, but 13b [14b] is obscure. It reads, literally, "and after them, with their mouths, they will accept." The idea, in relation to 13a [14a], is likely that expressed by the NRSV, "the end of those who are pleased with their lot." Other versions (cf. KJV and NIV) take this phrase as saying that people in the future will approve this foolishness, while the NETS has the way of such people as their own pitfall, making their own rationalizations as

a postscript. The JPS is attractive, "Such is the fate of those who are self-confident, the end of those pleased with their own talk." The NRSV also ignores the "selah" (סֶלָה) at the end of this verse (not original anyway) by making it begin rather than end a section, unlike most versions. The NETS translated it, "Interlude on strings."

Right Living Will Prolong Life (49:14–15 [HB 15–16])[1]
The psalmist was sure that God would keep alive those who trust in him rather than themselves.

49:14. In this section, the wise poet first observed that these rebellious (a "fool" is a moral rebel in biblical wisdom) rich people had been "set [שַׁתּוּ]" on a path toward the grave the same as sheep (49:14a [HB 15a], which have no choice about their future). Several aspects of this verse are controversial.

49:15. Yet the psalmist was confident or hopeful (אַךְ; "Surely!") that God would redeem "him" (lit., "my soul [נַפְשִׁי]," which merely means "my life" or "me"; v. 15a [HB 16a]). The reference was to his physical not immaterial being. The particle (אַךְ) can also be used for "only" or "however; but" (NIV; NETS, "on the other hand"). Either way, he believed God would help him, unlike those who are arrogant (v. 13 [HB 14]), since neither he nor they could save themselves.

He has concluded already that all men, wise or wicked, will experience death. So, his hope here had to do with deliverance from a specific threat of death ("from the hand of the grave-world"; מִיַּד־שְׁאוֹל). He would die eventually, but he had confidence that he would be preserved for now because he was not like those who were both wealthy and wicked. Still, the words that follow may or may not support this view. We

---

1   Verses 14–15 were sectioned off by the Hebrew editorial scribes ("selah" [סֶלָה] before and after) but seem to be no more structurally than a continuation of the previous pericope about humans destined for death, and the same is true for the last pericopé (vv. 16–20 [HB 17–21]).

recognize the irony of this verse, in Anderson's words, as both the climax of the psalm and "far from clear" (Anderson 1995, 379). In 49:15b [HB 16b] he adds, "because ['that'; 'when'?, כִּי] he will take me." Some, perhaps best, take "that" (כִּי) as emphatic (also NIV) and propose to place the major break in the verse after "my life" rather than "from the realm of death." This provides the solution, "But God will redeem my life // From the grave he will certainly take me" (Anderson 1995, 379). Regardless, the phrase is simply "he will take me," but some versions have "receive me" (cf. NETS, NRSV, Vulgate). Some suggest a parallel with God's taking (same word) of Enoch (Gen. 5:24) or Elijah (2 Kings 2:3–5), but nothing concrete in the context indicates this. Von Rad noted that nothing in Israel's thinking would make such ideas a priori impossible, and Wolff saw this verse as a confirmation of continued communion with God (Kraus 1993, 483, citing von Rad 1975, I:204 and Wolff 1974, 109).

Psalm 49 is thought to at least hint at the afterlife or even resurrection after death; however, the basis for this is only the somewhat vague expression in verse 15b [HB 16b], "for he [God] will take me." The parallel line in verse 15a [HB 16a] speaks of being ransomed from death, but in context this may only refer to being rescued from being killed, so the following comment about being received by God could be no more than restatement. Regardless, there is a contrast between the wicked wealthy and the psalmist as, presumably, relatively poor but righteous. These rich people trust in their wealth to the point of assuming that they are guaranteed a long life, being protected from an early grave by their powerful positions. They think their possessions and honored professions are proof of their importance. The psalmist sees they are no different than poor people or animals and are destined to die, while the poor and pure will be preserved beyond the grave in God's presence.

Kraus has proposed that the meaning of verse 15 [HB 16] should be viewed as a response to verses 5–6 [HB 6–7], which speaks

of deliverance from a circle of enemies, which is often described as the circle of "Sheol" (שְׁאוֹל). He can expect safety from death as one who is upright. But a very different approach is to compare verse 15 [HB 16] with verse 7 [HB 8] (since both begin with אַךְ—MT has אָךְ in verse 8, but some Hebrew manuscripts have אַךְ). This would mean that verse 15 [HB 16] has to do with rescue from the fate of death. While the wealthy cannot buy their way out of a deadly situation, the poor are rescued from death and removed ("received"). Some see this as an explanation of the "riddle" of verse 4 [HB 5]. Kraus questions L. Wächter's strict denial of any afterlife theme, who understands the verse as only about preservation from an early death in light of the parallels. In support of a resurrection undertone, Kraus mentions the views of J. J. Stamm and G. von Rad (Kraus 1993, 483–84, citing Stamm 1940, 16, and von Rad 1975, I:406). No scholarly consensus exists on the meaning of verse 15 (HB 16) or the structure of Psalm 49. We cannot prove or disprove that the poet was thinking about eternal life (especially as we use "eternal" in evangelical and traditional ways). But if God can save from potential death, he can save from perpetual death.

Trusting in Wealth Is Foolish (49:16–20 [HB 17–21])

In these final verses, the psalmist focused on why the rich should not be envied.

49:16. The psalmist began with the advice "not to fear" (אַל־תִּירָא) when the rich obtained even more power and possessions. While some translations suggest "do not be afraid" (KJV, NET, NASB, ESV, NRSV), the NIV best captures the psalmist's meaning: "do not be overawed" or perhaps "don't be dismayed" (NLT). This is because the psalmist appears, contextually, to have been concerned with envy or jealousy of the wealthy, rather than mere "fear" of them. The next verse (17 [HB 18]) begins with "because" (כִּי) and applies this caution to the understanding that riches are only temporal. Even a long earthly life is a flash compared to the afterlife.

49:17. Then the poet perhaps boasted that, while God would take him (v. 15 [HB 16]), the rich person cannot take (same Hebrew word) all his goods with him when he dies (v. 17a [HB 18a]). His "glory" or "splendor" (same word as in the previous verse; כָּבוֹד) will "not go down [לֹא־יֵרֵד]" after him (v. 17b [HB 18b]). One wonders why the psalmist is taken (up?) to God but the wicked wealthy person goes down. Yet this has to be understood in light (no pun intended) of verse 19 [HB 20], which says he will join his ancestors, but also not see the light. Technically, the comment about God taking or receiving the psalmist says nothing about direction, although it could be implied. All who die in the OT go to "Sheol" (שְׁאוֹל) or the grave world, which is related to the ANE concept of the underworld or netherworld, below the earth. So, at death all "go down," the righteous and the wicked, and join their departed ancestors. Yet the psalmist in some way believed he, as one not wealthy and arrogant, would be received by God. His concern in these final verses, however, was with the reality that people, no matter how rich or reputable in life, still die and enter the darkness of death like animals (vv. 18–20 [HB 19–21]).

49:18–19. The versions read very differently due to the difficulty of the Hebrew in this final passage. Regardless, the point made was that rich people like all people cannot escape death and its perpetual darkness.

"Soul" in the OT and Psalms

The word often rendered "soul" (נֶפֶשׁ) should seldom if ever be translated "soul" in modern and contemporary versions, as is typically done. This is because the way we use "soul" currently (a disembodied spirit being) does not correspond to its use in the OT (cf. Gen. 2:7, where it is translated as a "living being," and 1 Kings 9:4, where it means "life"). This word should not be confused with the later concepts of an "eternal/immortal soul" (which concept is problematic anyway since the NT speaks of a resurrected body not just an incorporeal being, consistent with the OT concept that keeps the life force connected to a body; but this is not the case in some Egyptian and Mesopotamian documents; but cf. 1 Sam. 28:13). In a related Semitic language to Hebrew (Akkadian) the cognate term *napashu* "refers to the neck or throat and by extension to breath" (Walton 2000, 537). Usually the Hebrew term is used in the OT in reference to a living person or one's emotional state as a person, and often can be left untranslated without changing the meaning of a statement or can be substituted with the pronoun "I" or "me." The parallel poetic line usually clarifies how this word is being used in a verse in a psalm.

49:20. The psalmist closed the psalm by discussing the rich who are immoral: "people who have wealth but lack understanding" (NIV) or "Mortals cannot abide in their pomp" (NRSV). The word "man" (אָדָם; cf. KJV et al.) is best translated as "humanity" (= "mortals"). The NIV's "wealth" here is not the same word as used earlier (חַיִל; "strength," vv. 6, 10) but means "precious" (יְקָר; cf. v. 12). "He will understand" (יָבִין) is "endure" (יָלִין) in a few Hebrew variant manuscripts, thus corresponding to the parallel in verse 12 [HB 13]. The LXX (cf. NETS) and Vulgate agree with the NIV's "understanding," yet also with NRSV's "pomp" (having "honor" instead). The bottom line is that people with honor in life do not live forever, but like beasts eventually are "ruined" or "cut off [נִדְמוּ]."

THEOLOGICAL FOCUS

The exegetical idea (the psalmist summoned people from every economic level to remember that those who are oppressive, prideful, and prosperous should not be envied, for even the rich cannot purchase extended life) leads to this theological focus: People are mortal and, like animals, must die; and not even the wealthiest is exempt or can bribe God to grant freedom from the grave, where the godly do find life.

The theological focus of Psalm 49 revolves around a riddle or one of life's perplexities: how to react when the ungodly have riches and are rulers. The psalmist cautions against fear. A good cross-reference is Ecclesiastes 9:11–12 and 10:1–7, where the author (Solomon, many would say) recognizes that God allows people to have the consequences of their choices. What is expected (like the psalmist's hope that good is always rewarded and bad punished) is not what happens in life. Life is not a formula. The wise person understands that very wicked and foolish people can obtain riches and positions of leadership. Their power has to be respected because your life can be cut short if you anger them. But you should not be afraid or allow their temporary "success" to create doubt about God and his promises. Only God is to be feared (trusted and obeyed completely). Wise people learn how to navigate life with fools in charge, maintaining an impact while not being corrupted by wicked, wealthy rulers. The author of Psalm 49 also instructs his audience about being righteous and brave even when surrounded by deceptive rich people (vv. 5–6). Wealth and power are often combined, but the psalmist emphasizes the limits of luxury. No amount or wealth can keep a person from death's door and the grave (afterlife; vv. 6–20). Eventually the righteous will rule (v. 14), and the psalmist expects God to protect him from death when attacked by a wicked, wealthy person (v. 15).

PREACHING AND
TEACHING STRATEGIES

Exegetical and Theological Synthesis

It is common in wisdom literature for the sage to issue an invitation for all to pursue wisdom. In this wisdom psalm, the psalmist does just that to both the rich and the poor (vv. 1–4). The universal nature of wisdom points to the universal nature of God's truth in general and a great reminder to the absolute truth–denying ethos of our present age.

Another characteristic feature of wisdom is its concern for the basic issues of life. And here Psalm 49 shows its wisdom roots in addressing wealth, power, life, and death. A rhetorical question in verses 5–6 is used to point out that one need not fear the rich and powerful because death is the great equalizer, and neither prosperity nor power can prevent it (vv. 6–13). Indeed, the rich and powerful are shepherded to the grave by death, and ultimately the righteous, whom the Lord will redeem, will rule over them (vv. 14–15). Verses 16–20 put the final nails in the coffin of the folly of trusting in riches. The wise should not be impressed (lit., "fear") by the prosperity of the wealthy, the temporal admiration that goes with it, and those who do not understand who are like beasts that perish (vv. 12, 15).

Preaching Idea

The universality of death means that one must live wisely knowing that God, not wealth, delivers from the grave.

Contemporary Connections

What does it mean?

What does it mean to live wisely in light of the universality of death? First, one must accept the universality of death. Many try to delay it through activities like healthy living. (Not that living healthy is a bad thing, but an obsession can be problematic.) A few try to defeat it through things like cryogenics. Yet ultimately, most accept death as part of life even if there is no consensus about what death actually is. But whether we accept it or understand it, the fact is death comes to all people.

Second, one must realize that wealth and its temporal perks that go with it are unable to deliver from death. Financial resources may make it possible to receive the best health care that money can buy, but it cannot prevent the inevitable. Similarly, having the applause and approval of others might offer some encouragement, but it does not change the reality of death.

Third, in light of the first two points, one must understand that God, not wealth, is the only way that one can be delivered from the grave (v. 15). Verses 7–9 are theologically significant in two ways: (1) They assert the inability of one human to redeem another (vv. 7–8). (2) Verse 9 refers to life beyond the grave, a concept that some Bible interpreters doubt is present in the OT in any significant way.

If these three truths are accepted, realized, and understood, then the wise person need not fear (v. 5) or be overly impressed with the exploits of the rich and famous (v. 16).

Is it true?

A number of the salient points in Psalm 49 stand undisputed. The universality of death is accepted in most, if not all, cultures and religions. For Hindus and Buddhists, human life is cyclical with the idea of reincarnation. For Judaism and Christianity, life is linear, and death is part of that trajectory. Yet even though there might be differences of opinion over what death is and if there is life after death, most do not deny that death is part of the human condition. Also, commonly accepted today is the notion that material riches cannot prevent death, nor can they be taken with one to be utilized or enjoyed in the life hereafter.

Now what?

Live in light of both death and eternity. Most people don't want to think about the former, and others give little thought to the latter. This a grave mistake (pardon the pun).

Learn to trust God for the future. As Hebrews 9:27 reminds us that "it is appointed for man to die once, and after that comes judgment." Take an honest look at what you are trusting in for both your life and impending death. If it isn't God, it isn't good.

If you have not done so already, join the redeemed by placing your faith in Christ. If you are already counted among the redeemed, examine your life to see if you are investing for eternity. Jesus calls us to "lay up for yourselves treasures in heaven, where neither moth nor rust destroys and where thieves do not break in and steal" (Matt. 6:20).

Creativity in Presentation

Tim McGraw's 2004 song "Live Like You Were Dying" could be used to introduce or illustrate the need to live in light of death and eternity. According to the song, life in light of death basically entails treating people better and checking items off one's bucket list, with a brief mention of finally reading the "Good Book." The song provides a way of comparing and contrasting how the singer and the psalmist view life and death.

In the R-rated movie *Slumdog Millionaire* (2008, codirected by Danny Boyle and Loveleen Tandan), we are introduced to Salim Malik, the older brother of the protagonist, Jamal. The tragic choices Salim makes in life are driven by the pursuit of wealth. Near the end of the movie, when Salim realizes that his life is about to be over, he fills a bathtub with money and sits in it. His actions are not explained but may symbolize his attempt to take his money with him or his inability to do so. The futility of Salim's actions is tragic and sobering either way.

In a 2012 interview in *The Talks* online magazine, the actor Morgan Freeman was asked, "Do you have those earrings just for fun or do they serve a purpose?" Freeman responded, "Yeah these earrings are worth just enough to buy me a coffin if I die in a strange place. That was the reason why sailors used to wear them." Use this quote to illustrate how little wealth can do in light of death.

The limitations of wealth can be illustrated by John D. Rockefeller, considered by some to be the wealthiest American who ever lived, who is purported to have said, "Who is the poorest man in the world? I tell you, the poorest man I know of is the man who has nothing but money."

Songs related to Psalm 49 are relatively sparse, but two good ones are "Psalm 49" by Jason Silver and "Psalm 49" by Ian White.

No matter how you choose to present this sermon, the idea that the universality of death means that one must live wisely knowing that God, not wealth, delivers from the grave needs to shine forth. Because death is universal . . .

- We need to look at what God's Word has to say about it (49:1–4).

- We need to accept that we are going to die (49:5–12).

- We need to plan for death's inevitability by trusting in God alone (49:13–20).

DISCUSSION QUESTIONS

1. Does the author believe goodness, rather than gold, can lead to a long life? Explain.

2. How does Psalm 49 compare to other wisdom texts in the OT?

3. What does the psalmist mean when he says, "[God] will receive me"?

4. How much does one need to make or be worth to be considered wealthy?

5. In what sense can people be no better than animals when it comes to death (vv. 12, 20)?

PSALM 73

EXEGETICAL IDEA
Although the ungodly seemed to succeed while the godly suffered, the psalmist was satisfied that Israel's God would bring about their downfall.

THEOLOGICAL FOCUS
While the godless person appears to prosper and godly people suffer, God will eventually judge the ungodly.

PREACHING IDEA
God is good even though bad things happen to good people and good things happen to bad people.

PREACHING POINTERS
The superscription of Psalm 73 links it to Asaph, a Levite and music leader in the time of David (1 Chr. 15:17, 19; 16:4–7; 2 Chr. 29:30). This is one of twelve psalms associated with Asaph (Psa. 50, 73–83). Whether Asaph is speaking of himself or someone else is uncertain. But the psalmist touches upon an inequity—in *Star Wars*-ian terms, "a disturbance in the force." It is a world where bad things happen to good people and good things happen to bad people. The problem is exacerbated by the knowledge that this world is ultimately ruled by a sovereign, righteous, and most importantly a good God. So, the psalmist cannot simply attribute this inequity to mere luck, fate, or fortune.

Bart Ehrman, a biblical scholar and former evangelical, left Christianity altogether over issues similar to that raised by our psalmist. As Ehrman (2008, 3) puts it, "But I came to a point where I could no longer believe. It's a very long story, but the short version is this: I realized that I could no longer reconcile the claims of faith with the facts of life. In particular, I could no longer explain how there can be a good and all-powerful God actively involved with this world, given the state of things. For many people who inhabit this planet, life is a cesspool of misery and suffering." But while the psalmist would likely acknowledge Ehrman's "cesspool of misery and suffering," he thankfully reaches a different conclusion. Rather than denying God because he does not understand him, the psalmist clings to the parts of God that he does understand, namely, his faithfulness even in the midst of trials and his ultimate judgment of the unrighteous.

DO NOT BE ENVIOUS WHEN
THE WICKED PROSPER

LITERARY STRUCTURE AND THEMES

The psalmist began with a confession about how he struggled with envy over God prospering sinners. He believed that God rewarded goodness so was troubled when he saw bad people with health and wealth (vv. 1–3). He then considered how some wicked people prosper while giving no thought to God. This created mental and emotional anguish, until he understood their fate (vv. 4–20). Consequently, he was able to rest and rejoice, and praise God for his spiritual provisions for the righteous and punishment for the unrighteous (vv. 21–28).

- *Confession (73:1b–3)*
- *Reflections on the Wicked and Righteous (73:4–20)*
- *Confession and Praise and Profession of Faith (73:21–28)*

EXPOSITION

Psalm 73, according to its superscription (73:1a), is a "psalm [מִזְמוֹר]" about (by/for?) Asaph (לְאָסָף; see Psalm 50 superscription comments). The next ten psalms (74–83) are also related to Asaph. Commentators connect this psalm to Psalms 37 and 49 as well as to Job for didactic reasons. As to genre, however, many have not considered this a didactic poem, and have regarded as either a Confession of Trust or a "Thanksgiving" Song (= Testimony).

In light of verse 28, it could have been part of a worship liturgy. The debate is also over whether the king is or is not the speaker, whether it is individual or national, and whether its date is pre- or postexilic.

Regardless, since the psalm is not lament or praise per se, it is here treated under wisdom because it has a focus on the fate of the wicked in contrast to the righteous, and specifically on the wisdom puzzle over the suffering of the righteous and the success of the unrighteous (see Kaiser 2010, 98–106). Therefore, although the ungodly seemed to succeed while the godly suffered, the psalmist was satisfied that Israel's God would bring about their downfall.

Confession (73:1b–3)

The psalmist confessed how he almost sinned due to envy over wealthy people who were also wicked.

73:1. The psalmist began with his conclusion (what he finally came to realize with more certainty): that "surely [אַךְ]" God was good to those whose intentions were pure (73:1b). He then explained how he did not always think this way (vv. 2–3). Psalm 73:1b, however, has an odd parallel. That God did (the verb is implied) "good things [טוֹב]" for Israel (לְיִשְׂרָאֵל; v. 1bi) was restated as doing goodness (implied) for those who had a pure heart (v. 1b). This reads as if Israel as a whole or consistently had pure motives. The meaning could be that God was good to Israel, or Israelites, when the nation acted, or the people acted, with the proper attitudes and aims. He went on to reflect on how wicked people could experience strength, yet obedient people (as he) could have problems; so, his opening statement probably meant that he realized God's people (who seek to follow his ways) may suffer bad times, but also, they eventually would be rewarded with good times. He said this now, but at a previous stage he had come close to leaving the path of obedience to, and faith in, "Elohim" (אֱלֹהִים).

73:2. This is stated and restated as "almost having lost his footing." The NETS (cf. LXX) speaks of being "shaken."

73:3. This happened because he became jealous when he witnessed wicked people constantly boasting (ptc.) about their "well-being" (שָׁלוֹם).

Reflections on the Wicked and Righteous (73:4–20)

Although some wicked people had health and wealth, and were godless, they would eventually experience divine displeasure and judgment.

73:4. The psalmist opened with a description of wicked people and their prosperity (vv. 4–12). The poet observed that sometimes ironically the unrighteous prosper while the righteous suffer. He next described this "peace" over which these wicked people were so proud. First, they had "no pains unto their death" (v. 4a; אֵין חַרְצֻבּוֹת לְמוֹתָם). The word "to their death [לְמוֹתָם]" may can be conjecturally redivided to read "for integrity" (לָמוֹ תָּם; BHS, 1154); but most versions do not follow this (NET being an exception). Translations vary with "they have no struggles" (NIV) and "no bands in their death" (KJV). While somewhat unclear, the following parallel line of verse 4 reads "their bodies [are] fat/healthy." The observation made was that they stay healthy until the day they die.

73:5. Second, for example, the psalmist observed, among these sinners, those "without human troubles" (v. 5a), who are "not touched by man" (v. 5b). The JPS likely captures best what this implies: "They have no part in the travail of men; they are not afflicted like the rest of mankind."

73:6. As a result, the poet claimed that "pride has embraced them [as a necklace], and [with] a garment [made] of violence they envelop themselves."

73:7. Third, their imaginative iniquity knew no bounds (but the Hebrew of this verse is difficult).

73:8. Fourth, "they mock ['scheme' in the Greek and Syriac texts; Latin 'laugh at,' *inriserunt*], and they speak 'about terrible' [בְרָע] oppression" (73:8a) // "they speak from heights" (73:8b; meaning perhaps they speak arrogantly; see NIV, JPS); but the LXX interprets it as "against the sky" (NETS). It may also be better to ignore the placement of the strongest divisional accent (under עֹשֶׁק) as do a number of versions (but not KJV), e.g. NIV, "They scoff, and speak with malice; with arrogance they threaten oppression."

73:9. Finally, the psalmist noted an unbecoming description of the Israelites: "they place their mouths in the heavens [sky]." The psalmist's metaphor may be better rendered as "and their tongue walks in the land." Some translate this as "travels throughout [תִּהֲלַךְ]," "take possession" (NIV), "struts through the earth" (NCBC; Anderson 1995, 532) or propose that the speaking is "against heaven" (NETS; and other versions). Regardless of the translation, the main accusation is that the wicked are arrogant.

73:10. Consequently (לָכֵן), the poet then said, "his people will return here; and abundant water will be drunk by them." The NETS (cf. LXX) has "Therefore my people will return here, and full days will be found for them." But the JPS reads, "So they pound His people again and again, until they are drained of their very last tear." In context, the psalmist still seems to be reflecting on the ironic good fortunes of the ungodly. So, this verse seems best understood as continuing the previous perspective on how these proud sinners devour the land and God's people, and even defy God.

73:11. The psalmist continued "and they said" (וְאָמְרוּ = "they wondered"): "How can 'El' [אֵל = God] know? Does 'Elyon' [עֶלְיוֹן; 'the Most High God'] have knowledge [of what we have done]?"

73:12. Postscript: "Behold this [describes] the wicked: always at ease and 'getting richer [הִשְׂגּוּ־חָיִל]' [all the time]."

73:13. The psalmist then moved to a description of righteous people and their sufferings (vv. 13–17). The poet began with what is sometimes designated as a protestation of innocence. While it's bad enough that unbelievers are healthy and wealthy, the psalmist is doubly troubled as a believer whose life is full of difficulties and dilemmas. Then he decides, "Certainly in vain I have [maintained] a 'heart' [= desire] to be clean; I have washed my hands in innocence." The psalmist wondered what the point was of being good when bad people prospered as well.

73:14. And although innocent, he "was 'continually stricken' [ptc.] every day; [that is] reproved every morning." He was experiencing what ungodly people deserved.

73:15. Then the psalmist realized that his thoughts were improper: if he "had said 'I may report this,' I would have acted with treachery against a generation of 'your sons' [= 'your children'?]." The NETS translates this "family of your sons," but the JPS has, "circle of Your disciples." The verb is "betrayed," "been faithless," or "been false" in various English texts; but one Greek manuscript has "you" as the subject.

73:16. He complained next that when he racked his brain (strong form of חשׁב) to understand (all) this, it was trouble "in my opinion" (lit., "in my eyes"). "It [הִיא]" in verse 16b means "this mystery." He was faced with the challenge of how to reconcile this reality regarding the ironic experiences of godly and ungodly people. His popular theology seemed to promise a different reality.

73:17. He had no answer "until he entered the sanctuary of 'El' [אֵל]" (v. 17a). The word for "sanctuary" (מִקְדְּשֵׁי) is plural but singular in the Greek OT (LXX). Only after being in God's presence did he understand their [the ungodly's] destiny (v. 17b).

73:18. The psalmist closed with a solution to his crisis of (vv. 18–20). "Surely" (אַךְ) "you [God] will set them on a slippery slope" (v. 18a; not the same word translated "slip" in v. 2). Perhaps this can be read as an imprecation. He then added, "You 'have made them fall' all the way to their ruin" (v. 18b). In a poetic line, this completed action verb can be read as future since the initial verb set that tone. Poetry allows for more fluidity in verb forms than historical narrative.

73:19. Then he exclaimed, "[Look] how, in a moment, they have come into desolation; they have come to an end, they are finished, 'from terrors' [מִן־בַּלָּהוֹת]," which in the Greek OT (LXX) is "because of their lawlessness" (διὰ τὴν ἀνομίαν αὐτῶν). The NIV and JPS have "swept away by terrors." The psalmist hoped or believed that God would not let them escape punishment forever.

73:20. As one having a dream, the psalmist believed God would wake up and (come to his senses) and then "intentionally rise up" and despise these "shadows" ("phantom" in NETS; cf. LXX; "image" in JPS; and "fantasies" in NIV).

Confession and Praise and Profession of Faith (73:21–28)
In these concluding verses, the psalmist reflected on his past and present perceptions of God's work in the world.

73:21. The psalmist opened with a confession of trust (vv. 21–24). He confessed that his "heart" and his "kidneys" (i.e., his emotions) had been "sour" (יִתְחַמֵּץ) and "disturbed" (אֶשְׁתּוֹנָן; cf. HALOT, s.v. "I חמץ" and "I שׁנן," pp. 329, 1606).

Literally in Hebrew these verbs are "leavened" and "sharpened," which exposes again how meanings in translation have to be contextualized. As often in OT poetry these verbs are a combination of an incomplete and complete action, but they are translated with the same tense since the second verb is controlled by the first.

73:22. He also confessed that he had acted like an "uneducated person [בַּעַר]," who lacks knowledge (v. 22a); that is, he says, "I was [like] beasts 'with' (= in relation to) you" (v. 22b). The past tense verb in verse 22b (הָיִיתִי) supplies it as understood in verse 22a. This is an example of reverse parallelism (cf. Isa. 1:3, where "owner's manger" in the second line shows that "master" in the first line was intended as "master's manger"; see Freedman 1985, 42–43).

73:23–24. The psalmist realized that he was "always" (תָמִיד) with God, who (always) has held his right hand (v. 23) and would lead him with godly advice (v. 24a; restated literally as, "and later 'glory,' 'you will take/receive me' [תִּקָּחֵנִי, v. 24b]). The NIV's "you will take me into glory" reflects a modern anachronistic reading. The NRSV and JPS are more likely, with renderings that speak of the psalmist being honored. The word (כָּבוֹד) often translated "glory" has to do with the significance or value of something or someone. The LXX suggests a prefixed preposition "in, with." The psalmist believed that God would keep aiding him with valuable guidance.

73:25. He concluded with the recognition of his utter dependence on God, making a profession of faith (vv. 25–26). In verse 25a, he asked "Who [is (LXX inserts a verb 'exists' ὑπάρχει)] in the heavens/skies for me?" The next line is difficult, literally, "and with you never I have delighted on earth" (v. 25b). The intended sense seems to be as the NRSV has it, "And there is nothing on earth that I desire other than you" (the Greek and Syriac versions have "who," where the MT has "not.").

73:26. The poet then extolled God by saying that although he (the poet) is "finished" (כָּלָה; to complete) in body and spirit (lit., "flesh and heart"), God will always be his "rock of heart" (= his basis for mental/emotional stability) and all that he will ever need ("my portion forever").

73:27. The psalmist then requested that God notice those who are distant from him and unfaithful (lit., "are harlots") and that "they may perish" (volitional mood); restated as, "[that] you might destroy [them]." This qualifies as an imprecation, followed in the next verse with a promise to give a testimony.

73:28. Finally, he vowed to recount all of God's (marvelous) works (on his behalf; v. 28b) because (in contrast to those who are unfaithful; וַאֲנִי, "but I") for him "to stay close" (LXX, προσκολλᾶσθαι) to God is good (v. 28ai; MT has "nearness of God"); so he has set (= "made") the Lord Yahweh as his refuge (v. 28aii; the KJV has the best paraphrase: "I have put my trust in the Lord GOD"). He promised that when God protects him from these ungodly people, he then will testify before his own people. The psalmists almost never praised God "in advance," only after the fact.

THEOLOGICAL FOCUS

The exegetical idea (although the ungodly seemed to succeed while the godly suffered, the psalmist was satisfied that Israel's God would bring about their downfall) leads to this theological focus: While the godless person appears to prosper and godly people suffer, God will eventually judge the ungodly.

The theological focus of Psalm 73 is threefold. First, the godless appear to prosper while godly people suffer. God seemingly allows wicked people to enjoy life and go unpunished (vv. 4–12), while the godly often suffer from injustice and illness (vv. 13–14). Naturally, this could lead to envy of sinners and discouragement. This is similar to the wisdom themes found in Job and Ecclesiastes, where a believer suffers severely or observes suffering among those who do right, raising questions and doubts about how God is governing life on earth (e.g., Job 31; 33:8–10; Eccl. 7:15; 8:9–10, 14–17).

Second, there is the questioning of God's fairness. He was troubled theologically by the reality of the wicked prospering and not being punished (v. 16). But, like Job's wife, he doubted God's loyalty to a (presumed) absolute promise that obedience leads to blessing and disobedience to a curse, or that right living produces happiness and health, while wickedness leads to death and disease. But such a promise was never made. It was a tradition not truth. It was true in principle and in ultimate reality but was not a guarantee for life on earth. This misunderstanding caused the psalmist to think perhaps his righteousness was in vain (v. 13).

Third, God will judge the ungodly. Every choice has a consequence. People are free to make choices and to be just or unjust. The world is full of broken people of whom some trust God and others do not or trust false gods. God has provided a way of forgiveness and renewal, but perfection is not possible on earth. Wisdom in the OT in general and the Psalms in particular teaches that a wise person avoids wicked behavior because the odds are, the way of ungodly people will culminate in physical or emotional damage, and shorten or end one's life. That someone "gets away with murder" is not a good basis for choosing a life of crime. On the spiritual level, however, ultimately the wicked are judged with death but the righteous with life (abundant life on earth and "eternal life" after physical death).

PREACHING AND TEACHING STRATEGIES

Exegetical and Theological Synthesis
God is good, even though bad things happen to good people and good things happen to bad people. Four theological points are made clear in this psalm.

First, the psalmist makes it clear that we live in a fallen world where bad things happen to good people and good things happen to bad people. The former can be seen in verses 2, 8, and 14, and is implied in verses 4–5. The latter is expressed in verses 3, 4, 5, and 12. The universal nature of this discrepancy can be seen in the fact that Asaph's observations here echo those already made by David in Psalm 37.

Second, it is clear that in this fallen world, sinners sin against both God and other people. The sin against God takes the form of rebellion against God's laws and questioning God himself (v. 2). The sins against others include pride and arrogance (vv. 3, 6a, 8b), violence (v. 6b), and malicious speech (v. 8a).

Third it is clear that any prosperity that the wicked enjoy is strictly temporal. They are on slippery ground about to be cast down to ruin, destroyed, and swept away (v. 18). They will ultimately perish and be destroyed (v. 27)

Fourth, it is also clear that God is good and that he will deliver his people. God's goodness introduces the psalm (v. 1) while the status of being near God concludes the psalm (v. 28), forming "bookends." The ability for God to deliver is underscored by the fact that he is ever-present (v. 23), he gives guidance (v. 24a), he is a refuge (v. 28b), and ultimately, he will take his people into glory (vv. 24b, 25, 26). Indeed, failure to recognize these truths about God is akin to being a senseless beast (v. 22).

Preaching Idea
God is good even though bad things happen to good people and good things happen to bad people.

Contemporary Connections

What does it mean?
If Psalm 73 teaches us anything, it is that one's situation in life is not a reliable indicator of

divine blessing or one's relationship with God. Bad things happen to good people and good things happen to bad people. Since circumstances are unreliable, every one of us must place our trust in the one who is reliable, the God who is good and the one who will ultimately deliver his people.

Is it true?

Is it true that bad things happen to good people and good things happen to bad people? The answer seems patently obvious to anyone who has lived much life.

A harder question to ask and answer relates to how we can square this seeming inequity with the existence of a good, loving, and powerful God. Theologians, philosophers, and the man in the street all wrestle with this issue with varying degrees of sophistication. For theologians, the technical term is theodicy, which basically means the defense of God's goodness in light of the existence of evil. An extended discussion of the issue would go beyond the parameters of this commentary; indeed, it is interesting that the psalmist does not really seem all that interested in vindicating God. God's goodness is presumed rather than defended. In fact, the psalmist sees the problem in himself rather than God (v. 21).

Now what?

Stop viewing circumstances as the lens through which you see divine favor or God's goodness. Then and now, circumstances (bad things happening to good people and good things happening to bad people) are not reliable. They can only reveal "what is" and not "who is."

Recognize that it takes faith to see God's goodness when bad things happen to good people and good things happen to bad people. Philosophical arguments are fine, and perhaps to some degree helpful, but ultimately, we must come to the point that we can say "God's presence is my good" (v. 28).

Find comfort in God's presence. Notice how the psalmist does just that in verse 23: "I am always with you." We often talk about God being with us and that can be true. But it is not simply that God is with us, but that we are with God.

Look to the cross. The cross shows us that bad things happen to good people (i.e., Jesus) and evil can appear to triumph. Yet, the cross also demonstrates that God can still be good and bring about good even, and perhaps especially, in such circumstances.

Creativity in Presentation

Consider using the song "Psalm 73 (My God's Enough)" by the group BarlowGirl. Although the song does not directly reference the words of the psalm, the lyrics capture the essence of it. For a song based on the text of the psalm, a good one is "Psalm 73" by the Sons of Korah, an Australian-based band devoted to giving a fresh voice to the biblical psalms. For other psalm-based songs in general, consider the songs available from EveryPsalm (www.everypsalm.com), a ministry of Christian folk band Poor Bishop Hooper, a husband-wife duo who over three years are releasing a new song every week with the goal of working through the Psalter (150 songs). They may complete their project before we complete our commentary! But you may find their work helpful, along with other Scripture-based albums and artistic and musical projects, for illustrating and experiencing various psalms in your preaching and teaching. Perhaps the work of others will inspire musicians, singers, and songwriters in your church to take up similar efforts as the Lord leads and the Spirit gifts them.

Psalm 73 could be illustrated by discussing the idea of multitasking. In 2014, *Psychology Today* had an article entitled "The Myth of Multitasking" by Nancy Napier, emeritus faculty and leadership coach for the Boise State Executive MBA Program in Idaho. According to the article, "Research in neuroscience tells us that the brain doesn't really do tasks simultaneously, as we thought (hoped) it might. In fact, we just switch tasks quickly. Each time we move from hearing music, to writing a text, or talking to someone, there is a stop/start process that goes on in the brain." Our psalmist probably wasn't familiar with the concept of multitasking, but he did know that he could either focus on the circumstances of his life and the lives of others or he could focus on God. What he could not do was both at the same time.

Due to similarities in themes, one might also consult this section in the discussion of Psalm 37.

In any case, the truth that needs to be hammered home is that God is good even though bad things happen to good people and good things happen to bad people.

- God is good, but the bad look good to me (73:1–3).

- God is good and the bad are bad even if they look good (73:4–20).

- God is good, so I will praise him even when things are bad (73:21–28).

DISCUSSION QUESTIONS

1. Why does God allow wickedness to flourish for so long?

2. Is the expected downfall of the wicked earthly, eschatological, or both?

3. Is it true that no good deed goes unpunished? Explain.

4. Why does the poet say he will speak in riddles and then say these are things known (Ps. 78:2)?

5. Is it significant that the psalm begins and ends with the concept of goodness (vv. 1, 28)? If yes, why?

PSALM 78

EXEGETICAL IDEA
The poet taught that remembering God's past interventions for Israel should strengthen present and future faithfulness.

THEOLOGICAL FOCUS
God is faithful to intervene on behalf of his people in order both to punish and preserve them.

PREACHING IDEA
History matters because rehearsing the past can expose the dangers of disobedience and also remind us of the faithfulness of God.

PREACHING POINTERS
Psalm 78 is another one of the psalms attributed to Asaph (Psa. 50, 73–83), a Levitical music leader in the time of David (1 Chr. 15:17, 19; 16:4–7; 2 Chr. 29:30). The psalm uses the generic address "my people" (v. 1) and concerns itself with passing on the faith from one generation to the next primarily through Israel's history. The appeal to this historical reiteration suggests that perhaps some in Asaph's day had either neglected or forgotten their past. This might not be all that different from today. The study of history doesn't seem to capture the imagination these days as it may have done with past generations. Just a few years ago, an article in *Forbes* magazine by J. Maureen Henderson asked the question, "Just How Clueless Are Millennials When It Comes to Popular History?" Even as this was being written, *The New Yorker* posted an article by Eric Alterman entitled "The Decline of Historical Thinking" (Feb. 4, 2019). Perhaps this decline is due in part to our being so focused on living in the moment, capturing it in a selfie, and posting it on the latest social media platform that we hardly give much of a thought to what happened last week, much less hundreds let alone thousands of years ago.

For God's people, this popular disinterest in history and the events of the past in recent times and antiquity is not only unfortunate but spiritually dangerous. It fails to understand that history is not merely about what happened to "them," but it is about what might happen to "us." This truth is at the core of the Scriptures (e.g., 1 Cor. 10:6), and Psalm 78 in particular clearly demonstrates how rehearsing the past can reveal the dangers of disobedience while reminding us of the faithfulness of God.

WHY IT IS WISE TO REMAIN FAITHFUL TO GOD

LITERARY STRUCTURE AND THEMES

The psalmist wanted the Hebrews to learn from their history, especially from their mistakes, and to recall how God was always faithful when they were not (vv. 1–4). He followed this purpose with, first, a reminder of God's provisions and powerful deeds on their behalf (vv. 5–16); and, second, with a long litany of Israel's rebellions and God's responses (vv. 17–72).

- *The Psalmist's Plea and Plan (78:1–4)*
- *God's Power and Purposes (78:5–16)*
- *Israel's Failures and God's Interventions (78:17–72)*
  - *Israel's Impertinence (78:17–33)*
  - *Israel's Intentions (78:34–39)*
  - *Israel's Impiety (78:40–55)*
  - *Israel's Impertinence Redux (78:56–72)*

EXPOSITION

Psalm 78, a very long psalm (only outdone by Ps. 119), has one of the shortest editorial headings, "A 'maskil' (מַשְׂכִּיל) of Asaph." This suggests some connection to pedagogical prudence. Some of the early Christian commentators remarked how this psalm is so long as to be tiresome (Goldingay 2006, II:479). Its concern is with the need to pass on information to future generations about God's awesome acts for, and fearsome acts against, his people (see Leonard 2008, 241–65, regarding Psalm 78 as a proving ground for principles of inner biblical allusions in the Psalter; and see Leonard 2008, 264n63, citing Margulis 1969, 496, regarding Psalm 78's possible influence on Psalm 105). The emphasis is on how God intervened to punish his people in response to stubborn resistance to his regulations, followed by

compassion and deliverance. The wise aphorism that those who fail to learn the lessons of history are doomed to repeat its mistakes was suggested by this psalm long before stated by the philosopher Santayana. Of the seventy-two verses, thirty-nine deal with God's responses (suffering or salvation) to Israel's insistence on being morally independent and idolatrous.

Remembering Israel's history was essential for Jewish people in the past and present. The tenth plague in Egypt, where God passed over all the firstborn Hebrews in Egypt, was to be remembered during Passover (Exod. 12:1–16). God's protection of Hebrews during the time of Esther was to be remembered during the Feast of Purim (Esther 9:23–28). It was also equally important to remember the failures of the exodus generation (e.g. Exod. 13:3; Deut. 6:20–25; 29:1–29; Pss. 29:3–4, 10; 78:43–51; 105:27–36; cf. Heb. 4:1). Consequently, the poet taught that remembering God's past interventions for Israel should strengthen present and future faithfulness.

The Psalmist's Plea and Plan (78:1–4)

The people were summoned to listen to wise instruction, to be passed down through, and as vital for, future generations.

78:1. The psalmist opened with a plea. He called on his fellow Hebrews to pay close attention to "my torah" (תּוֹרָתִי), meaning not his "law" (as often used), but instruction (v. 1a); to "what I am saying" (v. 1b). "Give ear!" (v. 1a) is restated as "stretch out your ear!" (v. 1b). In each case the same root (אזן) is used, first as a verb (הַאֲזִינָה; impv.) then as a direct object (אׇזְנְכֶם; "your ears").

78:2–3. The psalmist then moved to a plan (vv. 2–4). His developed advice included regulations, and was deemed essential knowledge or wisdom, because he planned to propound proverbs (מָשָׁל) and ancient riddles (חִידוֹת). A "proverb; parable" had to do with making a comparison; that is, he would teach lessons for successful living verified by repeated experience. Proven principles that were heard and now known from reports handed down from their forefathers were considered sound advice.

78:4. The psalmist then included his audience and determined that "we will not hide these testimonies about 'Yahweh' (יְהוָה) by telling about his power and the wonders he performed from the next generation of their fathers' descendants." The construct pair "praises of 'Yahweh' [תְּהִלּוֹת יְהוָה]," as the object of the verb "recount," indicated God's praiseworthy deeds to which testimony would be given. The verb (מְסַפְּרִים; ptc.) indicated a testimony that they would "keep recounting." The same idea appeared in verse 3 ("told to us"; סִפְּרוּ־לָנוּ) in regard to what the forefathers had recounted.

God's Power and Purposes (78:5–16)
The psalmist hoped that future generations, unlike the previous, would respond with greater obedience by remembering God's past proven power and help.

78:5. The psalmist continued by directing attention to God's power. For example, God erected (קוּם "to stand") statutes, i.e., established a law code (תּוֹרָה; same word in v. 1) in Jacob (rephrased as "in Israel"), which God commanded the forefathers "to teach" (לְהוֹדִיעָם; lit., "make them know"; infin. of purpose; v. 5). Because Jacob's name was changed to Israel, eventually the nation and more specifically the northern kingdom, after civil division, became "Israel" (one who struggles with God).

78:6. The purpose of this was "so that" (לְמַעַן) the next generation of yet-to-be-born children "might know [these instructions]" (v. 6a; cf. the verbal tenses in the LXX). Also, the purpose was that they will rise up and recount (this testimony; v. 6b; same verbs as in vv. 3 and 5, respectively) to their children. Verbs with indicative forms at times need to be interpreted with a volitional mood due to the context. The inspired text only had consonants, so the spelling tradition with vowels (MT) can at times be read with some flexibility.

Israel in Egypt by Edward Poynter (ca. 1867)

78:7–11. The psalmist believed that, as a result of such testimony, they (the next generation) would put its confidence (כִּסְלָם) in God and not forget God's works (v. 7a); and, therefore, they would keep his commandments (v. 7b); and they would not be like the older generation, which was "constantly" (mood of each ptc.) stubborn and rebellious (v. 8a), and which did not "make firm its heart," meaning it did not set its affections wholly on God (v. 8bi). In other words, "its spirit" (רוּחוֹ) or "emotions" or "intentions" were not entrusted toward God (v. 8bii). For example, some Ephraimite archers retreated in battle (v. 9); they did not keep his covenant, (meaning) they "steadfastly refused" (stem of מאן) to follow his laws (v. 10). Also, they forgot the wondrous works that he had "displayed" (causative stem of "see" ראה; v. 11).

78:12–16. The psalmist recalled that God performed marvels before their fathers in the fields of Zoan in "the land that is [appos.] Egypt." Yet translators need only say "Egypt" since "land/country of/being" is understood. He also recalled that God split apart the sea and "enabled them to pass over [it]" (וַיַּעֲבִירֵם, v. 13; cf. Exod. 14:29, "walked through"). He made (verbal causation form) the water stand up like a "dam" (v. 13; but NETS, cf. LXX, has "wineskin"; HALOT, s.v. "נֵד," p. 671). He led them with a cloud in the daytime and with the light from a fire during the night (v. 14; cf. Exod. 13:20–22). He split apart rocks in the desert and "enabled [verbal causation form] them to drink" from (ocean-like; lit., "abundant") depths (v. 15; cf. Exod. 17:6). He made streams come out from a rock and made water flow (verbal causation) down like a river (v. 16).

Israel's Failures and God's Interventions (78:17–33)

Next the psalmist gave a lengthy review of the ways Israel rebelled and how God intervened.

Israel's Impertinence (78:17–33)

78:17–18. Despite previous miracles, Israel was impertinent. They (frequentative verbs) "repeatedly" (וַיּוֹסִיפוּ עוֹד) sinned and rebelled (against) "the Most-High," (עֶלְיוֹן; cf. LXX, ὕψιστον) in the desert. They "frequently tested" God "intentionally" (lit., "in their hearts" = "mentally" as a Hebrew idiom) by asking for food "for themselves" (לְנַפְשָׁם; correctly in the JPS; but "for their souls" archaically in the NETS; even the KJV avoids this and has "for their lust"; v. 18). The NIV has "food they craved."

78:19–20. They spoke against God by questioning if he could really set a table in the desert. Although he once made water flow from a smitten rock, they wondered if he could really provide food for his people.

Moses Striking the Rock by Jacopo Tintoretto (ca. 1563)

78:21–24. When God heard this, because they did not trust in his salvation (vv. 21a, 22), he intervened. God became very angry and his fiery wrath burned against Israel (v. 21b); so (to teach them a lesson): he commanded "doors" in the sky to open and rained down "manna" [מָן], the "grain [דָּגָן] from the sky/heavens," for them to eat (vv. 23–24).

Hebrew Cosmology (Ps. 78:23)

The psalmist's reference to "doors" in the sky indicated a shared view of the cosmos in the

ANE. The consensus has been that the ancients perceived a flat earth overarched by a sky dome under the starry "heavens," held up by pillars, with waters above and below the earth, and the world of the dead also below the land. This verse and others in the OT (like the floodgates ["windows" in KJV] of heaven and the waters above and below in Genesis 1–2; 7:11) suggest the authors of these texts had a cosmology at least somewhat like their neighboring cultures. However, some oppose this interpretation (e.g., Keel 1985, 157–61; Weeks 2006, 283–93; Houtman 1993, n.p.). Yet, whatever cosmology was held by the Hebrews, such passages in the OT do not intend to make scientific statements or propositions about the actual nature of the universe. Such observations were only necessary supportive references, relative in terms that contemporaries would understand, as parts of texts focused on certain absolute theological and practical truths. Divine revelation came through human instrumentality in an ancient historical and cultural context. Divine communication (the message) is housed in a human container (the messenger; although guided by God). Only the former is timeless and universal. If written today, the message (theology) would be the same, but its manner of expression (culturally, linguistically, and technically) would be different.

78:25. Each person ate abundant provisions of mighty bread that God sent to them (Exod. 16:4).

78:26. God sent forth by his power (a wind storm) in the sky in the east and south (the initial verb in the MT is a jussive, suggesting "may he send out," but the parallel verb is a past tense; therefore, the opening verb was probably originally some past tense form. The Greek OT (LXX) has an aorist verb both times and also has "south" rather than "east" in the first line).

78:27–30. God rained down birds for meat upon them like dust or the sand along the sea, making them fall down among their camp, all around their tents. So, they ate and were stuffed since he had given them their desire (vv. 27–29); and this happened while they had not become estranged from their desired (food) and it was still in their mouths (v. 30).

78:31–33. And in anger God rose up and killed and humiliated (lit., "made bow down") the fattest and youngest (= healthiest and strongest) Israelites (v. 31; NETS, cf. LXX, "he killed among their sleek ones, and the select of Israel he shackled"). But in spite of this, they still rebelled (against God) and did not believe in his wonders (v. 32), so he filled the rest of their life with futility and terror (v. 33).

Israel's Intentions (78:34–39)
Although God's people had good intentions, they lacked the resolve or "spirit" to obey faithfully.

78:34–37. The Israelites fell into a lazy pattern of pretending to repent each time God punished them. The verb used is "killed them" (הֲרָגָם; v. 34). This was both literally and figuratively the case. They indicated they wanted to return to repent (v. 34), and they remembered (= acknowledged) that God Most High (was) their rock and redeemer (v. 35). But in reality, they were not truthful or sincere (v. 36). They had no intention of remaining committed or faithful to his covenant (v. 37).

78:38–39. Still, despite Israel's false intentions, God intervened. God (has) compassion, covers iniquity, and does not destroy (v. 38a; NETS, cf. LXX, says "will atone . . . not destroy them"). Also, he repeatedly turns back his anger (lit., "nose") and does not stir up his wrath (v. 38b; NETS, cf. LXX, has future tenses, "will increase . . . [will] not ignite"), and he remembered (past tense verb) that they (are only) human (lit., "flesh"), a (mere) passing breeze that will not return (once it is gone; v. 39).

Israel's Impiety (78:40–55)

The Israelites rebelled against God and failed to remember his power to redeem as displayed to them and the Egyptians in the ten plagues, his shepherding guidance in the desert, and his giving of the land of Canaan to his people as their promised inheritance.

78:40–43. The psalmist underscored Israel's impiety when he said they often (frequentative verb forms) "fostered rebellion and grief" (מרה and עצב II) in the wilderness wasteland (v. 40; NETS, cf. LXX, has the adverb "how often[?]," ποσάκις, for the initial "how" [כַּמָּה]; but the Syriac translators took it as "they" [הֵמָּה]). The former is closest to the MT. They returned, and "tested and provoked" (frequentative verbs) Israel's "holy" (unique) God (v. 41). They forgot his intervention (lit., "hand"), when he redeemed them from the adversary (the Greek OT has "from the oppressor's hand"; cf. NETS), when he displayed (lit., "set") his (wondrous) sign in the fields of Zoan in Egypt (vv. 42–43; two words for "sign" are used, but NETS, cf. LXX, has "signs . . . wonders"; and Zoan is Tanis).

78:44–50. As a result, God intervened (vv. 44–55). God made them suffer.

78:44. The psalmist exemplified God's intervention and the suffering of the Egyptians by recalling that God turned their River (lit., "rivers") and streams into blood so (that from them) they could not drink (Exod. 7:20–21). For the psalmist, "not they will drink," contextually, was a continuous action, set in the past by the previous verb ("then he turned").

78:45. God kept sending (frequentative form of שלח) a swarm among them (Exod. 8:21 [HB 8:17]; but note that for the swarm, this verse uses the strong form מְשַׁלֵּחַ) that then devoured them, and frogs (cf. Exod. 8:2 [HB 7:27]) that devastated them. The expression "struck by" (נָגַף) in Exodus MT 7:27 is the verb "plague" in the NIV. "Flies" as in the NIV (Ps. 78:45) is not in the MT. The NETS (cf. LXX) has "dog-fly"; the parallelism could be static, and the "swarm" of verse 45a could be repeated as frogs in verse 45b (see v. 46).

78:46. God gave over their harvests (lit., crops and labor) to locusts (lit., grasshopper and locust; NETS has "rust . . . grasshopper"; LXX's ἐρυσίβη is "mildew"; JPS has "grubs . . . locusts"; cf. Exod. 10:12–15).

78:47–50. He (God), literally, "slays" (= kept ruining) their vines with hail, their sycamores (fig-trees) with frost (v. 47). He shut (down) (וַיַּסְגֵּר; form = agency [i.e. God] and past tense) their animals with hail, their cattle with flashes (v. 48; the MT's use of prefixed preposition ל on "hail" [לַבָּרָד] conflicts with the previous "with hail" (בַּבָּרָד), and several Hebrew mss. have the ב prefix. But ל also is used with "flashes [= lightning; לָרְשָׁפִים]," so the intention of the verse originally was likely that God "gave the livestock over to hail storms" (vv. 48–49a; see NIV, JPS, NETS, KJV, all with this same idea for the verb). He sent against them the heat of his anger (lit., "nose"): (his) wrath, indignation, and distress (= "hostility"); that is, a company of bad messengers (probably illness; v. 49b). He cleared a path for his anger (v. 50a), which included even death through pestilence (or plague; v. 50b). The JPS says accurately, "He did not stop short of slaying them, but gave them over to pestilence" (v. 50b). Even so, he saved them (78:51–55).

78:51. God smote the firstborn of all the Egyptians (who are rephrased and defined as the beginning of their strength in the Hamitic tents). The Egyptians were viewed as descendants of Noah's son Ham (Gen. 10:6).

78:52–55. But like a flock of sheep he led his people out (of Egypt) and through the desert

(v. 52), and he led them in safety so that they were not afraid, while the sea covered their enemies (v. 53); and thereby he brought them to the border of his holy (place), to the hill his right hand took (lit., "bought; acquired"; v. 54). The poet focused on the promised land in terms of its most prized possession, the holy hill Zion, the sight of Jerusalem. He drove away the (enemy) nations sharing the land, and "made fall" (לפנ, causative form) a region to them as a possession (v. 55a); so, he settled the Israelites in their tents (v. 55b). The allotted region is not the entire land in verse 55ai, but the tribal portions (JPS, "He expelled nations before them, settled the tribes of Israel in their tents, allotting them their portion by the line" [which approach inverts the lines]). The enemy was defeated and then the territory divided.

Israel's Impertinence Redux (78:56–72)

The Israelites added insult to injury by rebellion joined with the audacity to test God.

78:56–58. The psalmist highlighted Israel's impertinence by recalling their testing of the Most-High God by rebelling against him, (meaning) they did not keep his decrees (v. 56). Just like their forefathers, they backslid and were treacherous; they were bent like a faulty bow (v. 57; i.e., they were unfaithful and unreliable). They made God mad (כעס, causative form) and jealous with their (worship of) graven images on sacred (Canaanite) hill tops (v. 58).

78:59–61. The psalmist underscored God's intervention by recalling his decision to make Israel suffer for their disobedience (vv. 59–64). He became very agitated (reflexive form of עבר II) and utterly rejected Israel (v. 59); then he forsook the tabernacle tent at Shiloh, (where) he dwelt among humans (v. 60; NETS, cf. LXX, has "he encamped"). Then he gave his strength and beauty into the captive hands of the adversary (v. 61). The NETS, cf. LXX, has "[he] gave their strength" and the Syriac version has

the equivalent of "His people." Based on Psalm 132:8, this "powerful glory" is thought to be the ark (box) containing the covenant (NIV, "He sent the ark of his might"; 78:61); however, the Greek OT did not follow this interpretation; cf. NETS, "and gave their strength over to captivity and their comeliness into an enemy's hands."

78:62–63. He relinquished (same verb as v. 48; וַיַּסְגֵּר) his people to slaughter (lit., "the sword") because he was very upset (reflexive form of עבר II) with his possession (v. 62). The JPS reads, "He gave His people over to the sword; He was enraged at His very own." For example: his young men were devoured by fire and "his virgins [וּבְתוּלֹתָיו] were not praised [הוּלָּלוּ]" (v. 63). Here the counterpart term in the parallelism is "young men," so most versions have the translation "maidens." The NIV has "their young women had no wedding songs"; but the NETS (cf. LXX) has "their girls were not bewailed."

78:64. The priests fell by the sword and the widows "were not able to weep" (past continuous action). Why they did not cry is curious, so the LXX (OT Greek) is probably right to interpret it as "their widows will not be lamented" (NETS; Jerome and the Syriac version agree). "They could not weep" remains a mystery, and the context seems to be focused on some way in which they were abused. However, eventually he (God) saved them (78:65–72).

78:65–69. The Lord woke up like someone asleep from having been overcome by wine (v. 65), and then, he routed (lit., "smote back") his enemies and handed (lit., "gave") them (lit., "it") "perpetual" (עוֹלָם) shame (v. 66). Then he rejected and ignored (lit., "did not choose") Jacob's tent and Ephraim's tribe (v. 67); but rather, he choose Judah's tribe, (the location of) Zion's hill, which he loved (v. 68). Note how in the past God loved (chose) Jacob but hated (did not choose) Esau (Mal 1:2–3);

then he constructed his sanctuary (lit., "holy place"), like the skies and like the land he established to (be) "perpetual" (עוֹלָם, traditional "everlasting"; v. 69). How we use "everlasting" today in popular terms does not conform to this context. The phrase, however, in the parallelism is obviously the counterpart to "the earth; land," which in some Hebrew mss., as well as the Greek and Syriac versions, is "in the land" (in contrast to the MT's "like the land").

78:70–72. Also, the Lord chose David (to be) his servant, so he took him from a sheep pen; he brought him from tending (lit., "nursing") (them) to shepherd Jacob/Israel his people and possession (vv. 70–71). Consequently, he (David) shepherded them with heartfelt integrity, and led them with "understanding hands" (v. 72; JPS and NIV, "skillful hands"; NETS, cf. LXX, "cleverness of his hands"). The idea seems to be "with integrity and insight."

THEOLOGICAL FOCUS

The exegetical idea (the poet taught that remembering God's past interventions for Israel should strengthen present and future faithfulness) leads to this theological focus: God is faithful to intervene on behalf of his people in order both to punish and preserve them.

Psalm 78 is concerned with God as a Rock and Redeemer. Whenever his people rebel against his love and law, he is steadfast to make them suffer for their sins, and at the same time save them from extinction in spite of their sins. Such suffering may be directed by God or come indirectly from God through natural disasters or natural consequences of unwise, risky, or dangerous behavior. The psalmist believed that remembering the past (God's wrath and rescue) can empower his people to live more obediently in the present and future. The psalm, therefore, is drawn out (*ad tedium*) due to his many examples.

A question for theology proper is engaged here in regard to the focus on God's anger. Does

God really lose his temper? Such wording may be viewed as consistent with (1) an ancient worldview and a time when verbal and written divine revelation was in its early stages, (2) the ANE religious and cultural context, and in light of this (3) an ancient Hebrew poet's attempt to represent God in anthropomorphic terms (with which an ancient human audience was familiar and could identify). The intention was to communicate a bottom line about God's nature, that he cares about his people and will chastise those he loves if necessary, to ensure renewed and continued relationship and redemption.

PREACHING AND TEACHING STRATEGIES

Exegetical and Theological Synthesis

It seems appropriate that the second longest psalm in the Psalter would retell the long story of Israel's unfaithfulness and judgment and the equally long story of God's faithfulness. It seems equally appropriate that the psalm begins with a call to hear the lessons of history. History shares certain affinities with wisdom, and this call echoes wisdom's appeals (e.g., Prov. 1:8–9; 4:1, 10). For example, wisdom like history is grounded in the past. In wisdom, those who have gone before us share their life experiences, their history as it were, so that we might learn from them. And wisdom like history, although grounded in the past, functions to affect the present. This rationale is unpacked in verses 5–8. We are to teach and tell the next generation so that they might know what God has commanded (v. 6), set their hope in God (v. 7), not forget his works (v. 7), keep his commandments (v. 7), and avoid making the same mistakes as their forefathers who were stubborn and rebellious (v. 8).

The remainder of the psalm is a survey of Israel's history. This history highlights two main themes: the unfaithfulness of God's people (and the dangers that result) and the faithfulness of God. Commentators outline this material in different ways, but basically it is the story of the exodus to the Promised Land, with some material extending into the period of the monarchy (vv. 9–11, 56–72). The theme of Israel's unfaithfulness can be seen in verses 9–10, 11a, 17–20, 22, 32, 36–37, 40–43, and 56–58. The resulting judgment can be noted in verses 21–22, 31, 33–34, and 59–66. Nonetheless, God's faithfulness is highlighted in verses 11b–16, 23–30, 38–39, 44–55, and 69–2.

Preaching Idea

History matters because rehearsing the past can expose the dangers of disobedience and also remind us of the faithfulness of God.

Contemporary Connections

What does it mean?

What all this means is that history matters, and this is particularly true as it relates to our relationship with God. The significance of history for the person of faith is at least threefold.

First, history is one way that God reveals himself. He reveals himself through his-story. Since much of the Bible is historical narrative, much of our doctrine about God derives from the history recorded there. This is not to deny that there are no theological assertions or statements in the Bible. There are obviously such statements, but they are often fleshed out in the stories of Scripture.

Second, history provides a powerful and memorable way of seeing ourselves and our circumstances. The historical accounts in the Bible provide a mirror that can reflect our own actions, attitudes, and choices. Paul's statement in 1 Corinthians 10:11 is interesting in this regard: "Now these things happened to them as an *example*, but they were written down for our *instruction*, on whom the end of the ages has come" (my emphasis). Note that God acted in time and space for the original benefit of his people and he recorded that action for the benefit of those who would follow later. In this way

a later generation would be able to see themselves and God even though they were not physically present in the original event.

Third, and very importantly, this understanding of history means that our preaching, teaching, and use of history is not merely history for history's sake. Occasionally someone will remark that they love it when a preacher or teacher gets into the historical background. And frankly, many preachers and teachers enjoy laying out the historical table from which their sermon or lesson will dine. The danger in doing so, however, is that we can camp in the relative safety of the *then* without being personally challenged in the *now*. We can cluck our collective tongues at the shortcomings of the people in our stories without recognizing that more often than not, their stories are our stories.

Is it true?

Is it true, that history in general, and biblical history in particular, is really that important? Psalm 78 and much of the Bible seem to think so. About 80 percent of Psalm 78 focuses on the past (sixty-four of its seventy-two verses). Old Testament scholar C. Hassell Bullock identifies no less than twenty-five historical places or events in the psalm (Bullock 2017, 47). Likewise, although estimates will vary, a very conservative guess would be that more than 50 percent of the Bible consists of narratives. What should be abundantly clear to anyone who has spent significant time in the Bible is that it is not formatted as a doctrinal statement or systematic theology. Much of it is theology expressed through narratives of the past.

The importance of biblical history is also evidenced by the fact that most people probably know more biblical stories than biblical statements. Some Christians can recite Psalm 23 or John 3:16 from memory, but many more can retell biblical stories such as Adam and Eve in the garden, David and Goliath, and Jesus feeding the five thousand. Simply put, biblical history is important because they have a way of implanting in our consciousness and motivating us in ways that statements, even slogans, do not.

Now what?

Now that we have established the importance of biblical history, four personal challenges can be put forward.

First, learn the historical accounts in the Bible. One of the best ways to do this is to commit to reading through the entire Bible in a year. There are many different plans, approaches, and even apps available to help you get started and to stay on track. A quick search online should reveal a number of them.

Second, look for parallels between the past and the present. Like the psalmist, use biblical history to inform and challenge your life and those with whom you interact.

Third, avoid the faithlessness that too often characterized the story of Israel. This is not complicated, but it is also not easy. Commit yourself today to living in obedience to the God who loves you, because of the Son of God who died for you, and the Spirit of God who empowers you and indwells you.

Fourth, be grateful for the faithfulness of God. Such is the mystery of grace that even when we fail, God is still faithful. This grace is not to be abused, but it is to be believed and to give voice to our praises.

Creativity in Presentation

Consider beginning your message by referring to the two articles mentioned previously: J. Maureen Henderson's article in *Forbes*, "Just How Clueless Are Millennials When It Comes to Popular History?" (August 26, 2014), and Eric Alterman's article in *The New Yorker* entitled "The Decline of Historical Thinking" (February 4, 2019). You can also search the internet for one of Jay Leno's "JayWalking" clips where he asks people historical questions. You may also find more contemporary interviewers questioning people on the street. The key is to make sure the humor involved in

exposing people's ignorance of the past serves to illustrate why history matters.

DNA tests are another way of introducing the psalm and seem to be all the rage at the moment. One of the companies offering this service speaks in terms of unlocking your past and inspiring your future, and apparently many have signed up to do just that. But even if such tests can tell you about the ethnicity and geographical location of your ancestors, it is hard to see how they can unlock or inspire. Though the Bible can't help you discover your ethnicity or locate your geographic origins, it can help you to see God, see yourself, and inspire you to live more faithfully.

Another way to introduce the psalm is referencing Sam Wineburg's 2018 book, *Why Learn History (When It's Already on Your Phone)*. Although this book is not written from a biblical perspective and really addresses a broad range of educational issues, one could piggyback off of the title with something like, "Why Learn the Bible (When It's Already on Your Phone)?" Another suggestion would be to utilize a baton like those used in running relay races as a prop to remind the audience of the need to pass the baton to the next generation. One way to do this is by passing on the rich legacy of God's faithfulness to his often-wayward people (see esp. vv. 4–8).

Make sure to reinforce the idea that history matters because rehearsing it exposes the dangers of disobedience and remind us of the faithfulness of God. This can be expressed in three commitments.

- Be committed to retelling what God has done (78:1–4).

- Be committed to recalling what God has done (78:5–16).

- Be committed to revisiting past failures (78:17–72).

DISCUSSION QUESTIONS

1. Why does the poet say he will speak in riddles and then say these are things known (Ps. 78:2)?

2. Why is the same word used in the OT for praise of God also used for praise of unmarried girls (Ps. 78:63)?

3. How should we explain the psalmist's description of God as waking from a stupor like a drunk (Ps. 78:65)?

4. What is the relationship in verse 7 between setting one's hope in God, not forgetting the works of God, and keeping God's commandment?

5. How many people, events, and places from the OT can you identify in verses 9–72?

PSALM 127

EXEGETICAL IDEA
Israelite pilgrims rejoiced in Yahweh's essential involvement in building and protecting a city to avoid futility, and his provision of sons to ensure strength against opponents.

THEOLOGICAL FOCUS
Unless God is involved in a project, the venture is vain.

PREACHING IDEA
True security and lasting significance in life is found in God alone.

PREACHING POINTERS
It seems that security is on everybody's mind these days. The average person is concerned about pandemics, terrorism, mass shootings, global-warming, identity theft, and zombies, just to name a few. (Well, maybe not zombies!) We want to feel secure. We also want to know that our lives matter, and that our lives are significant. I suspect that this is one of the major drivers in social media. If I post frequently about my life, then it must truly matter; thus, the seemingly endless pictures of our food, clothes, friends, parties, pets, and the like are shared.

The poet of Psalm 127 (Solomon, according to the superscription) had different concerns in his day, and he wouldn't be posting "selfies," but the desire for true security and lasting significance was just as real then as it is now. As one of the psalms that would be sung on the way to the temple associated with Solomon, one would be reminded of the Lord's protection over Jerusalem and the temple, and also of their families. This song highlights the intersection point between faith and family, and the psalmist has put his finger on something that many Israelites then and many Christ-followers today have failed to realize—namely, true security and lasting significance of both faith and family are found in God alone.

THE FRUITFUL BENEFITS OF RELYING ON GOD
(PSALM OF ASCENTS)

LITERARY STRUCTURE AND THEMES

The psalm follows a progression from self-reliance to relying on others. Whether you are a builder, soldier, or common laborer, if you do not rely on God, your work is "insignificant" (שָׁוְא) (vv. 1–2). This is often translated "vanity," but a different word (הֶבֶל) is the well-known "vanity" of Ecclesiastes, which has more the sense of something enigmatic or transitory. Working without relying on God makes the work a waste of time. One way God helps is by providing sons as a reward (v. 3, for trusting God). The more sons the better, and more are usually born when a man begins being a father when younger than older (v. 4). A man who has many sons is fortunate. The odds are increased that he will succeed when attacked by enemies or engaged with other adversaries or competitors (v. 5).

- **The Vanity of Self Reliance (127:1–2)**
  - *In Building a House (127:1a)*
  - *In Guarding a City (127:1b)*
  - *In Working a Job (127:2)*
- **The Value of Sons (127:3–5)**
  - *As Wealth (127:3)*
  - *As Weapons (127:4)*
  - *As Wisdom (127:5)*

EXPOSITION

In historical and cultural context, the psalmist most likely was concerned with the great blessing that was a son, especially many sons. Naturally, this is due to his male-dominated society. The word for "son" can also be translated "child" or "descendant" depending on context. Hermeneutically and theologically, the reader should not take this as a divine teaching that sons are

more important than daughters; this was just true culturally in that ancient and patriarchal situation. The "son" in wisdom texts should not be modernized to "child," since contextually a "son" was meant. This is not a gender discrimination. That the text *recognizes* the gender realities of its times does not mean it *promotes* the inferiority of women in principle. In context, the reality was that women were valued, due to cultural realities, mainly as wives, mothers, and homemakers, while men were expected to farm, fish, shepherd, soldier, etc. The Bible contains contextualized terms that the current audience could understand. We have to apply the timeless truths it affirms to our culture. As for God, the psalm stresses him as indispensable for activities like building, defense, or business, but God also provides sons ("children" today) as his way to enhance success in such endeavors. As a result, Israelite pilgrims rejoiced in Yahweh's essential involvement in building and protecting a city to avoid futility, and his provision of sons to ensure strength against opponents.

The Vanity of Self Reliance (127:1–2)

Work done in your own strength, apart from God's help, is a waste of time.

In Building a House (127:1a)

127:1a. The psalmist observed that if Yahweh (יְהוָה) is not he who will build a house, then "insignificance" (שָׁוְא) would characterize its construction.

In Guarding a City (127:1b)

127:1b. Also, if Yahweh is not the one who will watch (יִשְׁמָר) over a city, (then) futility (שָׁוְא)

characterizes the watchmen (שׁוֹמֵר) who "stand guard" (שָׁקַד).

In Working a Job (127:2)

127:2. Vanity (שָׁוְא) (it is) for you to keep being early (ptc.) to rise, to keep being late (ptc.) to sit (i.e., to rest), to keep eating (ptc.) (your) food (in) pain (v. 2a), for he will give sleep to his beloved (v. 2b). What is the logic of this statement? The idea seems to be that it is a waste of time to create agony and anxiety for yourself through overwork and lack of sleep because God (apparently) can be relied upon to provide effective rest or sleep to those for whom he cares (suggesting those who trust in him and not in excessive toil to avoid troubles). The JPS admits that the Hebrew here is unclear but gives the rendering, "He provides as much for His loved ones while they sleep." The NRSV (1989) suggests as an alternative "for he provides for his beloved during sleep", which probably makes the most sense.

> ### The Connection between Verses 1–2 and 3–5
> A Building a house without God is vain
>   B Guarding a city without God is vain
>   C Working a job without God is vain
> Aʹ But with sons as builders is rewarding
>   Bʹ But with sons as weapons is rewarding
>   Cʹ But with sons as coworkers is rewarding

The Value of Sons (127:3–5)

God favors the godly man with many sons as a reward, so he will succeed in his work.

As Wealth (127:3)

127:3. Some entitle this as being about family, but the focus is specifically sons. "Behold," the psalmist exclaimed, "sons [בָּנִים] are a possession [source genitive] *from* [נַחֲלַת] 'Yahweh' (יְהוָה)" (v. 3a) , and "the fruit of the womb a wage" (v. 3b). The idea of these sons as possessions and wages is "heritage . . . reward" in the NIV, "provision . . . reward" in the JPS, and "heritage . . . wage" in the NETS (cf. LXX, κληρονομία . . . μισθὸς). Sons (LXX, υἱοί) are valued as assets and a blessing

from God. The parallel expression in the second line, "fruit" (פְּרִי) (NIV has "reward"), is not "children" but another way to describe these "sons." The text does not teach that daughters are inferior but reflects the cultural situation, in which sons were vital for the father's business.

At the same time, in Psalm 17:14 בָּנִים means "sons" while עוֹלְלֵי means "children." Its meaning is ambiguous in a text like Genesis 10:1. Sometimes בָּנִים is distinguished from "daughters" (בָּנוֹת; cf. Gen. 5:22), but in a passage like Psalm 128:6 it could indicates children of either gender. Modern and gender-sensitive readers want Psalm 127 to mean "children," but exegesis is about what the author intended. Verse 3b technically is repeating "sons" in 3a, not expanding from sons to children, although that is not impossible. Still, the fact that the children being discussed are like arrows in verse 4 suggests sons. Even versions like the NIV that use "children" in verse 3b switch to sons in verse 4b. In verse 5b, these "arrows" are with the father when he meets enemies at the city gates.

As Weapons (127:4)

127:4. Sons, especially those born when the father is a young adult, also are like arrows in the hands of a mighty one (warrior). They can be "launched" as a way to protect and promote a family's fortune and force.

As Wisdom (127:5)

127:5. A father who has many sons (arrows in his quiver) is especially "fortunate [אַשְׁרֵי; cf. Ps. 1]" (v. 5a), which was a particular reality in the ancient world with high infant mortality and the need for farm hands and workers in the family business. "Fortunate [is] the man" is a typical wisdom expression, but here the "man/person" is not "man" (אִישׁ) but "strong man" (גֶּבֶר; ἄνθρωπος in LXX; cp. גִּבּוֹר "warrior" in v. 4). These sons will not be ashamed when they speak (do business?) with "enemies" (i.e., competitors?) at the city gate (v. 5b). But why not? What assures this success? Strength in numbers? Or is this a military motif, that they will increase the city's ability to defend itself in victory? In the immediate context, the issue would appear to be mainly about benefits of "sons" (בָּנִים) for business. A strong father with many sons is formidable in this ANE setting.

THEOLOGICAL FOCUS

The exegetical idea (Israelite pilgrims rejoiced in Yahweh's essential involvement in building and protecting a city to avoid futility, and his provision of sons to ensure strength against opponents) leads to this theological focus: Unless God is involved in a project, the venture is vain.

The author's main concern was the need to trust in God to achieve the most meaningful and fulfilling vocation. People without God could achieve a lot, but with God the potential for success and satisfaction was greatly enhanced. Work should be done for the right reasons as well as rigor. Also, working alone is risky, without God and/or coworkers. Many hands make light work. An OT wisdom book, Ecclesiastes, makes similar observations. The author described the sad state of a workaholic who had no family to assist him, because he sacrificed family for work (Eccl. 4:7–8). Working with partners ensures more productivity (4:9).

> ### Songs of Ascent
> Several of the songs of Ascent Pilgrim Psalms (120–134) are connected to David, but only this one, Psalm 127, is connected to Solomon. It mentions the building of a house, which may be a reference to God's house, the temple. Otherwise it has a wisdom theme in that it gives advice about the vanity of life, yet the word used (שָׁוְא) is not the same as in Ecclesiastes (הֶבֶל). Psalm 127's genre as a Wisdom Psalm is a mainstay of scholarship, although some think it originally was two separate poems. According to Anderson (1995, II:866), a Sumerian poem praises the goddess Nisaba as the guarantor of all construction and granter of children. This supports the speculation

involved in the notion of this psalm's original disunity. Still, Solomon as author is highly unlikely. Commentators propose the setting (*Sitz*) as building the temple or the birth of a child, but nothing is known for sure.

PREACHING AND TEACHING STRATEGIES

Exegetical and Theological Synthesis

Psalm 127 thematically breaks into two parts. In verses 1–2, security and significance are addressed by noting the vanity of self-reliance. The idea of security is expressed with images of watching over, watchmen, and sleep. The concept of significance is stated negatively in terms of vanity. But significance in the sense of leaving an enduring legacy, is possible when the Lord builds the house, and watches over the city. Most interpreters understand "house" in verse 1 to be a metaphor. But the referent is a bit ambiguous since "house" can be used metaphorically of a temple, dynasty, and a household, etc. The superscription to Solomon, the inclusion among the Psalms of Ascent, and reference to a city and watchmen (v. 1) seems to point in the direction of Solomon's temple. But the second half of the psalm seems to point in the direction of a household. So, it is likely that both faith and family are in view.

In the second part of the psalm, verses 3–5, the psalmist addresses security and significance in terms of children. The idea of significance is seen in the language of children as one's heritage, reward, and blessing. Children are a blessed reminder that we matter if for no other reason than that our children need us. In ministry, one often deals with very broken and damaged people. In talking with such people, those that are parents often confess that they believe that their children are the one thing right about their lives. And although it can be taken to unhealthy extremes when parents try to live too vicariously through their children, children do allow us to find significance in passing on a legacy to the next generation. The idea of children as a means of security seems a bit odd in our culture. After all, parents are to provide security for the child. But in the past and to some degree now, children were a means to provide security for aged parents in a world where social safety nets were practically nonexistent. In this sense, children were a means of security.

Thankfully this psalm not only surfaces the desire for security and significance, but it ultimately points us in the direction of God's providence as its source. It is God, and God alone, who provides true security and lasting significance. He does this by providentially overseeing our lives and by blessing us as his children.

Preaching Idea
True security and lasting significance in life is found in God alone.

Contemporary Connections

What does it mean?
What does it mean that true security and lasting significance in life is found in God alone? To this question, three answers seem appropriate.

First, the fact that the psalm raises the felt need for security and significance indicates that there is nothing wrong with desiring these things.

Second, the psalmist indicates that seeking true security and lasting significance apart from God is an exercise in vanity and will result in having neither. There is an old country-and-western song that spoke of looking for love in all the wrong places. The same could be said of the attempts of many to find security and significance in all the wrong places.

Third, writ large in this passage is the providence of God. God is not merely a source of true security and lasting significance; he is the only source. Variously attributed and oft repeated is the dictum that in every person there is a God-shaped vacuum that only God can fill.

Is it true?
Is it really the case that true security and lasting significance in life is found in God alone? For the person of faith, the answer seems obvious. But on what basis is the answer founded? The answer is at least threefold.

First, true security is ensured by the unmatchable power of God. Strength is often seen as a key component of security whether one is speaking of the military or passwords. If security is what you desire, then you want one who can ensure that security, like the one of whom Job speaks: "I know that you can do all things, and that no purpose of yours can be thwarted" (Job 42:2). Furthermore, this God offers an eternally secure salvation through his Son and our Savior.

Second, lasting significance is grounded in the eternality of God. One of the great enemies of lasting significance is the temporal nature of this life. People come and people go, monuments crumble, and memories fade but God is eternal. And it is out of that eternality that God extends the ultimate offer of lasting significance, namely, eternal life through Christ.

Third, both true security and lasting significance are found in God because he loves us. In the oft-quoted John 3:16, we have the trifecta of God's love ("God so loved the world"), security ("not perish"), and lasting significance ("eternal life") merging together.

Now what?
Some home security companies will do a free security audit of your home. They are hoping that such an audit will reveal an urgent need for the goods and services they offer. In any case, such an audit might be beneficial. But I (Charles) want to encourage you to do a different kind of security audit. *Take an honest and thoughtful look at your life to see where you have placed your security.* Is it in your job, family, bank account, education, something else, or is it in God? If it is in God, you are good to go. If it is in something or someone

else, I want to challenge you to reconsider and place your security in the hands of God either by accepting God's offer of salvation in Christ or living out that salvation if you have already done so.

Similar to the security audit, take a significance audit. Take an honest and thoughtful look at where you derive your significance. If it is in some thing or someone other than God, I want to challenge you to make a change. Root your significance in God by learning what the Bible says about you. For starters, the Bible tells us that we are created in the image of God and that God loved us so much that he sent his Son to pay the penalty our sins. But there is so much more to be discovered in God's Word.

Creativity in Presentation

Ask the audience to take out and look at their keys, wallet/purse, watches and jewelry, and cell phones. Then take a moment to explain how these common items are symbols of security and significance. Keys and passwords are means of security, but they can be duplicated or hacked. Keys, wallets/purses, watches and jewelry, and cell phones can all be status symbols proclaiming that we have arrived. But this only works until there are newer cars and more advanced cell phones. You can then transition into how true security and lasting significance in life is found in God alone.

Although it is less well known than some of Isaac Watts's other hymns, one might be able to incorporate the lyrics of "If God Succeed Not, All the Cost" (1806) into the message either in the introduction or conclusion.

> If God succeed not, all the cost
> And pains to build the house are lost;
> If God the city will not keep,
> The watchful guards as well may sleep.

> What if you rise before the sun,
> And work and toil when day is done;
> Careful and sparing eat your bread,
> To shun that poverty you dread;

> 'Tis all in vain, till God hath blessed;
> He can make rich, yet give us rest:
> Children and friends are blessings too,
> If God our Sovereign make them so.

> Happy the man to whom he sends
> Obedient children, faithful friends:
> How sweet our daily comforts prove
> When they are seasoned with his love!

A more contemporary musical treatment of Psalm 127 can be found in Jason Silver's "Unless the Lord Builds the House." Likewise, searching individual psalms by chapter (e.g., "Psalm 127") on Spotify or other web-based music players or apps is a useful way to discover many psalm-based songs and then evaluate the quality of the lyrics and music as appropriate for your preaching or teaching situation. Content specialist and trainer Kevin Halloran provides more specific suggestions in his blog post, "10 Artists with Worship Albums Based on the Psalms."[1]

The key point to emphasize is this: Unless God is involved in a project, the venture is vain. True security and lasting significance in life is found in God alone.

- The Lord builds houses so we can be secure (127:1).

- The Lord blesses our labor so we can rest (127:2).

- The Lord bestows children so we can have a legacy (127:3–5).

---

1   Kevin Halloran, "10 Artists with Worship Albums Based on the Psalms," Anchored in Christ (blog), October 22, 2019, https://www.kevinhalloran.net/worship-albums-based-on-the-psalms.

DISCUSSION QUESTIONS

1. How does Yahweh (יהוה) assist in building, defense, and business so as to stop vanity (as stated in Psalm 127)?

2. Why do you think Solomon was connected to this psalm?

3. What makes this a Wisdom Psalm—or not?

4. Are the sons beneficial for military or financial reasons or both? Explain.

5. Are these "sons" males only or children in general? Prove your answer.

6. How does Yahweh (יהוה) assist in building, defense, and business so as to stop vanity?

7. Why might this psalm have been included in the Psalms of Ascent or Pilgrim Psalms?

8. Where do you find your security and what is the source of your significance?

PSALM 128

EXEGETICAL IDEA
God prospers prayerful Hebrew fathers who fear and follow "Yahweh" with longevity and posterity, including many sons and grandsons.

THEOLOGICAL FOCUS
Those who prayerfully fear (follow) God receive long life and many descendants.

PREACHING IDEA
A blessed life comes from fearing the Lord and prayer.

PREACHING POINTERS
Now, in the southern United States, the word "bless" in its various forms is a common feature of the vernacular. It is usually used positively like it often is in the Bible ("I'm blessed"), but occasionally "Bless their/your heart" is used to question a person's competence or intelligence or both. In any case, those who speak of being blessed commonly view blessing solely in terms of being in a good state. And being blessed is simply something that happens to you. While both these sentiments are true, the writer of Psalm 128 is most interested in relating the *how* and *what* of blessing. It is not an exhaustive treatment of the topic but a poetic reflection on it.

The standard Hebrew verb for "bless" (*barak*) occurs around eighty times in the Psalms and nearly ninety times if you count the noun form. The verb and noun forms are used around four hundred times in the Old Testament and are found in twenty-nine out of thirty-nine books. It is literally used from the very beginning as God blesses what he has created (Gen. 1:22, 28). There is little question that the word and the concept was important in the Hebrew Bible.

THE FUTURE BENEFITS OF REVERENCING GOD (PSALM OF ASCENTS)

LITERARY STRUCTURE AND THEMES

Psalm 128 moves from past or present blessings or benefits that come from fearing God (vv. 1–4) to those that are anticipated (vv. 5–6a), ending with a benediction (v. 6b). Prosperity and productivity are the themes, first for family, then for posterity, and then for the surrounding population as well as for national peace. Fearing God is essentially obeying his precepts.

- **Benefits from Fearing "Yahweh" (128:1–4)**
- **Benefits for Those Who Fear "Yahweh" (128:5–6a)**
- **A Benediction (128:6b)**

EXPOSITION

Psalm 128 is a wisdom and ascent psalm, as is Psalm 127, but this one praises the man/male who fears Yahweh and mentions the rewards he will receive. Some see this as a blessing pronounced over the pilgrims at the temple for a religious festival (tabernacles?), just before departing (Anderson 1995, II:869), but not all scholars agree.

When the Israelites entered the land, half of the Jewish community stood on Mount Ebal and the other half stood on Mount Gerizim (Deut. 11:26–32). It was on those mounts that the nation went through a ceremony of curses for those who disobeyed God and a series of blessing for those who obeyed him. Psalm 128 draws attention to the blessing received by those who obey God. Thus, God prospers prayerful Hebrew fathers who fear and follow "Yahweh" with longevity and posterity, including many sons and grandsons.

Benefits from Fearing "Yahweh" (128:1–4)

Those who fear God will experience fruitful labor and family.

128:1. The psalmist opened with an exclamation. He heralded how fortunate were those who fear Yahweh, that is, those who "habitually walk" (הַהֹלֵךְ; ptc. = "live") according to his "ways" (= directives). And this is for "all" or "everyone" (כָּל). The bound construction of two nouns like "fear of Yahweh" (יְרֵא יְהוָה) needs to be translated. Hebrew has no word "of." When an expression "*x* of *y*" is seen in a translation, it signals this bound relationship between two nouns, which can be understood interpretively in one of a number of different ways. Here the idea is "fear" or "reverence" *for* God.

The psalmist validated (כִּי; "for"; v. 2a) this with two examples (vv. 2–3) followed by a summation (v. 4).

128:2. First, the psalmist said, "any one of those who follow 'Yahweh' [יְהוָה] will eat [what results from] the work of your hands" (v. 2a). Blessings or "benefits" (same word as "fortunate" in v. 1) and good (things will come) to you (v. 2b, meaning those who fear/follow God). There was a promise of agricultural prosperity that comes from hard work. The word for "blessing" (אַשְׁרֵי) speaks of God's favor or fortune. Another word in the OT often translated "bless(ing)" (II ברך) is sometimes interchangeable with words for "praise" and is used here in verse 4.

128:3. Second, the psalmist spoke of prosperity in the home. The God-fearer was promised a woman (= "wife" here) (who will bear children) like a fruitful vine hanging on the side of his house (v. 3a). Furthermore, his sons (will number or be productive) like olive branches/plants surrounding his table (v. 3b). In OT poetry, the major disjunctive accent is often the "above and below" mark seen with "your house" (בֵּיתֶךָ, called *'oleh veyored*) and not the one found under "olives" (זֵיתִים; called *athnach*). The latter is more prominent in prose texts.

128:4. Finally, to summarize, the poet returned to his opening sentiment (acknowledgement of how beneficial it is to follow God). "Look, this" (הִנֵּה כִי־כֵן; what has just been said in vv. 2–3) characterizes the man who fears Yahweh. In other words, pay attention, he said, to these ways that the "man" (גֶּבֶר) (with) "fear for Yahweh" (יְרֵא יְהוָה) "will be blessed/honored" (יְבֹרַךְ). This "man" is not one of the usual words (אִישׁ; אָדָם) but a word that describes a young, strong male (sometimes translated "warrior"; see comments on Ps. 127:5 above). This return to attention on benefits from obeying God suggest a chiastic structure:

A God blesses those who fear him (v. 1)
   B in their work (v. 2)
   B´ in their home (v. 3)
A´ God blesses those who fear him (v. 4)

Benefits for Those Who Fear "Yahweh" (יְהוָה; 128:5–6a)
The psalmist (and the pilgrims singing this song ascending to Zion) bestow such divine favors on all who reverence Yahweh.

128:5. The psalmist closed with a benediction or blessing of an Israelite's lucrative life. The verbs are volitional in mood: "may he bless you [יְבָרֶכְךָ] . . . and may you see/'experience' [וּרְאֵה]." The English reader may be confused by the NIV's use of "bless" in verse 1 and here, since the same Hebrew word is not used each time. Before, the idea was being fortunate, but now the idea (same word as in v. 4) is about being honored. Using jussive verbs, the poet wishes that from

Zion (Jerusalem; his residence) Yahweh might honor the God-fearer for the rest of his life (v. 5a), and that he might experience (lit., "see") "with/in (the) goodness of Jerusalem" (v. 5b). This last phrase is odd but seems to hope that he will profit from living in Jerusalem. The JPS translated it "share the prosperity of Jerusalem."

128:6a. The psalmist also underscored the long life for Israelites who obey God. Also, he urges such a father (ostensibly by fearing God) to "See! [impv.; i.e., make sure he experiences] grandsons (lit., "sons for your sons"], which implies living long enough to hold his children's children (although again in the patriarchal context the idea is specifically sons and grandsons). In wisdom literature, this implies obedience to God's commands, which normally leads to a longer life because the kinds of behavior that might cut life short are avoided. Although the NIV has "may you live to see" the verb is not volitional as in verse 5, although the same sentiment could be implied. The use of the imperative gives more confidence, "and you [can expect to] see!" your grandchildren.

The Use of the Masculine in the Psalm
The modern translator may be tempted by political correctness to say "person" instead of "man/male/father" in this psalm, but the context (literary and social) dictates that the exegete must convey that the author had fathers in mind. In light of the rest of Scripture, we can now apply this to parents, but context demands a meaning related to men/fathers. We might complain about the ancient parochial or chauvinist or patriarchal mindset, but the exegete must be true to the text and context. How this is applied is another matter. Christian women today can appropriate the principle that God honors those who fear him. Hermeneutically similar in principle, in the ancient world, people were afraid of, or terrorized by, God/gods. Today, with the progress of revelation thus providing more than the ancients had to work with, we want to or can soften this

to "respect," but in the ancient context this is too weak for what was the poet's intention.

A Benediction (v. 6b)
Hope for Israel's future welfare is proclaimed.

128:6b. The psalmist ended (although maybe added by a later editor) with the desire "[May] peace [be] upon Israel." The word for "peace" (שָׁלוֹם) has come into English as "shalom," and for the ancient Hebrews implied inner and outer health or wholeness (HALOT, s.v. "שָׁלוֹם," p. 1506).

THEOLOGICAL FOCUS
The exegetical idea (God prospers prayerful Hebrew fathers who fear and follow "Yahweh" with longevity and posterity, including many sons and grandsons) leads to this theological focus: Those who prayerfully fear (follow) God receive long life and many descendants.

Psalm 128 celebrates the favorable consequences that are expected to be experienced by those who reverence God by being obedient to his directives. (vv. 1, 4a). These outcomes or "blessings" are principally fruitful labor, outside and inside the home (vv. 2–3a), and numerous children (lit., "sons"; v. 3b), but here, unlike Psalm 127, the context does not specify "sons" (as males) per se. The main idea is that faithfulness to God ensures fruitfulness in life.

PREACHING AND TEACHING STRATEGIES

Exegetical and Theological Synthesis
Psalm 128 is not a detailed theological treatise on divine blessing. Rather it is a poetic reflection on it, most notably, the *how* and *what* of it.

The *how* of blessing is twofold. The first *how* involves fear, in particular, the fear of the Lord (vv. 1, 4). This seems counterintuitive because many people see fear as a negative rather than positive. In any case, although the structure of the psalm is somewhat debated (see the

commentary section) it is possible that verses 1–4 are a unit and "the fear of the LORD" forms an inclusio (a bookending type of effect). Whether there is an inclusio or not, the psalmist clearly points out the intimate connection between blessing and the "the fear of the LORD," which is basically the proper orientation of one's life to the Lord in terms of beliefs and behaviors, the former affecting the latter.

The second *how* involves prayer (vv. 5–6). It is possible that verses 5–6 might convey the idea of promise but the grammar seems to favor treating it is a prayer (as do most major English translations). These verses are also interesting in that they connect personal blessings with corporate blessings. The blessing of Israel as a theocratic nation expanded upon the blessing of its members.

The psalmist not only considers the *how* of blessing but also the *what*. This element could be missed by those who live in relative prosperity where materialism seems to be the default setting. Blessing here is tied to fruitfulness, the fruitfulness of hard work (v. 2), the fruitfulness of one's family (vv. 3, 6), and the fruitfulness of one's people (v. 5). The reference to children and grandchildren is especially poignant since mortality rates for children in the ANE seems to have been around 50 percent up to the age of five (King and Stager, 2001, 41).

Preaching Idea
A blessed life comes from fearing the Lord and prayer.

Contemporary Connections

What does it mean?
What does it mean that a blessed life comes from fearing the Lord and prayer? It is important to recognize at the outset that blessing cannot simply be reduced to a mathematical equation:

Fear of the Lord + Prayer = Divine Blessing

But neither can divine blessing be simply and solely reduced to a status as if we awaken to find that the blessing fairy visited us in the middle of the night. There is a connection between blessing and walking in his ways (v. 1). So ultimately it is not an either/or but a both/and. This both/and is illustrated nicely by the nine beatitudes in Jesus's Sermon on the Mount (Matt. 5:3–9). The poor in spirit, mourners, and the persecuted exemplify blessedness as a status, while the meek, merciful, and pure in heart evidence blessedness as a by-product of behavior. So, divine blessing is both an act of sovereign grace and also the result of a right relationship with the Lord. If God is willing to bless the good-for-nothings, how much more will he bless the nothings-who-seek-to-be-good?

One other aspect of the psalm merits some explanation, namely, the references to Zion, Jerusalem, and Israel. All three of these designations frequently have spiritual import in the OT and can mean more than a geographic designation. Such is probably the case here where the places serve as metaphors for God dwelling with his people. If this is correct, then we see that blessing is tied to God's presence and God's people. Or in other words, blessing has vertical (God) and horizontal (God's people) dimensions.

Is it true?

Is it true that a blessed life comes from fearing the Lord and prayer? Well, in a word association game, it is unlikely that "fear" would be the response of many to the word "blessing." And if one simply understands fear in the sense of "fright," then the disassociation is even more understandable. But the psalmist, in keeping with the wisdom tradition, points out that the fear of the Lord is a key element in living a life characterized by blessing. A life rightly aligned with God (walking in his ways, v. 1) will do much to help a person avoid the pitfalls and pratfalls that might keep one from experiencing or enjoying divine blessings.

One might also wonder whether prayer really has a role in blessing. But the connection of prayer to blessing is fairly easy to see in Scripture. For example, the well-known priestly benediction begins with "May the LORD bless you and protect you" (Num. 6:24). In 1 Chronicles 4:10, Jabez calls out for the Lord to bless him. Although he does not use the term "bless," Paul in Colossians 1:9–12 offers a wish-prayer for the Colossian saints that the Lord would bless their lives.

Earlier we noted that, blessing has vertical (God) and horizontal (God's people) dimensions. The vertical dimension is not controversial among the Lord's people even if it is often overlooked. The corporate horizontal dimension may be somewhat less obvious in an ethos that prizes individuality, the "bless us four and no more" mentality. But in the ANE, the idea of "it takes a village" was the default. Blessing and judgment in the Scriptures more often than not has corporate dimensions. One can think of Achan's individual sin that led to a national defeat (Josh. 7). Or, more positively in Paul's epistle to the Ephesians where he states, "Blessed be the God and Father of our Lord Jesus Christ, who has blessed *us* in Christ with every spiritual blessing in the heavenly places" (Eph. 1:3, emphasis added).

Now what?

If a blessed life comes from fearing the Lord and prayer, how should we respond to this idea and apply it in the activities it involves? Here are several suggestions.

Prayerfully consider what you think a blessed life should look and feel like. If your life does not match that, consider whether you have the right criteria. If your life fits a life of blessing, take a moment to thank the Lord.

Cultivate a robust theology of the person and work of God. Do you treat God with reverence? Or do you treat your spouse, coworkers, and friends with more respect and consideration? The fear of the Lord happens when our attitudes and actions run into God's holy and wholly transcendent otherness.

Develop (or continue) the habit of praying that the Lord would bless others. It is all too easy to be focused on mine and ours, and not so much yours. But this psalm teaches that our blessing is often tied to the blessings of others. Applied in the family life of the church and living in one's culture and society, biblical wisdom does not deny the need to look to one's own interests, but to curb "selfish ambition or conceit" we are directed to look "also to the interests of others" (Phil. 2:3–4). This puts into practice the idea in God's covenant with Abram in which he blessed Abram and his family to be a blessing, even that in him "all the families of the earth shall be blessed" (Gen. 1:3).

Creativity in Presentation

Begin your message with a word association game where you state a word and ask the audience to reply with the first word that comes to mind. An example would be saying the word "snow" and someone replying with "cold." You can try this with several words and then say the word "blessing." Use the responses as an introduction to the topic and a transition to the psalm.

Use a social media platform to ask your audience to text (SMS) in their answer to the prompt "Blessing is . . .". If you don't want to use your own phone or device, there are a number of group-messaging tools designed for teachers. Use the answers to introduce the topic and as a transition to the psalm.

Another way of introducing the topic of a blessed life is through the current emphasis on human flourishing. Harvard University's Human Flourishing Program has identified five areas that relate to flourishing: (1) happiness and life satisfaction, (2) health, both mental and physical, (3) meaning and purpose, (4) character and virtue, and (5) close social relationships.[1] It

is interesting to note that a case can be made that Psalm 128 addresses all five of those areas.

For older and newer renditions of Psalm 128 put to music, consider using the song entitled "Psalm 128" by Ian White and "Psalm 128" by Jason Silver, respectively. Various online psalms playlists on Spotify or similar web players or apps may include other suitable selections.

The key point to emphasize is this: Those who prayerfully fear (follow) God receive long life and many descendants. Make sure that you keep the idea that a blessed life comes from fearing the Lord front and center. When we follow the Lord . . .

- He blesses what we do (128:1–2).

- He blesses those we love (128:3–4).

- He blesses where we live (128:5–6).

DISCUSSION QUESTIONS

1. What does it mean to fear God?

2. Why is this man/father a גֶּבֶר rather than just an אִישׁ?

3. Is the poet focused on children or just sons? Explain your answer.

4. How is such a paternalistic text authoritative today?

5. Can one be blessed without children or grandchildren? If so, how?

6. How should we understand the references to Zion and Jerusalem (v. 5) for today?

---

1   Tyler J. VanderWeele, "On the Promotion of Human Flourishing," *Proceedings of the National Academy of Sciences* 114, no. 31 (August 1, 2017): 8149, https://doi.org/10.1073/pnas.1702996114.

PSALM 133

EXEGETICAL IDEA
An Israelite pilgrim and poet celebrated the sacred nature of family fellowship and faithfulness to covenant commitments.

THEOLOGICAL FOCUS
God is pleased with and blesses family members who remain loyal to their obligations.

PREACHING IDEA
Unity of family and faith is wonderful and involves God's blessing of "life forevermore."

PREACHING POINTERS
Some of our fondest road trip memories involve snacking, stops at roadside attractions, bathroom breaks, and for many, singing. We sing as we travel (no talent required) because it helps us to pass the time and it helps us to bond. Spouses and siblings also find it harder to bicker when there is a melody to be proclaimed. Simply put, singing brings us together.

It seems Israel understood this and so the Psalms of Ascents (Psalms 120–134, aka the Pilgrim Psalms) provided a means to pass the time and bond as they traveled up to Jerusalem to worship. So, it seems fitting that one of these Psalms of Ascents, Psalm 133, pictures the blessedness of unity in family and faith. The family that walks together worships together and vice versa.

THE WISDOM OF FAITHFUL FAMILY FELLOWSHIP (PSALM OF ASCENTS)

LITERARY STRUCTURE AND THEMES

Psalm 133 begins with the recognition that unity among family members is indispensable (v. 1). It provides healing like oil (v. 2) and refreshment like morning dew (v. 3a). Yahweh commanded this so life could be continually benefitted by family fellowship. The key idea is how essential family unity is for success.

- **Commitment to Family Fellowship (133:1)**
- **Characterizations of Family Fellowship (133:2–3a)**
- **Consequence of Family Fellowship (133:3b)**

EXPOSITION

Another of the few Ascent Songs related to David, and another very short one (three verses), Psalm 133 celebrates togetherness among brothers or family members. Commentators differ widely on the psalm's purpose and the historical setting or occasion. Its proverbial or instructional nature places it within the wisdom genre. A postexilic date is the consensus, but nothing proves it. Perhaps it was a time when national or spiritual disunity was rampant. The psalm suggests an intense longing for the soothing benefits of unity. So, an Israelite pilgrim and poet celebrated the sacred nature of family fellowship and faithfulness to covenant commitments.

Commitment to Family Fellowship (133:1)

Unity among a family is essential.

133:1. The psalmist opened his poem with an exclamation. He exclaimed "Look! How good, how pleasant, [for] brothers also to dwell together" (מָה can be used for "what," "how," or "why"). The infinitive (שֶׁבֶת) expresses a state of being. The poet does not explain what prompted this reminder. "Community" (יַחַד) basically indicates "togetherness," so the translation "unity" may be misleading and allow the modern reader to color the ancient context with concerns of the reader rather than the author. The question is what kind of "unity" did the psalmist have in mind? Why did he feel the need to say this? The NIV's "when" is not in the Hebrew text and may be gratuitous, suggesting an unintended comment about a division being healed. It could be that the values of community are at stake rather than a reunion after some social split (hence, Anderson's title, "The Blessings of the Covenant Fellowship"; Anderson 1995, II:885). This would be consistent with a pilgrimage praise song. Still, the national or just relational/family covenant may be in view. Some see a connection to sharing a family inheritance. The focus on "brothers," however, could indicate that the mending of a family feud was the psalmist's concern, such as reflecting on the story of Cain and Abel or Jacob and Esau or Joseph and his brothers. The serious negative ramifications of hatred among brothers is frequent in the OT. The ancient author is unlikely using "brothers" generically as more currently in terms of "men and women" (as when brothers are addressed in the NT churches and the speakers likely only have men in mind, although the proper application today is to all believers; however, words like "man" [אדם] were used for both genders collectively or "humanity").

While the Hebrew text speaks grammatically and ostensibly of a male person ("he"), this can be the common feature of many languages in which the masculine gender is used generically for any human, male or female. Context is the key and in Psalm 133:1, males are in focus. The translation "those/they/them" (for masculine forms) is accurate functionally in many texts but does not mimic the Hebrew words literally or formally. The third masculine singular form at times can signify "a person." Psalm 133:1 reflects a patriarchal cultural context in which women were thought inferior in some ways.

but the suggested emendation to the singular is perhaps correct). This picture, however, is odd or unrealistic because Hermon is located in Aram or Syria, so its dew could not drip down on Mount Zion in Jerusalem. Some suggest "Hermon dew" is figurative for heavy dew (Anderson 1995, II:886).

Consequence of Family Fellowship (133:3b)

Unity is commanded because it maintains a constructive existence.

133:3b. "Because there 'Yahweh' [יְהוָה] commanded the blessing: ongoing lives." The key exegetical issue is the location intended by "there [שָׁם]." Commentators mainly suggest Jerusalem or the context of brotherly (or family) fellowship while sharing an estate (v. 1). Regardless, fellowship is favored by God's decree. The expression "lives until the always" (חַיִּים עַד־הָעוֹלָם) is not about eternal life gained by each family member but the outcome of extended family influence (long lives or many descendants).

Characterizations of Family Fellowship (133:2–3a)

Unity like an anointing fosters vitality.

133:2. Recognizing the importance of fellowship, the psalmist considered it special or sacred. He first describes it as like oil. Fellowship is described or pictured as "the best [הַטּוֹב] oil ['poured,' understood] on the head" (v. 2ai). This is then further pictured as "running down [ptc.] Aaron's beard" (v. 2aii) and restated as "which [oil is] running down [ptc.] the edge of [lit., 'mouth of'] his measurement" (v. 2b). The edge or collar of a measure likely refers to the priest's garments. This "good oil" signifies something costly or fragrant (spiced) and is described as being used in a sacred anointing ceremony for a priest (which would seem to contradict interpretations of this oil as common). The idea appears to be that covenant fellowship is deemed sacred.

133:3a. Continuing his perspective of the sacredness of fellowship, the psalmist then described it to be like dew. Also, this can be compared to Mount Hermon's dew running down (same ptc.) Zion's hills (MT is plural,

THEOLOGICAL FOCUS

The exegetical idea (an Israelite pilgrim celebrates the sacred nature of family fellowship and faithfulness to covenant commitments) leads to this theological focus: God is pleased with and blesses family members who remain loyal to their obligations.

Psalm 133 underscores God's concern for, and high estimation of, a covenant or family fellowship. Commitment to verbal agreements is the glue that binds family relationships and enables them to last through the storms of life. This outcome is good and pleasing, as well as sacred. A lasting union is anointed. Brothers are bound by covenants as a priest is by his calling. God's covenant with his people may be implied along with family fellowship. The principle is easily adapted to the NT church.

PREACHING AND TEACHING STRATEGIES

Exegetical and Theological Synthesis

As one of the Psalms of Ascent, Psalm 133 should be read in the context of pilgrimage and worship. In this setting, "family" probably refers both to actual members of one's family but also the broader "family" of those who might not be otherwise related but still includes those who worship the same God. There is religious terminology to be noted in "Aaron" (the first high priest), the "mountains of Zion" (which seems more than a geographic reference), and the Lord's blessing of "life forevermore." The term "brother" might have connotations that go beyond familial relationships. It is in this context of pilgrimage and worship that one proclaims a wonderful picture of the unity of family in faith and a family of faith as they share in the divine blessing of "life forevermore."

Preaching Idea

Unity of family and faith is wonderful and involves God's blessing of "life forevermore."

Contemporary Connections

What does it mean?

What does it mean that the unity of family and faith is wonderful and involves God's blessing of "life forevermore"? Let us begin by trying to understand that unity and uniformity are not exactly the same. Though unity usually involves some measure of uniformity, the beauty of unity is when disparate elements (e.g., personality, gender, nationality, etc.) come together in a shared vision, mission, work, and/or devotion. For the psalmist, unity is an intersection between the horizontal dimension of family ("brothers") and the vertical dimension of faith ("Aaron," "mountains of Zion," and the Lord's blessing of "life forevermore"). Such unity is "good and pleasant" and involves "life

forevermore." It is tempting to view "life forevermore" in the redemptive eternal life sense but most commentators see it in reference to a prolonged earthly, life extended through one's posterity, or in the sense of one's legacy. Regardless of the specific understanding, unity is tied to life and life to unity.

Is it true?

Is it really true that the unity of family and faith is wonderful and results in God's blessing of "life forevermore"? The blessing of unity is readily apparent. Given the choice most would choose unity over disunity, and peace over conflict. That unity involves horizontal (among people) and vertical (with God) aspects is also taught consistently in Scripture. It can be seen in the United Kingdom of David and Solomon that consisted of twelve tribes in theocratic unity. It can be seen in our Lord who expressed this bi-dimensional unity in what is called his high priestly prayer that "they may be one even as we are one" (John 17:22). Similarly, Paul emphasizes unity within church (e.g., 1 Cor. 1:10; Eph. 2:15–16; Phil. 2:2).

Now what?

If the unity of family and faith is wonderful and results in God's blessing of "life forevermore," how should we respond to this idea and apply it to our lives? Here are a couple of suggestions.

Take a moment to reflect on the blessing of unity and thank the Lord for it. It is all too easy in our world of hatred, conflict, and misunderstanding to miss the examples of unity that are part of our lives. The occasional flashes of unity we experience now gives us a foretaste of the perfect unity to come.

Be a person who is a peacemaker, a unifier. Such people are blessed by the Lord (Matt. 5:9). Those who divide and cause dissension are a dime a dozen but peacemakers are a rare breed.

Creativity in Presentation

If you have military experience or have any active or retired military people available, you could share or have them share their experiences with marching cadences, the calls and responses used in drill instruction and the importance of such exercises to instill unit cohesion, that is, how an exercise of singing can bring people from diverse backgrounds together.

Ask the audience for their favorite road-trip songs and interact with those before segueing into the Psalms of Ascent generally and Psalm 133 particularly. If the audience is too large or unwilling to respond, you can simply do an internet search for favorite road trip songs (there are many such lists available) and go from there. Psalm 133 has been linked to communion in the Christian tradition. The Lord's Table provides a beautiful picture of the horizontal and vertical dimensions of unity. So, consider incorporating the Lord's Supper into the preaching of this psalm.

For a song based on the text of the psalm, a good upbeat one is "Oh, How Good It Is" by Keith and Kristyn Getty. Two others are "Psalm 133" by Jason Silver and "Psalm 133" by Ian White.

The key point to emphasize is this: God is pleased with and blesses family members who remain loyal to their obligations. Unity of family and faith is wonderful and involves God's blessing of "life forevermore."

- Unity is really good (133:1).

- Unity is really beautiful (133:2–3a).

- Unity is really living (133:3b).

DISCUSSION QUESTIONS

1. Why does the psalmist only mention brothers (Ps. 133:1)?

2. Is this psalm about "unity"? Why or why not?

3. What is indicated by the comparison to oil running down a priest's head (Ps. 133:2)?

4. What is the nature of the life Yahweh bestows, where does he bestow it, and on whom (Ps. 133:3)?

5. How does knowing that Psalm 133 was one of the psalms sung by Israelites going up to Jerusalem affect how we might understand this psalm?

PSALM 145:
RIGHT AND WRONG WAYS TO LIVE CONTRASTED

Not usually considered a Wisdom Psalm, 145 does contain a few parallels with Psalm 1, making it at least a psalm with wisdom features or a wisdom theme. It is discussed in volume 3, *Praise Psalms*, of this commentary.

PSALM 145:20	PSALM 1:6
[Because] "Yahweh" (יהוה) "keeps watching" (שׁוֹמֵר; ptc.) over all who love him,	Because (כִּי) "Yahweh" (יהוה) "knows" (יוֹדֵעַ; ptc. = stays aware [of]) the way of the righteous,
but all the wicked "he will destroy" (יַשְׁמִיד).	but the way of the wicked "it will perish" (תֹּאבֵד).

FOR FURTHER READING

Bailey, Christopher W. (2012). "Psalm 1." Accessed October 3, 2019. https://www.imdb.com/title/tt2319999.

Bateman IV, H. W. and D. Brent Sandy, eds. (2010). *Interpreting the Psalms for Teaching and Preaching*. St. Louis: Chalice Press.

Boice, James Montgomery. (1994). *Psalms 1–41*. Vol. 1. Grand Rapids: Baker.

Bullock, C. Hassell. (2015) *Psalms 1–72*. Teach the Text. Grand Rapids: Baker.

Charry, Ellen T. (2015). *Psalms 1–50*. Brazos Theological Commentary on the Bible. Grand Rapids: Brazos.

Goldingay, John. (2006). *Psalms 1–41*. BCOT. Edited by Tremper Longman III. Grand Rapids: Baker Academic.

Hill, Kim. (1988). "Psalm 1." Uploaded October 8, 2011; accessed October 3, 2019. https://www.youtube.com/watch?v=xFTIfoBOb9I.

Kaiser Jr., Walter C. (1993). *The Journey Isn't Over: The Pilgrim Psalms for Life's Challenges and Joys*. Grand Rapids: Baker.

_____. (2010). "Psalm 73: The Prosperity of the Wicked and the Perspective of the Believer." In *Interpreting the Psalms for Teaching and Preaching*, 98–106. Edited by H. W. Bateman IV and D. B. Sandy. St. Louis: Chalice Press.

Lloyd-Jones, D. Martyn. (1953). *Faith Tried and Triumphant*. Grand Rapids: Baker.

Motyer, J. A., ed. (1994). *IVP New Bible Commentary*. University and Colleges Christian Fellowship. Electronic Hyper-text version, Accordance 2.1.

Stedman, R. C. (1973). *Psalms of Faith: A Life-Related Study from Selected Psalms*. Ventura, CA: Regal.

Swindoll, C. R. (2012). *Living the Psalms: Encouragement for the Daily Grind*. Brentwood, TN: Worthy.

Taylor, J. G. (2010). "Psalms 1 and 2: A Gateway into the Psalter and Messianic Images of Restoration for David's Dynasty. In *Interpreting the Psalms for Teaching & Preaching*, 47–62. Edited by H. W. Bateman IV and D. B. Sandy. St. Louis: Chalice Press.

Walton, John H., Victor H. Matthews, and Mark W. Chavalas, eds. (n.d.). *IVP Bible Background Commentary: Old Testament*. Electronic Hyper-text version, Accordance 2.1.

WISDOM PSALMS
ABOUT GOD'S WORD / REVELATION

This second section of Wisdom Psalms focuses on five psalms (Pss. 19, 91, 111, 112, 119) that are labeled "Torah" or "law; instruction(al)" because they focus, in whole or part, on the psalmist's reverence for God's verbal and written revelation of his will to his people. Another frequent theme of OT Wisdom (besides what is right and wrong) is wise guidance. These psalms speak of God's "word(s)" (from roots דבר or אמר) as divine revelation including what had been recorded to date (such as the Mosaic laws or instructions/teachings) as well as what the psalmist believed he heard God say to him (directly through prayer or indirectly through a prophet). The term "word" (which is usually plural) should not be read as "Word" as if the poet was thinking of a Bible as we have today. To him, God's "word" is what God has communicated.

Of course by extension and application, believers today can think of the Bible as God's revealed will or divine revelation. They understand that it contains God's own dictates and directives as well as Spirit-guided literary creations of human authors eventually agreed upon as Scripture by the church. Therefore, these are God's "words" in the indirect sense of divine speech as well as religious writings that reflect thinking and stories divinely and humanly approved as indispensable for spiritual and theological belief and behavior. Consequently, the NT deems all that is "written" (Scripture; γραφή) as θεόπνευστος or "God-breathed" (2 Tim. 3:16, in which "breathing out" is translated "inspired," although strictly the English equivalent would be "expired," but this term has come to mean "died"). When we say that the Scripture is inspired, we mean the text, not the author. The Bible never speaks of inspired speakers, only writings. But this does not require that the words were copied verbatim as God spoke audibly to various prophets or apostles. Some people in the Bible do claim having heard God's voice, but this may include various means. The biblical texts exhibit the styles of the different authors, so we know what resulted (through whatever means) as the original documents of the Bible came through a dual process: God revealing directly or indirectly his desired texts through human authorship that involved the skills, personalities, perceptions, and experiences of the authors, yet somehow guided to write what God willed. This is sometimes called confluency. Peter added to this process by saying that no "prophecy of scripture" (προφητεία γραφῆς) resulted from personal interpretations and no prophecy originated by human will; rather, these men spoke from God by means of being moved by a spirit/wind/breath of holiness (or, the Holy Spirit; 2 Peter 1:20–21).

Today, evangelicals debate the precise nature of the "inerrancy" of the biblical text, and that debate will not be solved here; the bottom line is that the original OT and NT can be trusted to be what God led the authors to write, regardless of the methods or circumstances. Christians do not have a Scripture that "fell from heaven"; yet, although humans had a hand in its development, God governed the entire process. We have the fearsome duty not just to read these texts as authoritative but to read them critically and reverently. Rather than just being mindless, robotic readers, we have been favored and challenged with the privilege and responsibility to translate and interpret God's revelation. We might wish we did not have this duty, only the seemingly easier task of blind or uncritical obedience; but the reality is that we do. God for whatever reasons thought it best to hand us his revelation in a human vessel (as was Jesus). This demands our utmost intellectual and spiritual muscles. To walk away from this calling is to be content to have theology based purely on secondary and tertiary sources and what (hopefully trustworthy) teachers tell us. The prayerful yet persistent and penitent attitudes of the authors of the following Torah psalms serve as a great example to all who personally engage God's written revelation.

This major section of Wisdom Psalms about God's word contains five preaching units:

1. Creational and Verbal Revelation Contrasted (Ps. 19)
2. Wisdom of Relying on God's Promise (Ps. 91)
3. Wisdom Comes by Prioritizing Divine Revelation (Ps. 111)
4. Obeying God's Revelation Leads to Wisdom and Well-Being (Ps. 112)
5. What It Means to Love God's Laws (Ps. 119).

PSALM 19

EXEGETICAL IDEA
God's existence and significance was revealed in creation; and his express will was revealed in verbal communication.

THEOLOGICAL FOCUS
God wants to be known, and has made himself, and his will, known through cosmological creation and anthropological communication.

PREACHING IDEA
The revelation of God's glory and his word challenges us to evaluate the way we live.

PREACHING POINTERS
Psalm 19 is attributed to David although the particular occasion is not identified. Presumably, the idea of spiritual self-examination was as important then as it is now. You have probably witnessed one of the television exposés where a reporter armed with a blacklight inspects hotel rooms to see how clean (or unclean) they really are. The blacklight reveals spots and stains that one might not otherwise see. Presented with this unsightly and unsanitary evidence, the hotel manager often confesses that such conditions fall short of their standards, and then apologizes and pledges to correct the issues.

But, what would happen if we would examine the rooms of our lives with the divine "blacklight" of God's person and his word? What would be revealed about our thoughts, attitudes, and actions? In Psalm 19, the psalmist considers how the revelation of God's glory and his word challenges us to evaluate the way we are to live.

CREATIONAL AND VERBAL REVELATION CONTRASTED

LITERARY STRUCTURE AND THEMES

Psalm 19 moves from information about general (vv. 1–6) to special divine revelation (vv. 7–11) and concludes with an application (vv. 12–14). The first topic is about how certain aspects of the created world communicate something about God. The second, and more important, is how God has spoken his will verbally to humanity. There is no excuse not to fear, reverence, or bow before God. There is no need to be afraid of, or in terror of, him (as if powerful yet not good) because his laws are rewarding and reliable, highly valuable and satisfying. They expose divine exhortations and condemnations so people know what is right and wrong and what needs to be changed in order to be more healthy and holy.

- **General/Creational Revelation (19:1–6 [HB 2–7])**
- **Special/Verbal Revelation (19:7–11 [HB 8–12])**
- **Reflection/Application (19:12–14 [HB 13–15])**

EXPOSITION

Superscription: The reader understands that something is "for the [musical] director," but what exactly is "for him" is not explained. Again, this is "a psalm pertaining to David" (מִזְמוֹר לְדָוִד; cf. Anderson 2016, 167). Psalm 19 may be considered a mixed psalm, combining praise of creation with the nature of God's laws or commands. Alternatively, each part may be viewed as a describing divine revelation in, first, creational or natural revelation, and, second, in terms of relational or supernatural verbal revelation. Some have proposed that each poem was originally independent. Notable distinctions in substance and style have been observed, suggesting different authors. One such difference is that while "El" (אֵל) is the reference to God in verses 1–6, Yahweh is the subject of verses 7–14; however, the former is not necessarily the name of the early God of Israel but may just refer to "Yahweh" as God. In any case, God's existence and significance was revealed in creation; and his express will was revealed in verbal communication.

General Revelation: Creation Speaks (19:1–6 [HB 2–7])

How the creation tells us something about God is indicated.

19:1–2. The psalmist explained that God has revealed himself through the "language" of creation in the sky. It "speaks" day and night (v. 2) about God's "glory" or "importance" (כְּבוֹד in v. 1a, which has to do with the value or weight, i.e., the "heaviness" or "significance" of something or someone). Specifically, this is defined in 19:1b as the (wondrous) works of creation in the sky. Every day and night, people can "hear" (experience) how the heavens "recount" (מְסַפְּרִים in v. 1a) and "declare" (מַגִּיד in v. 1b) information or knowledge about God (v. 2). Every different linguistic community on earth can understand this universal language of creation.

19:3–4a. "There" and "where" (KJV) is not in the Hebrew text. The text says the "sound" (lit., "their voice"; קוֹלָם) of both speaking and words are not regularly heard (pass. ptc.; נִשְׁמָע). The distinction may be between "talking" and "languages." A creator is indicated through the realities of creation but not through vocalization. While verse 2 said "speech [אמר] pours forth," verse 3 says "no speech [אמר; happens]." The first is figurative about the "revelation" of creation, while the second is literal, about how no actual verbal communication is involved. The heavenly bodies generally point to a God but cannot specifically profile him. This information is accessible to everyone, everywhere (v. 4a).

19:4b–6. Then the psalmist observed the sun. More specifically within the heavens, the sun testifies to the Creator's significance as it moves with such determination, like a bridegroom or a warrior in pursuit along a path. It travels from one end of the sky to the other, shining on everyone and everything along its course. This phenomenon evidences consistency or faithfulness for all time.

Special Revelation: God Speaks (19:7–11 [HB 8–12])

That God has communicated his will verbally is celebrated.

19:7–9. Next, the psalmist spoke about the nature of God's law in particular. More precisely and objectively (v. 7a), God also has verbally revealed his moral will for humanity. It not only has an informative or intellectual quality, his moral will also has practical and life-changing power. God's "law" (תּוֹרָה) is "complete" (תְּמִימָה; just as it should be) and is able to "revive" or reinvigorate a person's (spiritual) life (מְשִׁיבַת נָפֶשׁ). The rendering "soul" (for נָפֶשׁ) is misleading since the idea is that of a renewed person in the flesh not a disembodied spirit. A "soul" is a living being (cf. Ps. 49:19; see also "'Soul' in the OT and Psalms," p. 77).

19:7b–8. "Law, ordinances, etc. of 'Yahweh' (יְהוָה)" means "given by 'Yahweh' (יְהוָה)." The NETS ([18:8] reflecting the LXX, ἄμωμος)

has this law as "faultless." In verse 7b (HB 8b), God's "statutes" (עֵדוּת) are "reliable" (נֶאֱמָנָה), helping naive or inexperienced people be wise (i.e., morally skillful at life). The root of "reliable" (I-אמן) is related more to reliability than the modern, philosophical concept of "truth" (cf. Marlowe 2010, *in toto*). In verse 8ai, God's "precepts" (פִּקּוּדֵי) are "right; straight" (יְשָׁרִים) as opposed to wrong or misdirected, in terms of moral and ethical direction. The NETS says "upright." This causes rejoicing (19:8aii). "Rejoicing of heart" (מְשַׂמְּחֵי־לֵב) is an idiom for happiness. "Heart" in the OT combines mental and emotional realities. In verse 8b, God's "commands" (מִצְוַת) are "pure/radiant" and "enlighten the eyes"; i.e., they provide clear guidance for life.

19:9. "Yahweh's fear" (fear given by God?)—perhaps an idiom for God's instructions (see translation analysis of verse 9a below)—is "clean" (טְהוֹרָה) so it "stands/endures" over the ages. Editors of the Hebrew text have suggested that the word "fear [יִרְאַת]" perhaps was originally "sayings" (אמרת), since "fear" seems an odd way to refer to God's words. Support for this is found in Psalm 119:38, which is translated in the LXX (cf. NETS) as "Establish for your slave your saying [אמרת], for fear [יראת] of you." Apparently, a strong mental link existed between God's speech and human submission. In verse 9a we read about "the fear of 'Yahweh' (יְהוָה)" being pure or clean and enduring.

Fearing God

The genitive expression "fear of God" is usually taken as "fear directed at God" (objective), but it could be at times "fear from God" (agency or source). In Psalm 111:10, this fear is defined as following his precepts. In Proverbs 1:7, it is the source of knowledge. In Isaiah 11:3, the root of Jesse will delight in this fear. Isaiah 11:2–3 may be a chiasm, and if so, then "wisdom" in verse 2a is re-expressed by this "fear" in verse 3a (cf. Marlowe 2014, 44–57).

This (being afraid or terrified of God, if that is what this means) sounds strange in a context about the nature of God's verbal communication or laws, especially when the parallel line (see v. 9b) restates this "fear" as "the ordinances of [מִשְׁפְּטֵי 'judgments of'] 'Yahweh' (יהוה)." All of this suggests a close relationship between this fear and God's verbal revelation. The statement is not "fearing Yahweh" but operates as a subject or object, "the-fear-of-'Yahweh' is [x]" or as in "understand the fear-of-'Yahweh'" (Prov. 2:5). The translation "fear of Yahweh" indicates to most readers "being afraid of God," but it may, in light of these data, suggest God's revelation, something like "God's fearsome or awesome [words]." Obedience is related to fear of consequences for disobedience. Yet too much terror erodes relationship (v. 19:9b). The parallel line in 19:9bi is that God's "ordinances/judgments [מִשְׁפָּטֵי]" are "firm/reliable/sure (אֱמֶת; some have "true"; the NETS [cf. LXX] has "valid"; but cf. נֶאֱמָנָה above in 19:7); this is restated in 19:9b as "altogether just [or 'justified']" (Marlowe 2010, 24–42).

19:10. Then the psalmist spoke about the value of God's laws in general. Such laws are not or should not be received as distasteful or problematic. Rather, they are positive gifts from God. They are more valuable than gold and sweeter than honey, as moral and ethical currency and nutrition.

19:11. They provide God's servants (same word as the NETS "slave" in Psalm 119:38) with rewarding advice in terms of moral guidance for a successful life.

Reflection/Application (19:12–14 [HB 13–15])

With all this in mind, the psalmist concluded that such laws allow people to discover unknown faults, enabling more thorough confession and cleansing, and thereby, moral and spiritual growth.

19:12. In light of God's "fear" (v. 11; perhaps a reference to his laws, in parallel with v. 9, "rules/ordinances," מִשְׁפָּטֵי), the psalmist was aware of his inability to discern his sins and failures apart from verbal revelation (cf. vv. 9b–11a; God's commands are certain and precious, therefore and because they warn about how to live and be rewarded, or not live and be punished [implied]).

19:13. He asked God to keep him from being controlled by "pride [מִזֵּדִים]," which seems to suggest presumption or willful rebellion. Then he can be "complete/blameless" (אֵיתָם; same root as in v. 7 regarding God's laws being "perfect/complete") as well as "innocent/free [וְנִקֵּיתִי]" of great transgression.

19:14. He prayed that his own "speaking [אִמְרֵי־פִי]" and "thinking," literally, "heart talking" (הֶגְיוֹן לִבִּי; NETS, cf. LXX, has "meditation") receive God's "favor" (רָצוֹן). Yahweh is his rock (protector or sure foundation) and "redeemer/avenger [וְגֹאֲלִי]."

THEOLOGICAL FOCUS

The exegetical idea (God's existence and significance was revealed in creation; and his express will was revealed in verbal communication) leads to this theological focus: God wants to be known, and has made himself, and his will, known through cosmological creation and anthropological communication.

God has revealed himself to humanity through general and special means; nonverbally through creation, which still "speaks," and verbally through commands as contained in laws, which have been transcribed and which are guaranteed guides to godliness and goodness (cf. Rom. 1:18–20). People consciously and foolishly choose to ignore this God and worship creation instead in the form of manmade idols (1:21–23). Perhaps behind Paul's words was a reflection on Psalm 19, which emphasizes the essential nature of God's revelation in nature and in Scripture for right belief and behavior.

PREACHING AND TEACHING STRATEGIES

Exegetical and Theological Synthesis

A key concept in Psalm 19 is revelation. In theological terms one can speak of general (or natural) revelation and special revelation. The former includes what can be known by God through things like nature, while the latter includes supernatural acts of revelation like Scripture. Here the psalmist highlights both general and special revelation and how both can provide insight into one's life. This can be seen in the New Testament book of Hebrews where the revelation of the Son of God seeks to motivate Christ-followers to persevere and press on in the faith.

Preaching Idea

The revelation of God's glory and his word challenges us to evaluate the way we live.

Contemporary Connections

What does it mean?

What does it mean that the revelation of God's glory and his word challenges us to evaluate the way we live? The revelation of God's glory (vv. 1–6) and his word (vv. 7–11) helps the person of faith to examine his or her life, resulting in a more righteous life (vv. 12–14). In sum, the psalmist gazes upward into the cosmos and sees the transcendence of God, focuses downward upon the perfect Word of God, and then inward to the very thoughts and intentions of the heart.

Is it true?

Is it really true that the revelation of God's glory and the Scripture can help a person of faith to examine his or her life and as a result live more righteously? The answer seems patently obvious. Most of us have been challenged in positive ways by learning about great women and men. Being exposed to people like Mother Teresa and Martin Luther King Jr. has inspired many others to live more selflessly and justly. So,

it should not be altogether surprising that the greatness of God has a similar effect.

Neither should it come as a shock that a text can have a life-transforming effect. Even less than Pulitzer–prize winning tomes have made profound impacts on those who read them. Self-help resources are legion whether one is seeking to gain confidence or lose weight. And it seems indisputable that the Bible has transformed more lives in the annals of human history than any other book, self-help or otherwise.

Now what?

If the revelation of God's glory and the Scripture can help a person of faith to examine his or her life and as a result live more righteously, how should we respond to this idea and apply it to our lives? Here are several suggestions.

Consider what nature might teach you about God. Go to your favorite nature spot (e.g., lake, woods, garden, etc.) and read Psalm 19 and reflect on how God's glory is manifested there.

Reflect on the value of the word of God. Look at all the adjectives used to describe it in Psalm 19. For example, verse 7 describes God's word as perfect, refreshing, sure, and able to make one wise.

Memorize Psalm 19:14. C. S. Lewis writes of Psalm 19, "I take this to be the greatest poem in the Psalter and one of the greatest lyrics in the world" (Lewis 1958, 63). It is worth noting that my "rock" and my "redeemer" reveal God in natural and special terms, respectively.

Creativity in Presentation

Use beautiful images from the Hubble Space Telescope to introduce Psalm 19 or in discussing its contents. NASA's extensive image and video galleries available online (nasa.gov) generally are not subject to copyright in the United States and may be freely used (with source acknowledgment) for education or informational purposes.

In discussing the perfection of God's word (v. 7), one could refer to Ed Sheeran's song "Perfect," one of the biggest musical hits of 2017.

Talk about how the term "perfect" can be used in terms of a romantic relationship (as in Sheeran's song), a day, a job, a manicure, a latte, etc. This will allow a segue into the ways that the word of God is perfect. Numerous musical renderings of Psalm 19, both ancient and modern, are available. These could be used to introduce, illustrate, or conclude one's message. Some good contemporary options include "Psalm 19" by the Corner Room, "May the Words of My Mouth" by Shane Barnard (of Shane & Shane) on his *Psalms* album, the title song "A Greater Song" by Paul Baloche with Integrity's Hosanna! Music, and "Psalm 19 (The Heavens Declare)" by Chris Heesch with the Psalms Project.

The key point to emphasize is this: God wants to be known, and has made himself, and his will, known through cosmological creation and anthropological communication. The revelation of God's glory and his word challenges us to evaluate the way we live.

- God's glory is revealed in the world he created (19:1–6).

- God's glory is revealed in the word he inspired (19:7–11).

- God's glory is revealed in the way that we live (19:12–14).

DISCUSSION QUESTIONS

1. Does creation necessarily prove a single creator God?

2. What can be deduced about God based on the heavens?

3. Did Jesus expect love of the Law as much as love of neighbor?

4. How does the enormous size of the universe affect the way you view God and yourself?

5. How does God's word help one to discern his or her errors?

PSALM 91

EXEGETICAL IDEA
An Israelite psalmist in trouble placed his trust in Yahweh as his only hope and salvation, and believed that rescue could be expected from even the slightest level of harm.

THEOLOGICAL FOCUS
God promises his protection to those who trust fully in him alone as their refuge.

PREACHING IDEA
God is a refuge and source of protection for those who trust in him.

PREACHING POINTERS
Psalm 91 lacks a superscription, so identifying the specific occasion of the psalm is not possible. But the yearning for God's protection seems fairly universal.

I (Charles) used to live where there could be tornadoes and now, I live where hurricanes are a reality. Tornadoes and hurricanes are different weather phenomena, but both involve giving some thought to where to find refuge during these events. But whether we are looking for protection from natural disasters or other calamities of life, it seems we are constantly on the lookout for a place of refuge. For the author of Psalm 91, the best and ultimate storm shelter or safe room is God himself. This psalm is not a theodicy but rather an audacious declaration that God protects those who put their trust in him. For all those who are anxiety-ridden, Psalm 91 is an invitation into the divine safe room.

WISDOM OF RELYING ON GOD'S PROMISE

LITERARY STRUCTURE AND THEMES

Psalm 91 starts with the poet's perspective on "the God in whom I trust" (אֱלֹהַי אֶבְטַח־בּוֹ) as a safe shelter from life's storms (vv. 1–2). He then expresses his confidence in God as a protective cover against calamities in which countless others are victims (vv. 3–8), then explaining to whom this applies, why, how, and the result (vv. 9–16). A wise person will rely on God because of his promise of protection. The psalm has a chiastic arrangement:

- *A The Recipient of God's Protection: The Psalmist Speaks (91:1–2)*
- *B The Revelation of God's Promises of Protection (91:3–13)*
- *A´ The Recipient of God's Promised Protection: Yahweh Speaks (91:14–16)*

EXPOSITION

While Psalm 90 included a wisdom motif, Psalm 91 has more of a wisdom theme. This psalm also picks up the subject of God's protection (which began Ps. 90). Only the LXX has a superscription for Psalm 91, translated by NETS (cf. LXX; = Ps. 90), as "A laudation. Of an Ode. Pertaining to Dauid." An "ode" is described as a praise song without accompaniment in a NETS footnote. No consensus has been reached regarding its genre, and various theories have been proposed about its liturgical position or purpose. It most resembles a kind of Praise psalm. Most date it as postexilic and connected to the temple. It appears to answer the question, "Who can rely on God's promised protection?" and can be viewed as a chiasm with the last few verses returning to the theme of the opening verses

(the nature of the person whom God will safeguard). Therefore, an Israelite psalmist in trouble placed his trust in Yahweh as his only hope and salvation and believed that rescue could be expected from even the slightest level of harm.

The Recipient of God's Protection: The Psalmist Speaks (91:1–2)

God protects those who trust in him.

91:1. The psalmist started with the observation that "The one who dwells [regularly; ptc.] in 'Elyon's [עֶלְיוֹן] hidden place, lodges in 'Shadday's [שַׁדַּי] shadow." This opening claim echoes the sentiment in Psalm 90, where God is a dwelling place (90:1). God is now named as the most "High [עֶלְיוֹן]" and "Mighty [שַׁדַּי]."

91:2. Again, God provides a place of safety and shelter; but this time the psalmist rejoices in still experiencing this rather than lamenting its expiration. Consequently, he proclaimed that Yahweh is his refuge and stronghold, his God in whom he will trust.

The Revelation of God's Promises of Protection (91:3–13)

God will protect only the righteous from the most deadly dilemmas.

91:3. He then explained that this trust is deserved "because [כִּי]" this God delivers people from the hunter's trap (and) from (any) destructive thorn ("from a thorn" [מִדֶּבֶר] is "from a . . . word" in the NETS [cf. LXX and Syriac], suggesting the unpointed Hebrew text was interpreted as מִדַּבֵּר instead). These sources of harm are symbolic or illustrative of an enemy who would try to capture or kill others. In verse 2, "I will say [אֹמַר]" is "he will say" in the NETS (cf. LXX), which would switch the speaker to "the one dwelling" in verse 1. This alternative reading does not change the meaning. This poet may be praising God and postulating his plan to rely on Yahweh because of some recent and real threat. In Hosea 9:8 a prophet is described as one who is subject to hostile traps everywhere he goes, even in God's house.

91:4. The reader was then encouraged to "Let him cover you [jussive form; I-סכך] with his feathers" (v. 4ai). The parallel line reads, "and under his wings you will take refuge" (v. 4aii). The rest of the verse is unclear. "A shield and a buckler [or 'wall'] his reliability" (v. 4b). The NETS (cf. LXX) has, "with a shield his truth will surround you," and the JPS perhaps is to be preferred, "His fidelity is an encircling shield."

91:5–6. As a result of God's protection, the poet now lists a number of potentially frightening events of which no one ("you" in the text) trusting in God should be concerned. Absolute confidence is expressed with the use of the strong negative (לֹא) and the future form (the same used in the Ten Commandments with imperative force, "You must not!").

There is no need to fear (1) any nighttime object of dread "or" (not in MT but in a few alternate mss. and LXX) a daytime arrow that will fly (in your direction).

Nor was there a need to fear (2) a thorn/plague (same word as in v. 3, taken by NETS [cf. LXX] as "deed") that will arrive (lit., "walk") in the dark "or" (not in MT but in Syriac version) a destructive force bringing devastation at noon (the LXX and Jewish Greek versions read "and a demon" [יָשׁוּד] as if it were וְשֵׁד). In light of the next verse about thousands of people falling, these threats may all symbolize combat or sickness, or the former may be illustrated by the daytime attacks and the latter by the nighttime attacks. The picture of warfare is problematic, however, in that those falling are not comrades in arms (since they all should have the same protection as Hebrews seeking Yahweh's care). The poem so far seems to be about a particular faithful Israelite who is being hunted and who can find refuge in God. The NIV speaks of a "pestilence that stalks in the darkness" (v. 6a).

91:7. Even though tens of thousands may not escape, the person about whom the psalmist writes will not be touched.

91:8. Next, he clarified that only those who are wicked will be subject to this recompense, which the one who trusts God will avoid, only being an observer. "Wicked ones" (רְשָׁעִים; "sinner" is חָטָא) is translated as "sinners" by the Greek OT (ἁμαρτωλῶν) here as elsewhere in the LXX (e.g., Pss. 84:11, 92:8, 94:3, et al.). Again, the OT at times speaks of sinners as only those who are habitually disobedient (yet also recognizes that every human does wrong to some degree).

91:9. Then he clarified that such protection can be assumed only "when [כִּי]" someone has Yahweh as his or her refuge, employing a powerful conditional parallelism:

| If you | (say) | "Yahweh" (יְהוָה) | (is) | my-refuge | ("hope" in LXX), // |
| [If you] | set | "Elyon" (עֶלְיוֹן) | (as) | your-habitation | ("refuge" in LXX). |

91:10. (Only then) will "harm / tragedy / something terrible [רָעָה]" not fall upon you; and will an "affliction/blow/illness [נֶגַע]" not come near your tent.

91:11. How will God do this? According to verse 11, he will order his messengers regarding you, in order to guard you in all your circumstances (lit., "ways").

91:12–13. Examples of these circumstances are then listed, such as (1) being kept from stubbing your toe on a rock (v. 12), yet (2) you will tread (safely) on top of a "lion [שַׁחַל]" or an "adder/cobra [פֶּתֶן]" and trample a "young lion [כְּפִיר]" or a "serpent [תַּנִּין]" (v. 13). The real question is, to whom is this seeming unrealistic promise addressed, and why?

The Recipient of God's Promised Protection: Yahweh Speaks (91:14–16)

God promises to rescue those devoted to him, who call upon him.

91:14. Next, God explained that (from such danger) "I will deliver [וַאֲפַלְּטֵהוּ]" the one who "has been committed [חָשַׁק]" to God ("in me he hoped" in NETS; cf. LXX); and "I will protect [אֲשַׂגְּבֵהוּ]" the one who "has known" (= acknowledges) his name (meaning trusts in him; cf. v. 15, "call upon me" and "call on the name Yahweh" in the OT; Marlowe 2015, 6–27). The JPS says, "Because he is devoted to Me I will deliver him; I will keep him safe, for he knows My name." The NIV has "loves," but this (חָשַׁק) is not the usual word for love and is more related to being attached or joined to someone.

91:15. God promises that he will answer the one who calls on him; when he is in trouble, God will be with him (v. 15a). (God vows that) "I will extract him" (אֲחַלְּצֵהוּ) and "I will honor him" (v. 15b). These last two verbs use a strengthened form.

91:16. Finally, (God pledges that) "I will satisfy him" (אַשְׂבִּיעֵהוּ) with a long life ("length of days"), restated as "I will reveal" (וְאַרְאֵהוּ), literally, "make him see" salvation (verbs of causation). People who can expect God to protect or save (rescue) them are those who stay devoted to him, know him, and call on or hope in him (similar qualities are stated or suggested in vv. 1–9). Yet such people then and now are not always kept safe from little or large injuries or illnesses. Does God and/or the poet use hyperbole here for effect? If not, how do we interpret and apply such absolute divine dictates in light of contrary experience?

THEOLOGICAL FOCUS

The exegetical idea (an Israelite psalmist in trouble placed his trust in Yahweh as his only hope and salvation and believed that rescue could be expected from even the slightest level of harm) leads to this theological focus: God promises his protection to those who trust fully in him alone as their refuge.

What do we make of this divine promise to protect godly people from damage or death? In reality, we know that even some of the godliest people throughout history have suffered great harm and had no magic to avoid suffering or death. What's behind these unbelievable promises of protection in this psalm? Is it wishful thinking or poetic hyperbole? Psalm 91:9–10 ties this to those who dwell with Yahweh Most High. Moses reminded the Hebrews of the time when they camped at Rephidim in the wilderness on the way to Mount Sinai and demanded water (Exod. 17:1–7). Deuteronomy 9:22 says that this event made God angry (cf. Ps. 95:8). The people argued with and grumbled against Moses and were ready to stone him. In addition, they challenged God to show if he was with them or not. Moses asked God what to do and was told to strike a rock with his staff. When he did, water gushed forth; but he named the place "Massah" (test) and "Meribah" (quarrel). In Deuteronomy 6, Moses warned the people not to test God again as they did before (questioning the truth of his faithfulness to his promises and people).

The author of Psalm 91 wanted to stress God's nature as a protector of his people against potentially any harm, minimal or maximal. God is not obligated to save saints from all threats, but he offers his aid for all levels of injury, not just the tragic ones. What God promises, he will do; but the words of this psalm are hyperbolic and not intended to be absolutized in an absurd manner. The divine pledges made in this psalm are not meant literally and absolutely without exception, but they apply to the certainty of such divine care when God chooses to apply it to faithful followers. Everyone is subject to illness and injury, but those who do not place their faith in God have only human help available.

PREACHING AND TEACHING STRATEGIES

Exegetical and Theological Synthesis

Psalm 91 teaches that God is a refuge and source of protection for those who trust in him. Refuge and protection tend to involve at least two crucial elements: (1) concern/compassion and (2) power/strength. One could have compassion/care and yet lack the power/strength to provide either refuge or protection. Similarly, one could have the power/strength to provide refuge and protection but lack the concern or compassion to do so.

In Psalm 91, one can see that concern/compassion and power/strength are implicitly stated or implied in the imagery employed. For example, the mother (?) bird imagery (v. 4), the strength and toughness of a shield (v. 4), God's commanding the angels to intercede (v. 11), while all of verses 14–16 underscore the idea of concern and compassion. The motif of power and strength is evident in the titles used of God (Most High [vv. 1a, 9], Almighty [v. 1b]) and the absolute confidence that the psalm expresses throughout that God is able to protect and deliver.

Preaching Idea

God is a refuge and source of protection for those who trust in him.

Contemporary Connections

What does it mean?

What does it mean that God is a refuge and source of protection for those who trust in him? At its core, this means that (1) God is the ultimate source of our protection and (2) we must place ourselves within his protection. Whether we are using gloves or a hazmat suit, we are only protected by placing our hands in the gloves or our body in the suit.

Is it true?

Is it really true that God is a refuge and source of protection for those who trust in him? History, experience, Satan's misapplication of verses 11–12 (Matt. 4:6), and indeed other texts in the Bible itself would seemingly call that into question. After all, bad things happen to God's people (to borrow and adapt the title from Rabbi Harold Kushner's bestselling book, *When Bad Things Happen to Good People*). This issue was addressed in detail in the theological focus section so we will be brief here in outlining four explanations.

1. The tension could be eased by seeing the psalm as messianic and therefore not directly applicable to us. But even if this were true, our Lord Jesus was not always protected from harm; indeed, he was put to death on a cross.

2. The psalmist was talking of spiritual rather than physical protection. But the psalm seems to emphasize physical protection more than spiritual protection.

3. Perhaps the psalm is hyperbolic or is speaking in idealized terms. You will

commonly hear people say, "So-and-so was always there for me." The "always" is hyperbolic or general, for no one is "always" there for anyone. This approach is possible (given the wisdom elements present in the psalm), though it must be admitted that the psalm seems to have some rather specific acts of deliverance in mind.

4. The intent of the psalm is to highlight God's role as refuge and protector and not necessarily one's circumstances. As Broyles (1999, 363) notes, "one of the primary purposes of Psalm 91 is not to issue guarantees against misfortune but to promote faith in Yahweh as opposed to other ancient Near Eastern religions."

Maybe the best approach is to avoid seeing these views as mutually exclusive but as all contributing to our understanding of the claims of the psalm. The psalm spotlights God's role as refuge and protector in often hyperbolic or idealized terms that involve physical deliverance while implying spiritual vindication that is exemplified in the person and work of Christ.

Now what?
If God is a refuge and source of protection for those who trust in him, how should we respond to this idea and apply it to our lives? Here are several suggestions.

Place your trust in God as your refuge and protector. This is easier said than done, but it is essential if one desires to deal with anxiety and worry on our end. This also gives the Lord room to work on his end. The problem is, we are so busy trying to protect ourselves that we get in his way.

Move from fear to faith to faithfulness. According to Mark Futato (2009, 296), "The dangers—both real and imagined—of living

in this world can be the source of debilitating fears and anxieties. Psalm 91 has provided God's people 'through all the generations' (90:1) with an antidote to these fears and anxieties." Jesus's Sermon on the Mount echoes this thought in Matthew 6:25–34.

Memorize Psalm 91:14–16 and internalize the three truths about God made in these verses: (1) God delivers and protects; (2) God answer the prayers of his people in times of trouble; and (3) God is the author of life and the one who saves. All three of these truths find their ultimate and fullest expression in the Lord Jesus Christ.

Creativity in Presentation
This psalm could be illustrated using a pair of work gloves, which represents God's protection. Gloves only protect when we place our hands in them and use them. Similarly, if we want to experience God's protection, we need to dwell in his shelter and find refuge in his fortress. A more cumbersome but more visually striking approach would be to wear a hazmat suit to communicate the same point.

Psalm 91 is known as the "soldier's psalm" or "soldier's prayer," and camouflage bandanas are often given to US troops. This bandana could be procured and used to introduce, illustrate, or generate a conversation about the psalm.

Several recent songs are associated with this Psalm. Shane & Shane's "Psalm 91 (On Eagles Wings)" borrows language from Psalm 91, Psalm 18:2, and Isaiah 40:31. Those desiring more literal renderings of the psalm could consider Jason Silver's "Psalm 91, My God in Whom I Trust" or Esther Mui's Scripture song, "Psalm 91 (My God, In Him I Will Trust)." These songs could serve as an introduction or conclusion to the message.

The key point to emphasize is this: God promises his protection to those who trust fully in him alone as their refuge. God is a refuge and source of protection for those who trust in him.

- God is our refuge: The psalmist professes it (91:1–2).

- God is our refuge: The psalmist pictures it (91:3–13).

- God is our refuge: The psalmist's God promises it (91:14–16).

DISCUSSION QUESTIONS

1. Is it possible to be so holy that one can claim the promises of Psalm 91? Why or why not?

2. Is Psalm 91 intentionally about the future Messiah Jesus? Defend your answer.

3. Does this psalm unambiguously teach the ministry of angels for believers? Why or why not?

4. Do the promises of this psalm reflect a divine oath or a human hope. What are your reasons? If not literally applicable to all believers, about whom is the psalmist speaking? What is your evidence?

5. Does the reference to life in verse 16 relate to quantity, quality, or both?

PSALM 111

EXEGETICAL IDEA
The worshipping community was summoned to praise Yahweh for his faithful acts of redemption on behalf of his people.

THEOLOGICAL FOCUS
God is great, glorious, and gracious; and he gives to his chosen nation both land and wise laws.

PREACHING IDEA
God's *work* in our lives should produce *worship* from our lives.

PREACHING POINTERS
The English term *hallelujah* has taken on a rather pedestrian sense and tone in today's culture. It is often used as an interjection in response to perceived good fortune: "Hallelujah, I am getting a tax refund this year." Or it is used sarcastically: "The coach finally put in a new quarterback. Hallelujah!" Even Leonard Cohen's much-covered song "Hallelujah" has almost nothing to do with God. In fact, what all these uses have in common is they really have little, if anything, to say about God.

I (Charles) suspect that this is the very reason that many modern English translations do not often use the term *hallelujah* but rather translate it as "praise the Lord" (lit., "praise Yah"). In any case, from the very first word of Psalm 111, "Hallelujah," the Israelite then and the contemporary reader now is put on notice that God will be front and center and that the Lord's *work* in our lives should produce *worship* from our lives.

WISDOM COMES BY PRIORITIZING DIVINE REVELATION

LITERARY STRUCTURE AND THEMES

Psalm 111 begins with a summons for the assembled Hebrews to enter into a time of public proclamation over God's wonders and ways (v. 1). It continues with an enumeration of reasons their God deserves to be praised and testimonies given (vv. 2–9). It concludes with the results of praise, ending with the exhortation to continue with unending praise (because it is fosters wisdom; v. 10). An acrostic pattern has been recognized.[1]

- *Prologue to Praise (111:1a)*
- *Call to Worship (111:1b)*
- *Causes for Worship (111:2–9)*
  - *God's Character (111:2–4)*
  - *God's Conduct (111:5–9)*
- *Consequence of Worship: Wisdom (111:10a–b)*
- *Epilogue to Praise (111:10c)*

EXPOSITION

Psalm 111 is an individual Praise psalm ("Let me praise") with a wisdom or didactic theme included. It has no superscription in the MT or LXX and is anonymous (one of the so-called Orphan psalms). Since the second verb in the opening verse (ידה) clearly means something like "praise," this hymn is not properly a Thanksgiving psalm as some conclude. No specific setting or date can be identified (although some think its acrostic and wisdom features make it post-exilic), but the contents indicate that it followed some experience of God's power through the provision of food (following a famine?), of the conquest of neighboring nations, and of redemption for Israel. It contains the typical features of a praise song or poem of calls for and causes of worship. Therefore, the worshipping community was summoned to praise Yahweh for his faithful acts of redemption on behalf of his people.

Prologue to Praise (111:1a)

The people are summoned to acknowledge God's attributes publicly.

The worship leader opened this service with the command "Praise 'Yah'!" (הַלְלוּ יָהּ), traditionally Anglicized as "hallelujah." Today this has become, culturally, a response to God's goodness and treated as an act of worship rather than a summons to praise, as it always is in the OT. But technically, hallelujah is an order to begin a time of worship and specifically toward Yahweh and what this name signifies.

Call to Worship (111:1b)

The psalmist proclaims his intention to acknowledge God publicly.

111:1bi. [א] The request for worship continued with the psalmist's own intention, using

---

1 An acrostic pattern has been recognized but it causes some syntactical or lexical irregularities:

v. אוֹדֶה 1bi; בְּסוֹד v. 1bii; גְּדֹלִים v. 2a; דְּרוּשִׁים v. 2b; הוֹד v. 3a; וְצִדְקָתוֹ v. 3b; זֵכֶר v. 4a; חַנּוּן v. 4b; טֶרֶף v. 5a; יִזְכֹּר v. 5b; כֹּחַ v. 6a; לָתֵת v. 6b; מַעֲשֵׂי v. 7a; נֶאֱמָנִים v. 7b; סְמוּכִים v. 8a; עֲשׂוּיִם v. 8b; פְּדוּת v. 9ai; צִוָּה v. 9aii; קָדוֹשׁ v. 9b; רֵאשִׁית v. 10ai; שֵׂכֶל v. 10aii; תְּהִלָּתוֹ v. 10b.

a cohortative verb (II-ידה), saying "I want to confess Yahweh with a whole heart (v. 1b). The NIV has "with all my heart," but the possessive pronoun is not in the Hebrew text (although a number of versions feel it is implied). Either way, this indicates the psalmist's desire to worship without inhibitions or self-censoring for the fear of what others might say. Note that the verb the NIV renders "extol" (II-ידה) is the one it otherwise usually renders "give thanks" (giving doubt to the accuracy of this meaning).

111:bii. [ב] He wanted to give this testimony "in the council of [= composed of the] upright, and [the] assembly/congregation" (v. 1bii). But why is this in the "upright council"? "Council" (סוֹד) is not used in a formal sense but simply here indicates the worshipping community, composed of those who want to do what is right defined by Yahweh's directives. Then this group is further defined as the "congregation [הָעֵדָה]." The prefixed "waw" (ו) on this term is appositional, "[the upright community,] that is, the congregation." He will praise God in the assembly of Hebrew worshippers.

Causes for Worship (111:2–9)
The psalmist speaks of God's character (vv. 2–4) and conduct (vv. 5–9).

God's Character (111:2–4)
111:2a. [ג] The poet first focused on God's attributes (vv. 2–4), first his greatness (v. 2). "Yahweh's deeds [מַעֲשֵׂי יְהוָה] [are] great" (in influence; powerful).

111:2b. [ד] They are "constantly being examined [pass. part.] for all their delights" (לְכָל is בְּכֹל in another Hebrew ms. [the ב perhaps more expected for "by"]). "Seek" means investigate, enquire, or search out (HALOT, s.v. "דרש," p. 233). The grandeur of God's mighty acts in the past are worthy of repeated reflection or contemplation because this brings joy.

111:3a. [ה] Second, God's "glory" or "worth" was targeted (v. 3). "His [Yahweh's] activity [פֹּעַל] [is] splendid and majestic."

111:3b. [ו] "And his righteousness keeps standing [active ptc.] always." What Yahweh does is always right, awesome, and significant.

111:4a. [ז] Third, God's grace was observed. "He [Yahweh] has performed [עָשָׂה; same root in v. 2] memorable wonders [nominal ptc.]." What he has done in the past, he will do in the future.

111:4b. [ח] "Yahweh [is always] gracious and compassionate [or 'merciful']."

God's Conduct (111:5–9)
111:5a. [ט] Next, God's actions were named (vv. 5–9). First, he provides food (v. 5). "He [Yahweh] has given prey [= 'food'] to his fearful ones." The usual word for food is not used because a term staring with *tet* (ט) was required by the acrostic format. Those who are afraid are those who "fear" (i.e., faithfully serve or obey) God (see v. 10). The past tense verb is used to reflect on God's provisions of food in the past, as in the wilderness wanderings (implying that he will always do so).

111:5b. [י] "He [Yahweh] will always remember his covenant [promises, made to the patriarchs]."

111:6a. [כ] Also he provides foreign lands (v. 6). "He [Yahweh] has displayed [נגד] his powerful works [same word in v. 2a] to his people" (the construct כֹּחַ מַעֲשָׂיו, "strength of his works" = "power from/by his deeds," separative/source or agency genitive).

111:6b. [ל] He did this "in order to give [purpose use of inf. const.] to them [his people] [that] possession of [other] nations." The intended idea is that Yahweh *worked* on Israel's behalf to give them the land owned by neighboring nations. The construct "possession of nations [נַחֲלַת גּוֹיִם]" is a possessive genitive, "the nations' inheritance." The land Canaan was inhabited by numerous nations or tribes.

111:7a. [מ] Further, he provides firm statutes (vv. 7–8). "The works [same root in vv. 2, 6] of his [Yahweh's] hands are trustworthy and just." This rendering is contra the JPS and NETS (cf. LXX, ἀλήθεια), since "truth" as we use the term today is a misleading translation. Here (אֱמֶת) speaks of reliability (Marlowe 2010, 24–42; and ESV's "faithful"). Note the parallel term "trustworthy [נֶאֱמָנִים]" in verse 7b (cf. 8b). Often "judgment" (מִשְׁפָּט) in this situation can be "justice" (i.e., right judgments in context; v. 8b). The NETS renders the Greek OT word (κρίσις) as "justice."

111:7b. [נ] "All [some mss. say "for all"] his [Yahweh's] precepts are trustworthy." Whatever directions he gives or decisions he renders are right, reliable, and rewarding.

111:8a. [ס] "These precepts [are] kept firm [pass. ptc.] always."

111:8b. [ע] "[And they] keep being made [pass. ptc.] with reliability and rightness." The NRSV and ESV are probably best: "They are established forever and ever, to be performed with faithfulness and uprightness."

111:9a. [פ] God's provision of deliverance was then recounted (v. 9). "He [Yahweh] sent redemption to his people" (probably a global reflection on the exodus primarily; cf. Exod. 18:4–8).

111:9b. [צ] "He [Yahweh] commanded [= 'ordained,' JPS, NASB, and NET] his covenant as 'enduring' [לְעוֹלָם]."

[ק] "His name [Yahweh] is 'unique [קָדוֹשׁ],' so is being feared [pass. ptc.; i.e., is being reverenced with awe]."

Holiness

The Hebrew word קָדוֹשׁ is regularly translated "holy" in English versions. However, that word today in English carries lexical baggage that confuses its meaning in many OT texts. In current usage, "holy" has come to imply "sinless" or "pious." The Hebrew word basically had to do with separation or distinction, and in the OT it is often applied to being set apart from what is profane or common (cf. HALOT, s.v. "קָדוֹשׁ,", 1066). Yahweh was/is "holy" as uniquely distinct from all other gods, and not all but many of his laws were moral and ethical advancements in ANE religion.

Consequence of Worship: Wisdom (111:10a–b)

Fearing God leads to wisdom and is to be continued in all future generations.

111:10a. [ר] The psalmist then reflected on the benefits of fearing and worshipping God. "[The] beginning of 'wisdom' [חָכְמָה] [is this] fear of [submission to the precepts from] Yahweh" (cf. the parallel line). In some OT texts, Yahweh's fear seems to be linked to his laws (e.g., in Prov. 2:5 this fear appears to be restated by knowledge, and in 15:33 it teaches; and in Isaiah 11:2–3, delighting in this fear is in the context of understanding, knowledge, and counsel; in Psalm 19:9, "ordinances" restates this fear). Proverbs 1:7 has the same words except for the last, "The fear of Yahweh is the beginning of 'knowledge' [דַּעַת]"; however, this is restated as "wisdom [חָכְמָה]" in the second line.

111:10b. [ש] "Good insight [this wisdom] [comes] to all those who *regularly* perform [active ptc. of same root used in vv. 2, 6, 7] them [i.e., all the precepts mentioned in v. 7]."

Epilogue to Praise (111:10c)

Praise is a perpetual benefit.

[ה] Finally, the poem was ended with a call to continue praise. "His [Yahweh's] praise is standing [ptc. = 'endures'] for all time." The psalmist now calls on the people to continue praising Yahweh throughout all future generations. The JPS has, "Praise of Him is everlasting[/enduring]" (which probably corrects those versions that use "forever"). It is also possible that the hallelujah that begins the next psalm (Ps. 112; הַלְלוּ יָהּ) was originally an ending to this psalm (Ps. 111; see NETS) creating an inclusio(n) (i.e., a literary unit that begins and ends with the same or a similar feature that serves to "enclose" the contents).

THEOLOGICAL FOCUS

The exegetical idea (the worshipping community was summoned to praise "Yahweh" [יְהוָה] for his faithful acts of redemption on behalf of his people) leads to this theological focus: God is great, glorious, and gracious; and he gives to his chosen nation land and wise laws.

That the psalmist emphasizes Yahweh's provision of lands belonging to other people (v. 6) might raise some eyebrows. Why did God just not build the Hebrew empire in a region uninhabited? Why did he have to take land from the Canaanites, who were there first? Such questions might arise in our modern context of heightened sensitivities over how Western powers brutally and often dishonestly took land from less advanced people, even claiming it was God's will at times, and using the Israelite conquest of Canaan as biblical justification. What does this psalm tell us about God? First, Yahweh always does what is right (v. 3). The testimony of the psalmist here is that while his people were unfaithful, Yahweh maintains a gracious, compassionate, loving, and saving relationship with those who "fear" him. Praise, therefore, is appropriate and the wisdom of obedience will always be rewarding.

PREACHING AND TEACHING STRATEGIES

Exegetical and Theological Synthesis

As previously noted, Psalm 111 is built around an alphabetic acrostic structure where the first letter of the first word of each line of the Hebrew text follows the order of the Hebrew alphabet. The function of such acrostics in the Bible (e.g., Ps. 112; 119; Lam. 1–4) are debated and typically fall into three categories: (1) The function of the acrostics could be aesthetic; that is, it is literarily pleasing. (2) They are mnemonic devices to help people in a primarily oral culture to remember texts. (3) The alphabetic acrostics serve a didactic purpose, namely, to communicate the comprehensive nature of something. Someone might say, "from A to Z and everything in-between."

Dogmatism regarding these proposed categories is unwarranted and unnecessary. The acrostic inspires through its artistry, internalizes through its structure, and instructs in its comprehensiveness. Whether we are speaking of the Lord's works or our worship, we can do so "from A to Z and everything in-between." Or in other words, God's people could use a holistic view of God and a holistic view of worship.

Preaching Idea

God's *work* in our lives should produce *worship* from our lives.

Contemporary Connections

What does it mean?

What does it mean that God's *work* in our lives should produce *worship* from our lives? Two concepts merit some attention here.

First, while the meaning of the term "works" is not especially difficult, it is significant in this psalm. Two and possibly three different Hebrew words can be translated as "works" in verses 2, 3, 4, 6, and 7. We note that

God's works are "great" (v. 2), "full of splendor and majesty" (v. 3), enduring/forever (vv. 3, 5, 8, 9, 10), "wondrous" (v. 4), memorable (v. 4), powerful (v. 6), and "faithful and just" (v. 7). It is also worth noting that the works are corporate and done on behalf of the believing community. Note how the proclamation "his praise endures forever" (v. 10) seems to be a culmination of four previous references that include "forever" are connected to his righteousness (v. 3), his remembering covenant (v. 5), his precepts (vv. 7–8), and his commanding his covenant (v. 9). The psalm ends with His praise enduring forever (and it will with or without us), but our praise of him for forever is made possible because of *his righteousness* in works and precepts (vv. 3, 7–8) and *his faithfulness* in covenant (vv. 5, 9). The description of God's works, precepts, and faithfulness and the fact that they are done for the community suggest that *our praise and worship* is founded on the former and appropriate because of the latter.

The second term to consider is "worship." Worship can be defined as an expression of attitudes (reverence, adoration) and actions (service directed to and for God). That worship involves showing honor, devotion, and reverence is fairly basic. But what light does Psalm 111 shed on the topic? According to the psalmist, worship involves the "whole heart" (v. 1); it is primarily theocentric (centered on God; note the delight in Lord's works [v. 2]) and not anthropocentric (centered on people) (vv. 2–9); it is reverential ("fear of the LORD," v. 10); it is related to true wisdom (v. 10); and it is forever either in its practice or in its result (v. 10). These concepts seem foreign to much that is labeled "worship" today, which leans toward receiving not giving. People are more prone to say, "I enjoyed worship today" rather than asking "was the Lord pleased with our worship today?" This raises another point related to whether worship is communal or individual. The answer is surprisingly complex, but in short it is both/and. The book of Psalms generally, and this psalm in particular, assumes worship in community (vv. 1, 6, 9). But of course, community is made up of individuals, and we are not always gathered with our community. For example, note in verse 5 that the Lord provides food for those who fear him; clearly, we do not always eat in community.

Is it true?

Is it true that God's *work* in our lives should produce *worship* from our lives? The concept of works and worship has already been examined. But what remains is the relationship between the two. It has been suggested that the Lord's work in our lives *should* produce worship from our lives. Is the word "should" too timid? Perhaps, something more forceful like "must" or "will" are more appropriate. But the psalm itself suggests that "should" is appropriate.

First, the psalm begins with a call to praise. Such a call is needed because not everyone worships God. Second, the identification of the "company of the upright" once again seems to distinguish the psalmist and the upright from others (e.g., the wayward, unrighteous). Third, the reference to the fear of the Lord and the call to live wisely implies at the very least that not everyone will be part of the praise community. Finally, the extended listing of the works of God is no doubt intended to motivate the ignorant or reluctant to worship him. One final point, though it is not present in or implied by the psalm, is the idea that true worship is a choice. It is a permissive "should" of one who recognizes God for who he is and for what he has done.

Now what?

If God's *work* in our lives should produce *worship* from our lives, how should we respond to this idea and apply it to our lives? Psalm 111 is one of those biblical texts that basically applies itself. The very first word is a command to praise the Lord. But let's consider what principles and applications can be drawn from the psalm about worship. There are at least three.

First, true worship is tied to a robust view of God's works as revealed in the biblical record of those works. *So, know the God of the Bible so you will be able to truly worship the God of the Bible.*

Second, the default setting of praise and worship is communal because God often does his works in community. *Call others to worship with you and respond when others call you to worship.*

Third, praise is tied to reverence and wisdom. That is, worship is theological and practical. One who truly worships is wise, and one who is truly wise worships. *So, cultivate reverence toward God and wisdom toward life.*

Creativity in Presentation

Play a video portion of one of the renditions of Leonard Cohen's much-covered song (more than three hundred renditions) "Hallelujah" and discuss how the ideas conveyed in the song do or don't convey the meaning of the term "hallelujah."

Or introduce the psalm by using one of the more biblically faithful musical renditions of the psalm such as, Nathan Clark George's, "Psalm 111: Praise the Lord" or Jason Silver's "His Praise Endures Forever, Psalm 111." These are two of the better ones.

The communal nature of worship could be illuminated by the Newsboys' 2003 song "He Reigns," which repeatedly offers the refrain of "hallelujah" in a global context.

One could obtain a picture through Google Images of the Latin inscription of Psalm 111:2 that is over the door of the Cavendish Laboratory (home of the Department of Physics in the University of Cambridge). Use the picture and the story behind it to illustrate the idea that worship is not incompatible with intelligence.[2]

The key point to emphasize is this: God is great, glorious, and gracious; and he gives to his chosen nation land and wise laws. God's work in our lives should produce worship from our lives.

- Worship is intentional: look up (111:1).

- Worship is observational: look around (111:2–9).

- Worship is practical: look within (111:10).

---

2   For example, see "Physics and Psalms," The Faraday Institute, December 17, 2010, https://www.faraday.cam.ac.uk/churches/church-resources/posts/172. See also "The Research Scientist's Psalm," The Faraday Institute, March 1, 2012, https://www.faraday.cam.ac.uk/churches/church-resources/posts/the-research-scientists-psalm.

DISCUSSION QUESTIONS

1. Why are the Lord's works great?

2. What does it mean that the Lord has to "remember" the covenant?

3. How does "fearing" God begin wisdom?

4. Does the enduring praise in Psalm 111:10 relate to its practice (we continually offer praise) or its result (our praise has a lasting effect)?

PSALM 112

EXEGETICAL IDEA
This Israelite psalmist proclaimed praise because those who obey God's commands (unlike the lawless) will be prosperous, generous, confident, and celebrated.

THEOLOGICAL FOCUS
God rewards the righteous with success and satisfaction, while the wicked are dissatisfied even when their desires are obtained.

PREACHING IDEA
A blessed life is enriching, ethical, enduring, established, and even envied by the wicked.

PREACHING POINTERS
Like Psalm 111, Psalm 112 begins with a "hallelujah" ("praise the Lord") and shows that like us today, the Israelites were desiring to live a life of blessing. But what is the difference, if any, between living a charmed life versus a blessed life? According to the *Merriam-Webster's Online Dictionary*, a charmed life is "a life protected as if by magic charms: a life unusually unaffected by dangers and difficulties." Three aspects of this brief definition are noteworthy in what is omitted: (1) there is no mention of God; (2) there is no ethical component or corollary; and (3) a charmed life is one that avoids the trials and tribulations of life. On the other hand, a blessed life (at least according to the Bible) is integrally tied to God (one is not truly blessed apart from God), and ethics (a blessed person is righteous, and a righteous person is blessed), and blessedness does not avoid trials and tribulations (but is a status one has within them).

Scripture contains no promises about obtaining a charmed life, but it makes numerous proclamations about the blessed life. A charmed life is grounded in fate, luck, chance, destiny, and the like, while blessing is grounded in a sovereign God and living lives that reflect that God. So, it's great if you are living a charmed life, but if you are like the rest of us, then a blessed life is the best life. To that end, Psalm 112 helps to unpack what a blessed life looks and acts like.

OBEYING GOD'S REVELATION LEADS TO WISDOM AND WELL-BEING

LITERARY STRUCTURE AND THEMES

Psalm 112 starts out, as wisdom praise, with a summons for the people to acknowledge God's qualities as a lawgiver in public (v. 1a). This is followed by naming some of the advantages of obeying God's laws (vv. 1b–9), and then some of the disadvantages of disobedience (v. 10). The psalm ends also with a wisdom theme by contrasting the righteous and wicked.

- *Call to Praise "Yahweh" (יְהֹוָה) (112:1a)*
- *The Consequences of Obeying God's Commands (112:1b–9)*
- *The Consequences of Disobeying God's Commands (112:10)*

EXPOSITION

The "Hallelujah" (הַלְלוּ יָהּ; "Praise 'Yah'[יָהּ]!") that begins this psalm might belong to Psalm 111 as a closing inclusio(n) (that frames a poem, often praise) because Psalm 113 also begins and ends with this exhortation. That leaves Psalm 112 without this statement at beginning or end, but in both places for the preceding and following psalms. Otherwise we could postulate that "Hallelujah" only begins Psalms 111, 112, 113, and 114 (meaning that only the expression at the end of Psalm 113 is misplaced in the MT). As the MT stands, however, its placement is awkward (Pss. 111:1; 112:1; 113:1, 9), but perhaps only Psalm 113 has the inclusio(n) as intended. Regardless, Psalm 112 is another Praise Psalm. If "Hallelujah" is not allowed at the beginning, then we have no initial call to praise and only causes for praise. And Psalm 111 does have an equivalent call to praise. Whatever the case, this Israelite psalmist proclaimed praise because those who obey God's commands (unlike the lawless) will be prosperous, generous, confident, and celebrated.

Call to Praise Yahweh (112:1a)

The people are summoned to publicly and verbally recognize God's attributes.

Cf. commentary on Psalm 111:1, above.

The Consequences of Obeying God's Commands (112:1b–9)

Reasons why it is beneficial to fear Yahweh and follow his instructions are given.

112:1b. The consequence of or reason named first for obeying God's commands was God's favor. The "man [אִישׁ]" (= "person," not true just for males) fearful (adjective) toward Yahweh is "blessed" or "advantaged [אַשְׁרֵי]" (for אַשְׁרֵי = "fortunate/favored," cf. commentary on Ps. 1). In context, given the patriarchal and chauvinistic situation culturally, the author could have meant "male" because that was his focus. From the perspective of progressive revelation, however, the modern reader would understand that biblical theology affirms overall that both men and women are blessed when they fear and follow God. This "fear" is not mainly an emotional idea here but has to do with obedience due to great reverential awe of Yahweh (including respect for his power to give and take life as Creator). But in the ANE in general, due to the gods being "all-powerful" but not all-good, real emotional fear or terror of the gods was a widespread reality. The fact that fear for the Hebrews was more about obedience is demonstrated by the following parallel line of poetry: "[because] he has delighted greatly in his commands."

112:2. The second reason named was having successful children. His offspring [not just his male sons] will be mighty in the land (v. 2a). The parallel line is unclear: literally, "a generation of upright will be blessed" (v. 2b). The construct genitive has to be interpreted in context: "generation of upright" (which versions like the NIV leave literal and unexplained). The Syriac version has "in/with a generation." Whatever is meant is in some way related to verse 2a, that the person who obeys God gladly will have children who make a positive impact on society. The JPS interprets this as an upright generation (attributive genitive). The restatement is that these descendants will be strong in terms of the blessings or empowerment that comes from doing what is right.

112:3. A third reason for following God's instructions was economic security. "Wealth and riches [are] in his house; and his righteous [example] keeps standing [participle] for all time" ("forever" gives the wrong idea to a modern reader). God's ways will usually result in financial security. The point of these words is not the kind of excessive wealth we connect to a word like "rich" today (thinking of millionaires and billionaires). Only a few people like kings had such holdings in the ANE. A "rich" person in society at large was someone who was not poor and maintained a prosperous business by which he could provide adequately for his family.

112:4. The fourth reason mentioned was enlightenment. The psalmist says, "Light has risen in darkness for the upright; [for the] gracious, compassionate, and righteous [person]." The NIV's "Even in" is an interpolation but not impossible. The preposition "for" could also be translated "in regard to." In contrast to most versions (that are too literal and formal rather than functional), the point seems to be that people who are law-keepers are beacons of "light" (good examples of values like compassion and grace) in a "[morally] dark" world.

112:5. The fifth reason for following God's commandments was a good life. Such a good person, who is "habitually generous/gracious" (participle of I-חָנַן), "lending frequently" (ptc. of II-לָוָה), "will conduct" (future or durative of כּוּל) his "affairs [דְּבָרָיו] with equity/justice [בְּמִשְׁפָּט]." The NIV's beginning "Good will come" reflects a verb not present in the MT but which might have been intended. People who are generous promote justice or fair treatment of others.

112:6. The sixth reason offered was a memorable life. "Since [כִּי] he will never be moved [= 'waiver'; pass. future of מוֹט]" (i.e., he will be consistently compassionate). "A righteous person will be [= will produce] a lasting memory." A generous lifestyle will create positive, lasting changes for others who are disadvantaged.

112:7. The seventh reason for following God's laws was a confident life. "He will not fear a bad report; he [is] emotionally and mentally stable [lit., 'his heart is firm'], trusting in Yahweh" In other words, a law-abiding person who trusts God is not devastated by bad news. Although it may be troubling, he rests confidently in God's care.

112:8. The eighth reason was the prospect of a victorious life. "[He is] one whose 'heart' [i.e., his mind and passion] is always steady [passive ptc. of סָמַךְ], [so] he will never be afraid; until [the day comes when] he will look on his enemy." The JPS has, "in the end he will see the fall of his foes." Due to Yahweh's promises and power, a righteous Israelite could be confident that he would eventually be victorious over his adversaries in Canaan. The NIV and NRSV have, "in the end they will look in triumph on their foes."

112:9. Finally, a ninth reason to be obedient to God's instructions was for a generous life. This person is one who "has scattered, has given to the needy; [the results of] his righteous [deeds] are enduring [ptc. of עמד "stand"] [and] lasting; his horn [= power/influence] will be exalted in honor." In other words, he gives so widely to the poor, his importance and influence will be recognized.

The Consequences of Disobeying God's Commands (112:10)

The disadvantage of disobedience

112:10. The psalm was then concluded with an observation about the liability of ignoring God's laws. "[But] a wicked person will observe [lit., 'see'] [such generosity] and will get angry; he will gnash his teeth and he will be melted; the craving of wicked people will perish." The psalmist claims that lawless people will lose their composure over such selflessness, but what their selfish desires acquired has only temporary value. Wicked people do not believe that giving is better than receiving.

THEOLOGICAL FOCUS

The exegetical idea (those who obey God's commands [unlike the lawless] will be prosperous, generous, confident, and celebrated) leads to this theological focus: God rewards the righteous with success and satisfaction, while the wicked are dissatisfied even when their desires are obtained.

Psalm 112 offers rich material and spiritual rewards for living right according to God's commands. The problem for modern readers is that this is stated in a very black-and-white manner, similar to how Proverbs seems to promise a good life for the righteous and a bad life for the wicked. However, as Ecclesiastes reminds us, life does not work out this way in absolute terms. Righteous people can suffer and die young and be poor, while wicked people can be healthy and wealthy. Good fathers can have bad sons and vice versa (cf. Ezek. 18). If that is true, and we know it is from experience, what's up with OT passages that seem to guarantee good rewards for being good and bad results for being bad? Should we conclude that all who have negative experiences are really bad or wicked, contrary to appearances? And those who have positive experiences are ipso facto righteous, contrary to appearances? If a person is rich, do we just conclude he must have God's favor? Most would answer, of course not. So, how do we read these "promissory" notes?

The key is to understand the nature of wisdom literature. While many verses in the book of Proverbs sound absolute, they do not intend to ignore the "other side of the coin" (which Ecclesiastes and Job highlight); they merely want to encourage believers to do right, because (while the righteous can suffer) it remains true in principle that the best life possible is made possible by law-keeping. A lawbreaker might sometimes "get away with murder," but generally crime does not pay, and making foolish and faulty choices in life will, in most cases, lead to loss of life (physically and otherwise, in quality and/or quantity). The sayings of Proverbs are not absolute promises, but they are reliable principles. A wise person will trust God and his commands, while a foolish person will "lean on his own understanding" and what unbelieving people advise. The fear of God is the beginning of wisdom.

PREACHING AND TEACHING STRATEGIES

Exegetical and Theological Synthesis

It has already been noted that a blessed life is enriching, ethical, enduring (vv. 3, 6, 9), established (vv. 6–8), and even envied by the wicked (v. 10). But before examining the psalm's portrait of the blessed life, two important literary features need to be noted to ensure that the psalmist's theological vision is properly understood: (1) Psalm 112 is poetry, a genre that typically contains literal truths but truths that should not be viewed literally. (2) The psalm is influenced by the wisdom tradition (think of the book of Proverbs, for example), a genre, that tends to traffic in generalities and principles rather than absolutes and promises (see the discussion above in the theological focus section). Appreciating these two features will help to avoid two kinds of errors. One would be to view the psalm through the warped lens of prosperity theology. The other error would be to view the psalm as a pie-in-the-sky ideal that is divorced from the harsh realities of life. What the psalmist envisions seems to lie between the two. Rather than Joel Osteen's *Your Best Life Now*, you can live a blessed life now.

Preaching Idea
A blessed life is enriching, ethical, enduring, established, and even envied by the wicked.

Contemporary Connections

What does it mean?
What does it mean that a blessed life is enriching, ethical, enduring, established, and even envied by the wicked?

The enriching aspect can be seen in verse 3 where blessing is tied to "wealth and riches." One needs to be careful in understanding this as a kind of prosperity promise, but there is a sense in which those who follow God's ways are generally financially stable.

As previously noted, one crucial difference between leading a charmed life and living a blessed life is that the latter is tied to ethics. So, a blessed life involves fearing the Lord and delighting in God's commandments (v. 1), being gracious, merciful, and righteous (v. 4), being generous and just (v. 5), steadfast in righteousness (v. 6), and caring for the poor (v. 9). As John Goldingay (2008, 313) notes, "The psalm implies an analysis of good life, in two senses. It portrays the morally good life and the good life."

A blessed life is also enduring. Twice it is said of the blessed person that "his righteousness endures forever" (vv. 3, 9) and once that "he will be remembered forever" (v. 6). Interpreters wrestle over whether "righteousness enduring forever" in verses 3 and 9 refer to righteousness as a virtue or a work enduring forever, or that a reward/result of righteousness is that it endures. Regardless, the blessed life is one that makes or has a lasting impact. It is viewed in contrast to the wicked who does not ("perishes," v. 10).

A blessed life is an established life. The psalmist boldly declares that "the righteous will never be moved" and will ultimately triumph (vv. 6a, 8b). There might be a hint of the established and enduring nature of the blessed life in the presence of the alphabetic acrostic. The blessed life is complete from A to Z and everything in between. As such it is a life that does not fear bad news but rather is firm and steady in one's trust of the Lord (vv. 7, 8a). There are numerous calls in the NT to remain steadfast (e.g., 1 Cor. 15:58; 2 Thess. 3:5; 1 Tim. 6:11; James 1:3–4). As the old English proverb states, "Fear knocked at the door. Faith answered. No one was there."

Finally, a blessed life is even enviable to the wicked. Although envy is not directly stated, the idea seems to be implied by the wicked person's response to seeing the blessed life of the righteous. He resents what the righteous person has. One additional point is that the reference to the wicked in verse 10 seems a bit out of place. But as is often the case in wisdom literature, a quality or thing (in this case a blessed life) is highlighted by the use of contrast. In Psalm 112, the contrast is between the righteous and the wicked, between good works and bad (resentment and anger), and between one who endures and one who perishes.

Is it true?
Is it true that a blessed life that is enriching, ethical, enduring, established, and even enviable to the wicked is actually possible? Both life and the Bible would seem to answer with a hearty

yes. While the poetic and wisdom elements need to be properly understood, it is important to note that the poet begins the psalm with praise ("hallelujah," v. 1). If the praise is rightly associated with this psalm (see the commentary above), the hallelujah seems to function as a response to what is, namely, the reality of a blessed life. Furthermore, both Jesus and the NT seems to affirm the possibility of a blessed life now. Jesus can say, "Blessed *are . . .*" (Matt. 5:3–11). Similarly, Paul refers to those in Christ who are blessed (Rom. 4:7, 8; 14:22; Gal. 3:9; 4:15; Eph. 1:3, 6) as does James (James 1:12, 25; 5:11), Peter (1 Peter 3:14; 4:14), and John (Rev. 1:3; 14:13; 16:15; 19:9; 20:6; 22:7, 14).

Now what?

If a blessed life is enriching, ethical, enduring, established, and even envied by the wicked, how should we respond to this idea and apply it to our lives? Here are several suggestions.

Stop pursuing the elusive charmed life or bemoaning the fact that you don't have one. Focus instead on living a righteous life that leads to the Lord's blessings and one that will have a lasting impact. Can you say with the apostle Paul that "I count everything as loss because of the surpassing worth of knowing Christ Jesus my Lord" (Phil. 3:8)?

Live a life that is characterized by reverence and a love for the word of God. Live a life that is gracious, merciful, and righteous, generous, and just. Have a heart for the disadvantaged. Do not fret when those who reject the ways of God respond negatively to you.

Read Psalms 111 and 112 together and notice how these psalms work together. Having a right theology should lead to a right life. As Derek Kidner (1975, 431, 433) astutely observes, Psalm 111 pictures God at work and Psalm 112 presents godliness at work.

Creativity in Presentation

You could introduce Psalm 112 by bringing a cell phone out and talking about popular social networking services such as Instagram or TikTok where one can share photos, videos, and brief messages that some use to show the rest of us how interesting and fabulous their lives are. The places they go, the clothes that they wear, and the food that they eat are all real-time proof that they are leading charmed lives. (Now to be clear, not everyone who uses social networking uses it for this purpose, yet many do.) But how would the life of someone walking with the Lord, a blessed life, look as an Instagram post? Is righteousness frameable? Can personal generosity be posted in a way that is not a self-aggrandizing stunt to get "likes"?

Or consider using a sandwich and a couple pieces of toast to illustrate the difference between a charmed life (toast) and a blessed life (a sandwich). Toast is good and easy to make but basically it is just burnt bread. A sandwich is also good and also involves bread (maybe even toasted) but requires more effort and other ingredients to fill it out. So, it is with a blessed life. A blessed life is filled with blessings, righteousness, mercy, generosity, and so on. Maybe some of us have been settling for toast when we should have been going for a sandwich.

Musical renditions of Psalm 112 are available from 4Him ("Psalm 112"), Jason Silver ("Psalm 112"), and Mark Haas ("Psalm 112: The Just Man Is a Light")

The key point to emphasize is this: God rewards the righteous with success and satisfaction, while the wicked are dissatisfied even when their desires are obtained. A blessed life is enriching, ethical, enduring, established, and even envied by the wicked.

- A blessed life is an enriched life (112:1–3).

- A blessed life is an ethical life (122:4–5).

- A blessed life is an enduring life (122:6–9).

- A blessed life is an envious life (122:6–9).

DISCUSSION QUESTIONS

1. How does Psalm 112:1bii clarify the meaning of "fear" in verse 1bi?

2. What does it mean in practical terms to "delight" in God's laws?

3. What are the consequences of doing what God commands?

4. Does "righteousness enduring forever" in verses 3 and 9 mean righteousness as a virtue/work that will endure forever or a reward/result of righteousness that will be forever enduring?

5. Does the reference to "wealth and riches" in verse 3 ensure our material prosperity? Why or why not?

6. How does the lawbreaker's life differ from the law-keeper?

PSALM 119

EXEGETICAL IDEA
This ancient Hebrew poet expressed his love for and loyalty to the laws of Yahweh with the hope that he would experience divine deliverance from a deadly foe.

THEOLOGICAL FOCUS
A life regulated by, and devoted to, God's rules has the best chance for safety and success.

PREACHING IDEA
Devotion to God's word is the proper response to the challenges of life.

PREACHING POINTERS
It is said that Eskimos have fifty (or even a hundred) words for snow, and this rich vocabulary indicates that snow is truly important for these people. Cool, but untrue. Linguistic studies have pretty much defrosted this idea. It is the Scottish, in fact, who seem to have the richest winter vocabulary. What is beyond debate is that Psalm 119 uses eight different Hebrew terms to relate to the Law, or perhaps better, the word of God. What is also true is that the psalmist takes 176 verses to adequately express his devotion to the word. In musical terms, Psalm 119 is less like a song and more like a concept album.

While little is known of this psalm's historical context, the author's devotion to God's word seems so out of step with much of the culture. Americans are becoming less and less biblically literate, or to put it negatively, more and more biblically illiterate. This is true of even some Christ-followers who regard the Bible as mostly irrelevant or even a potential hindrance to their pursuit of Christ. When you throw in a healthy dose of postmodern skepticism in the mix, it seems that the sentiments expressed by Psalm 119 are quaint and simplistic.

WHAT IT MEANS TO LOVE GOD'S LAWS

LITERARY STRUCTURE AND THEMES

Psalm 119 (118 in LXX) is the longest psalm in the OT Psalter with 176 verses, and the longest chapter in the Bible. It also is a rare acrostic psalm with twenty-two sections or strophes (paragraphs; see Lam. 3) listed in successive order, one each for the twenty-two letters of the Hebrew "alphabet" (a term that comes from the first two letters, "aleph-beth" [א-ב], as the Greek "alpha-beta" [α-β], and is derived from Phoenician, Northwest Semitic as Hebrew). As a Torah psalm, it ranks as the representative *par excellence* of poems about the unequaled importance of God's verbal revelation or law. Consequently, it could be considered a hymnic praise to Yahweh as a lawgiver; yet others see it as a poem emerging from a wisdom school. As an acrostic, each section begins with a verse (bi-colon) of which the first word begins with a successive letter of the Hebrew alphabet (*aleph* [א] *to tav* [ת]). Each of the twenty-two strophes contains eight verses according to a clearly conscious poetic design (Anderson 1995, II:805–806, citing Deißler 1955, 71–74, regarding the possible significance for the eight strophes and eight different Hebrew words for "law" in Psalm 119). It contains little development of thought and is characterized by repetition but stands out for its size as much as its substance. Due to its unusual length, it may be outlined in summary and logically as follows:

- *Obedience Is a Blessing* (אַשְׁרֵי; "Fortunate") (119:1–8 [א])
- *How to Obey God's Laws* (בַּמֶּה; "How?") (119:9–16 [ב])
- *Why Desire More Revelation* (גְּמֹל; "Reward!") (119:17–24 [ג])

- *Keeping God's Laws Is Work* (דָּבְקָה; "[I] have clung") (119:25–32 [ד])
- *Lawful Obedience for God's Statutes Fuels Success* (הוֹרֵנִי; "Show me!") (119:33–40 [ה])
- *Obedient Witness Results from God's Rescue* (וִיבֹאֻנִי; "And may it come to me") (119:41–48 [ו])
- *Reliance on Divine Revelation Risks Ridicule* (זְכֹר; "Remember!") (119:49–56 [ז])
- *Obedience Welcomes God's Grace* (חֶלְקִי; "My portion") (119:57–64 [ח])
- *Divine Discipline Is Based on Good Laws* (טוֹב; "Good") (119:65–72 [ט])
- *Disobedience Should Be Disciplined but God's Enemies Destroyed* (יָדֶיךָ; "Your hands") (119:73–80 [י])
- *Divine Promises Are Certain but Not Immediate* (כָּלְתָה; "[I] have fainted") (119:81–88 [כ])
- *Divine Revelation Is Definitive* (לְעוֹלָם; "Always") (119:89–96 [ל])
- *Divine Revelation Leads to Skillful Reasoning* (מָה; "How/What") (119:97–104 [מ])
- *Obedience to God's Ways Increases Physical Safety* (נֵר; "Lamp") (119:105–112 [נ])
- *God's Ways Trump All Other Ways* (סֵעֲפִים; "Divided ones") (119:113–120 [ס])
- *Obedience Gives Confidence in God's Care* (עָשִׂיתִי; "I have done") (119:121–128 [ע])
- *Obedience Enhances the Odds of Divine Rescue* (פְּלָאוֹת; "Wonders") (119:129–136 [פ])
- *God's Laws and Loyalty Remain Despite Difficulties* (צַדִּיק; "Just; Right") (119:137–144 [צ])

- **_Longevity Is Opportunity for Obedient Service_** (קָרָאתִי; **_"I have cried"_**) **_(119:145–152_** [ק]**_)_**
- **_God's Reliable Revelation Gives Confidence of God's Help_** (רְאֵה; **_"See!"_**) **_(119:153–160_** [ר]**_)_**
- **_Law-Keepers May Feel They Deserve Not to Suffer_** (שָׂרִים; **_"Rulers"_**) **_(119:161–168_** [ש]**_)_**
- **_The Law-Keeper Expects God to Hear His Prayer_** (תִּקְרַב; **_"May it come near?)_** **_(119:169–176_** [ת]**_)_**

EXPOSITION

Some have proposed that Psalm 119 at one point concluded the OT Psalter as a kind of inclusio with Psalm 1 (also a wisdom or didactic poem based on the poet's delight in God's laws; Anderson 1995, 807, citing Westermann 1964, 338.; see also Botha 2012, 1–7). This is interesting in light of this psalm's current position, following Psalm 118, that ends a section of anonymous praise (Pss. 110–115, 117–118), and preceding Psalm 120, that begins the Ascent Songs (Pss. 120–134). The lone, awkward location of this Torah psalm suggests some special reason for its placement, that appears odd if Psalm 120 and following were already available at the time of arrangement. However, Psalm 119 could be called an extended yet simple lament in that the poet repeatedly complains about life-threatening persecution by an enemy and prays for protection. At times a justification for divine intervention is given. Thus, this ancient Hebrew poet expressed his love for and loyalty to the laws of Yahweh with the hope that he would experience divine deliverance from a deadly foe.

Obedience Is a Blessing [אַשְׁרֵי; _"Fortunate"_] _(119:1–8_ [א]_)_

The poet expresses his knowledge that law-keepers will be blessed, and vows to be more consistent, asking God not to abandon him.

119:1. Similar to Psalm 1, the psalmist began by describing those who follow Yahweh's laws as "blessed" (אַשְׁרֵי; v. 1), defined (cf. commentary on Ps. 1:1 and 26:4–5) as "fortunate" or "favored" (not "happy"). The fruit of delighting in God's revelation is not about being emotionally happy but spiritually competent and content (in terms of doing what is right because of knowing what is right). The use of the participle "those who walk" (v. 1b) suggests continual (consistent) behavior, which is first explained (v. 1a) as a "blameless direction" (תְמִימֵי־דָרֶךְ; a construct, objective genitive, lit., "blamelessness of way"). Some use the translation "perfect," but this is misleading because moral perfection is not biblically achievable, while a blameless life, or one free from open or hidden rebellion against God's kingdom values, is deemed obtainable).

119:2. Most favored are those who are fully devoted.

119:3. Still, from this OT psalmist's worldview, obedience is a means to success, and disobedience a cause of failure. This is why Job was perplexed over his suffering as a righteous person and is one of the aspects of this psalm that gives it an ANE sapience coloring. In verse 3a, he says that such a person "has committed no iniquity."

119:4. God commanded precepts to be kept fully.

119:5. The psalmist realized he has not met this standard.

119:6. If he could, then he would not feel ashamed.

119:7. He declared he would testify (verb II-ידה) about God as he is instructed (inf. of למד) by right judgments (rendered "laws" in some version; "Giving Thanks," p. 78–79.

119:8. He then vowed, "I will keep" your statutes, and pleads "may you not leave me" (with א ל) (as a weak, volitional impv.; v. 8). In this section, a number of words are used for God's instructions: way (דֶּרֶךְ), law (תּוֹרָה), decree (עֵדוּת), precepts (פִּקּוּדִים; פִּקּוּד in HALOT), statutes (חֹק), commands (מִצְוָה), and judgments (מִשְׁפָּט).

How to Obey God's Laws (בַּמֶּה; "How?") (119:9–16 [ב])

The poet wonders if he keeps God's laws and answers for himself.

119:9. He asked, "In what [way] may a young person keep his path clean?" (strong form of זכה; v. 9a) and restates this (although versions often take this as an answer) by saying, "[How is he able] to keep [his ways] according to your word" (v. 9b; but many variant Hebrew mss. and a Targum have "your words"). He was curious how to maintain consistent obedience to God's commands. God's "words" refer to his verbal communication, but in context the meaning is not equivalent to Scripture, since the author had no access to a "Bible" as we do now, but the priests had the laws of Moses from God. So, the idea is that he wonders how to be more obedient to God's commands regardless of the way he is made aware of them. By extension and application (but not exegesis) the Christian reader is able to receive God's will through the NT mainly, but also has to discern hermeneutically how to use the OT as Scripture in the church age.

119:10. Then he prayed: "Do not allow me to go astray" (with a precative/irrealis tone; although HALOT supports "do not lead me astray," s.v. "שגה", p. 1413); [because] with all my heart [= desire] I seek you" (probably = "to please you").

119:11. Then he confessed (what today is often memorized): "In my heart I have hidden your saying [אמר not the דבר of v. 9]) in order that I will not sin/rebel against you" (the verb is indicative not precative/irrealis as the NIV's "might

not sin," although a sense of purpose comes from the fronted לְמַעַן). The heart in the ANE could refer to the emotional or mental process. The reader should not make the mistake of interpreting this contextually as being about Bible memory. People in general had no access to written Scriptures at that time, so the verse has to do with how he treasures divine revelation (specifically the law he has been taught) and this will enable him to be obedient. Christians have the special privilege of personal access to Scripture, but keep in mind that believers were expected to succeed spiritually without Bibles until relatively very recent times.

119:12. The psalmist then "blessed [ברך]" Yahweh, beseeching him to teach (impv. verb) "his statutes [חֹק]."

119:13. And he expressed how "he has made known [ספר]" the just "judgments [מִשְׁפָּט]" God has spoken (some variant Hebrew mss., plus a Greek and Syriac ms., have the equivalent of "your justice" instead of "your mouth").

119:14. He was even more happy about following God's "decrees [עֵדוּת]" than having riches. Although he believed right living was a likely secure path to health and wealth; this is not to be taken as a promise for all believers. The text gives an accurate view of how the psalmist thought in his social and religious context.

119:15. He "meditated" (cf. Marlowe 2007, 3–17) on divine "precepts [פִּקּוּד]" that he "may look at" (cohortative) God's "ways [אֹרַח]" (cf. v. 23); that is, he pays attention to God's laws as a means to stay on the right path. But again, in his context, he (unless a priest) did not have personal use of a written Torah.

Meditation in Psalms

This idea of meditating on God's instructions was first encountered in this psalm in verse 15. It occurs here and also in vv. 27, 48, 78, 97, 99, and

---

148. In each case the word used (II שִׂיחַ) basically has to do with speaking but can also indicate consideration or pondering (HALOT, s.v. "II שׂיחַ," p. 1319). Earlier studies about its meaning related to motions are now discarded, and current scholarship defines it as (1) enthusiastic speech or (2) meditation with praise. The palmist has in mind how he will communicate or testify about God's laws. "Take to heart" may be the intention. Other verses in the OT with the translation "meditate" involve the Hebrew verbs הגה ("moan; mutter; speak; proclaim"; Josh. 1:8; Pss. 77:12; 143:5) or the strong stem of דמה ("compare; feel inclined; ponder"; Ps. 48:9; HALOT, s.v. "I הגה and I דמה," pp. 225, 237).

119:16. Still, he delighted in these "statutes [חֻקָּה]" and declared that he will not forget (future indicative; or "ignore") God's "word [דָּבָר]" (although many variant Hebrew mss., LXX, Syriac, and Latin versions have plural "words"). The plural is preferable in translation because the modern reader can mistake God's "word" for the Bible, but the idea is that he is vowing to follow any command God gives him.

Why Desire More Revelation (גָּמֹל; "Reward!") (119:17–24 [ג])

The poet prays that he would learn more of God's laws.

119:17. He pleaded for God to look after him (impv. of גמל + על) so that he may live and may keep ("obey" in NIV; both verbs have cohortative forms) God's word (דָּבָר; = 'commands'; again, many variant mss. and the ancient versions have plural "words"; see v. 16 and commentary).

119:18. Then he plead for God to uncover (impv. of גלה) his eyes so that he may (cohortative) look at (lit.,) "wonders from your law [תּוֹרָה]" (v. 18). This last phrase refers to what is in the law code. The NETS (cf. LXX) takes the verb as meaning "put my mind to." The JPS has, "perceive the wonders of Your Teaching." Somehow,

he seems only minimally knowledgeable about these laws, which he evaluates as supreme, and wants to learn more.

119:19. Next, the psalmist explained why he wants to learn more: he is only a stranger in the land, so he asks if God might not conceal (jussive; סתר) his "commands [מִצְוָה]" ("any longer," implied).

119:20. He confessed that he (lit., his נֶפֶשׁ) always had been worn down (גרס) with longing for God's "judgments [מִשְׁפָּט]."

119:21. He said this because he knows God "has rebuked" (גער) the proud, (who are) cursed (by God) and who are "always wandering" (ptc. שׁגה) from God's "commands [מִצְוָה]."

119:22. So, he then implored God to roll away reproach and contempt because he has kept God's "decrees [עֵדוּת]."

119:23. Even if people in power have sat down and "have spoken among themselves" (= plotting or slander; pass. of II דבר), as God's servant, he vowed to "meditate" on God's "statutes [חֹק]."

119:24. He said he delighted in these "decrees [עֵדוּת]" since they function like counselors (as he recalls their guidance). Naturally, at that time believers did not have personal "Bibles" that they could read and look up passages and reflect on as we do today. The psalmist's intention to "meditate" here has to do with his commitment to contemplation on, and careful alignment of his behavior to conform to, divine regulations. These were encountered through communal worship, prophetic pronouncement, or personal prayer.

Keeping God's Laws Is Work (דָּבְקָה; "[I] have clung") (119:25–32 [ד])

The poet asks God for renewed strength because he has followed God's laws.

119:25. The psalmist next elaborated on his condition just described. How his "being ['soul'; נֶפֶשׁ]" has clung to dust" (v. 25a) is unclear and debated in the commentaries. "My life [חַיֵּנִי]" in verse 25b is obviously the counterpart to "my 'nephesh' [נַפְשִׁי]" or "I/me" (not properly "soul"). The NIV's "preserve" is not in the MT, but some action is clearly implied. Since the psalmist is somehow experiencing humiliation (vv. 21–23, 25a), the LXX has "enliven me [ζῆσόν με]!," which the NETS takes as "quicken me" and the JPS as "revive me." This is to be done "according to your word," but the singular in the MT is plural in many other Hebrew mss. Again, in context this is not a "Bible" so to speak but has to do with being renewed in line with the promises or pronouncements God had made in the past (cf. v. 16). This section is like a lament in that the psalmist alerts God to a predicament and prays for divine deliverance.

119:26–27. Also, like some laments, he then announced that God has helped him. In verse 26a, the psalmist claimed that he has made known his ways (i.e., he enumerated his [negative] circumstances (strong form of ספר), and "then you answered me" (sequential past-action verb). Next, in what seems an odd parallel line the psalmist says, "Teach me! [impv. of למד] your statutes [חֻקֶּיךָ]" (v. 26b). This is restated in verse 27a as "Help me understand! [impv.] your precepts [פִּקּוּדֶיךָ]." The NIV makes it precative/irrealis, "Cause me," but the verb is stronger. This is followed by a mirror of verse 26a, making a chiasm: "so that I may 'meditate' [cohortative; = may talk about] your wonders."

A I have expressed my troubles and then you answered me (v. 26a)
  B Teach me your statutes! (v. 26b)
  B´ Give me insight regarding your ways (= your instructions)! (v. 27a)
A´ Then I will be able to ponder/proclaim the wonderful ways (you helped me) (v. 27b)

Cf. the JPS:

A I have declared my way, and You have answered me;
  B train me in Your laws.
  B´ Make me understand the way of Your precepts,
A´ that I may study Your wondrous acts.

119:28. He returned to his complaint, confessing that "his 'life [נֶפֶשׁ] had leaked" (see v. 25; but some mss. have "my eyes"). This meant "he wept" (I דלף) or had been sleepless (HALOT, s.v. "II דלף," p. 223) because of (מִן) (his) grief. So, he implored God to "enable me to stand" (strengthened form; impv. of קום) according to God's "word" (sing. in the MT; but plural in other mss.; see vv. 16, 25, and commentary; "word[s]" means God's previous covenant commitment).

119:29. He asked God to "turn me away from" (causative, impv. of סור) falsehood (v. 29a) and "show favor to me! your law" (v. 29b), which is a way to say as the JPS does, "favor me with Your teaching" (same in the Syriac version). He wanted divine guidance in how to avoid deceit.

119:30. He then claimed he had chosen the path of "reliability" (אֱמוּנָה; not "truth" as we use it today; Marlowe 2010, 24–42), that is (some mss. have a prefixed conjunction that can be appositional), he has "settled down with" (HALOT, s.v. "II שוה," p. 1436) "God's judgments" (מִשְׁפָּט). He would dutifully live by God's decisions. The NIV's "set my heart" is implied but not in the text.

119:31–32. He then said he "has clung" (same verb as in v. 25 with dust as the object) to Yahweh's "decrees [עֵדוּת]," so, he asked God "may you not shame me" (v. 31; jussive with weak negation אַל). Since he has been obedient, he expected God to give him victory over his enemy or problem. He would run along the path of God's commands (מִצְוָה) and expected that God would widen (רחב; causative form) "his heart," meaning that God would "broaden [his] understanding" (v. 32 JPS; cf. NRSV).

Lawful Obedience for God's Statutes Fuels Success (הוֹרֵנִי; "Show me!") (119:33–40 [ה])

The poet asks Yahweh to help him be obedient so he can have success.

119:33. The ponderous poet then invoked Yahweh, "Instruct me!" (III ירה) in the path of (= how to follow) "your statutes [חֻקֶּיךָ]" (v. 33a). This was so that he might keep (נצר volitive form) "it" (3rd fem. sg. object suffix, referring back to the common gender "path [דֶּרֶךְ]") "right to the end [עֵקֶב]" (v. 33b; but this closing comment may mean "as a reward"; Weiser 1962, 731, 738; and Kraus 1993, 416).

119:34. He then petitioned God "make me understand" (same verb as v. 27a) "so that I may keep" (same verb as v. 33a) your law and "so that I may keep/obey it" (cohortative/volitive form; שׁמר; "it" is fem. sg. referring back to the fem. sg. noun "law") "with all my heart" (this can refer to intentionality rather than feelings).

119:35. He next added, "Lead me along! [cf. ESV]" (causative impv. of דרך) "the path of 'your commands' [מִצְוֹתֶיךָ]" because "in it [masc. sg.]" (this path, also masc. sg.) the psalmist had found delight.

119:36. He also asked God to "Incline! [impv. of נטה]" his heart (= his desire) for his "decrees [עֵדְוֹת]" rather than unjust gain. Going back to verses 29–30, it seems he was struggling with being honest and honorable among his colleagues. His was not in practice what he wanted to be in theory.

119:37. He pleaded for God (since he lacked willpower) to enable his eyes to stop (causative impv. of עבר) in order not to see (inf. of purpose) what is "empty/frivolous [שָׁוְא]" (v. 37a).

In other words, he needed to lose his desire to engage in activities for which the outcomes have no moral value. As before, he wanted to be revived in line with God's promises (v. 37b; lit., "ways"; cf. v. 25, where he has חַיֵּנִי כִדְבָרֶךָ but now בְּדְרָכֶךָ חַיֵּנִי). The NIV's "preserve my life according to your word" takes a lot of liberties with the expression "make me alive according to your ways"). The term "word" (which should never be uppercase in the OT) is problematic for modern readers since it immediately brings up the image of the Bible. God's word for the psalmist was divine laws he had learned or what he gleaned through prayer or prophecy. By application, believers today can think of God's complete revelation (Bible) but should not read that idea anachronistically back into the ancient text's meaning.

The Word "W/word" in "God's Word"

Today we speak about "The Word of God" as the Bible. But the Bible itself never speaks this way about any book or collection of canonical texts. The best translations, even KJV, only use uppercase "Word" in some NT statements referring to Jesus as the "living Word of God" (e.g. 1 John 1:1). The expression "W/word of the LORD" occurs respectively in the NIV and KJV OT, 223 and 245 times; and "Word of God" 3 and 4 times (the former has "message from God" in 1 Sam. 9:27). When the Bible speaks about divine "word" or "words" it has in view something God communicated to a specific person or persons in a specific circumstance. The problem with the Bible as "God's Word" is that it gives the impression the entire book is a compendium of direct, divine pronouncements or precepts to be read apart from qualifications created by the historical and cultural settings or occasions (and being divided into verses only exacerbates this). Often versions translate/interpret "he spoke" as "promise" (there is no Hebrew word for "promise"). Exegetically or theologically, every verse should not be read out of context as a directive for every reader in all times and places apart from any qualifications.

Spiritually or applicationally, however, any passage (but not single verses since verses are artificial) can be read contextually for *personal* guidance in reliance on God's Spirit.

119:38. The poet, as a servant, wanted Yahweh to "raise up! [causative impv. of קוּם] your sayings [אִמְרָתֶךָ]" (i.e., bring about what he has told him in the past), that fear of (submission to) God may result ("for those who fear you"). Some see "fear[er] of you" as a restatement of "servant of you"; Dahood 1970, 178).

119:39. With the same verb as in verse 37a, the psalmist requested that God make the reproach that he has dreaded (יגר) pass away, because he realized that God's judgments/decisions are (always) good.

119:40. "Look," he said, "I have longed for your precepts [לְפִקֻּדֶיךָ]; so, make me alive in your justice" (not "righteousness"; since he is asking God to keep him alive, protect him from death, for the sake of divine צְדָקָה or justice).

Obedient Witness Results from God's Rescue (וִיבֹאֻנִי; "And may it come to me") (119:41–48 [ו])

The poet vows to be an obedient witness if Yahweh saves him.

119:41. The psalmist next asked if Yahweh's "loyal loves" (MT has plural construct of חֶסֶד) might come (jussive) to him; restated as, his salvation (might come to him, understood) in line with God's (previous) communications (כְּאִמְרָתֶךָ; note that whereas the NIV usually has "word" for this term in Ps. 119, it now has "promise").

119:42. If this happens, he added, "then I may answer" (cohortative) "the one who is taunting / making fun of me [ptc.; or nominal as 'my annoyance' from II חרף]" (v. 42a; but the Greek and Syriac versions are plural; the NETS [cf. LXX] has "those who reproach me," which is more

consistent with other similar texts in the Psalter; cf. the "Workers of Iniquity" in the Psalms, p. 79). The psalmist is confident about confronting his tormentors because "I have trusted [perf. verb in Hebrew and English] in your word [בִּדְבָרֶךָ]" (v. 42b; = "message"; again, the MT is singular here, but many Hebrew mss., the ancient Greek and Syriac versions, and a Targum are plural, "words"). Also, as before, he has in mind not sacred literature about God or Israel's history, but direct revelations from God via prayer or prophecy or the Mosaic and covenant precepts. The NIV's "word," as in most English versions, may mislead the reader away from the ancient context; and most likely "words/revelations" was the original wording. These assurances gave him boldness.

119:43. Consequently, he begged God not to allow the trustworthy (אֱמֶת) or "truthful" message (Marlowe 2010, 24–42; i.e., what he should say to his tormentors) to be taken (jussive) from him (lit., "his mouth"; v. 43a), because he has placed his hope (strong form of יחל) in God's right rulings (מִשְׁפֹּט; v. 43b).

119:44. If so, then he desired that he might "always [תָּמִיד לְעוֹלָם וָעֶד]" be able to follow (cohortative mood שמר) God's law (תּוֹרָה).

119:45. And the psalmist also wished that he might live in a spacious place (lit., "walk about [reflexive form of הלך] in a wide space"). The NIV's "walk about in freedom" seems a bit eisegetical, but the JPS's "walk about at ease" is perhaps more to the point.

119:46. He then hoped that he might repeatedly speak (strong frequentative verb) about God's decrees (עֵדוֹת; but the Syriac version has "about justice") before kings, and not be ashamed.

119:47. And he will delight (same verb as in v. 16) in God's "commands [מִצְוָה]," which he has loved (LXX adds "very much"; σφόδρα).

119:48. He desired to raise (cohortative) his hands (dual form) to these commands, which he has loved, and asks that he be allowed to "meditate" (cohortative; see v. 23; NETS uses "ponder") on the divine "statutes [חֹק]."

Reliance on Divine Revelation Risks Ridicule (זָכֹר; "Remember!") (119:49–56 [ז])

The poet seeks assurance of God's promises in the midst of mocking.

119:49. The psalmist then began with the statement (vague in the MT), "Remember! [impv.] a word/message to your servant" (v. 49a). The LXX (cf. NETS) adds "your" (possessive pronoun) to "word [דָּבָר]." He seems to be pleading with God to act on a previous commitment by which God had encouraged him (יִחַלְתָּנִי) in the past (v. 49b). One Hebrew and some Greek mss. read the equivalent of "your servants."

119:50. While suffering (this mocking) his only comfort was that this divine message or "promise" ("your word"; אִמְרָתֶךָ) had revived him (חִיָּתְנִי; "quickened" in the NETS; "preserved" in the NIV and JPS, translating the LXX, ἔζησέν).

119:51a. He needed this boost because his arrogant (enemies) had been ridiculing him (לִיץ) "endlessly [עַד־מְאֹד]" (but the LXX has παρηνόμουν ἕως σφόδρα, "transgress the law greatly").

119:51b. But still he boasted, "I have not moved away [נטה] 'from your law' [מִתּוֹרָתֶךָ]."

119:52. Instead, he remembered (same root word in v. 49) Yahweh's judgments/rulings (מִשְׁפָּטֶיךָ) and thereby he found rest (וָאֶתְנֶחָם).

119:53. Due to these wicked people, who keep ignoring (ptc. of I עזב), he confessed that "hot [anger] seized me [I אחז]" (although זַלְעָפָה [burning?] is a rare word; the NETS reads, "*Despondency* beset me"; cf. the LXX, ἀθυμία).

119:54. Yet no matter where he finds lodging, God's "statutes [חֻקֶּיךָ]" had been (soothing) like a song to him. However, some interpret "song" (זְמִרוֹת) as "strength" in light of comparative Semitic lexical data (Anderson 1995, II:824, citing Pope 1965, 228).

119:55. In the night, he said, I remembered (again זכר) your name (is) Yahweh, and then (consecutive verb) I kept a close watch on your law. God's essential nature as eternal and unchanging drew him back to a focus on God's regulations.

119:56. He explained that, therefore, observing God's precepts (פִּקֻּדֶיךָ) had become his (focus?; but the antecedent of זֹאת "this" is unclear). The JPS has "This has been my lot"; while the NETS (cf. LXX) has "This fell to me," and the NIV "This has been my practice."

Obedience Welcomes God's Grace (חֶלְקִי; "My portion") (119:57–64 [ח])

The poet prays for God's grace based on his obedience.

119:57. Yahweh apparently was described as his "portion [חֶלְקִי]," but if the LXX's use of the divine name as a vocative here is followed, the result could be that obedience to God's words is his "portion" (calling?) and commitment (אָמַרְתִּי). Translate "portion" as "share" (HALOT, s.v. "II 323," חֵלֶק). The MT/BHS has "your words" (דְּבָרֶיךָ), but other mss. and Jerome use the singular (the LXX has νόμον σου, "your law").

119:58. The psalmist said he has entreated (strong past form of חלה) God's presence (lit., "face") with intense intention (lit., "all my heart"), so he pleaded with God "be gracious to me [impv. of חנן]" according to his (God's previous) revelation (lit., "saying"; כְּאִמְרָתֶךָ; "promise" in several English versions).

119:59. He confessed next that "I have re-considered" (strengthened form of חשב) "my ways" (but "your ways" in NETS; cf. LXX), and "then I returned" (consecutive verb of שׁוב) (to moving) my feet in the direction of your decrees (רַגְלַי אֶל־עֵדֹתֶיךָ). But what about all his claims to strict obedience so far? Perhaps he protested too much. It seems at some point his frustrations led him off the straight and narrow path of obedience, but he quickly repented (Cohen 1945, 402). This misdirection happened before his suffering (see v. 67), so he may have interpreted his affliction as punishment for his wrongdoing.

119:60–61. As a result, the psalmist claimed that he had been quick and had not delayed in keeping God's commandments (v. 60). He argued (v. 61) that the "ropes" (i.e., the temptations) of the wicked "surrounded" (HALOT, s.v. "I עוד," p. 795) him, but he did not forget (past form) God's law (תּוֹרָה).

119:62. Now, he vowed that he will rise in the middle of the night in order to confess/testify (inf. of purpose; II ידה) to God about his just judgments (מִשְׁפְּטֵי צִדְקֶךָ). The NETS's "rise to acknowledge you" (cf. LXX) is preferable to the NIV's "rise to give you thanks" (the JPS has "I arise at midnight to praise You"; cf. Ps. 73).

119:63. Next he said he (is) a friend (nominal phrase, verb understood) to all who have feared God, meaning those who consistently follow (ptc.) his precepts (פִּקּוּד).

119:64a. Yahweh's loyal love (חֶסֶד) has filled the land (the palmist's known world).

119:64b. So, he compelled God to teach him (impv. verb; למד) his statutes (חֹק). But what does this mean? How does he expect God to do this? This likely infers the intermediacy of human teachers (Deut. 24:8; Job 36:22; Pss. 25:4–9; 27:11; 86:11).

Divine Discipline Is Based on Good Laws (טוֹב; "Good") (119:65–72 [ט])
God's goodness in disciplining is acknowledged.

119:65. He explained that Yahweh has done good to his servant in line with his (God's) "word" or previous promise (the MT is singular but several other Hebrew mss. have plural "words"; "word" must not be confused contextually or historically with the concept of God's written Word; see vv. 16, 25, 37, and commentary).

119:66a. So, the poet implored God to teach (impv. verb) him goodness (טוּב), discernment (טַעַם), and knowledge (וָדַעַת) (v. 66a). The first word may have been mistakenly repeated by a copyist. Regardless, these terms are "Kindness and discipline and knowledge" in the NETS (cf. LXX), but "good sense and knowledge" in the JPS. A question is if "good" is an adjective or separate quality. Most modern versions take it as modifying טַעַם.

119:66b. He wanted God to do this because he has trusted in God's commands.

119:67. Next, the psalmist confessed "I erred/went astray [or, 'I was a transgressor'] before I was oppressed" (v. 67a). But now, I have obeyed your (verbal) revelations (v. 67b). The MT has a participle, where the LXX has an indicative. The NIV reads a present/future form as past tense ("I was afflicted").

119:68a. He then told God that he (is) good (nominal phrase; the NETS [cf. LXX] adds the vocative 'O Lord') and that he brings about what is good (causative ptc.).

119:68b. Again, he implored God to teach (impv. verb; למד) him his "statutes" (חֻקֶּיךָ). The translation of the various terms used in the HB for God's "rules" or "laws," etc., are approximate and versions differ, but they usually attempt consistency. Current English usage makes the choice of a gloss difficult. It helps to consult a variety of versions and the latest Hebrew lexica.

119:69. Proud men had slandered him (lit., "smeared me with a lie"), but he would still keep God's precepts intentionally and/or passionately (lit., "with all his heart").

119:70a. By contrast he boasted that their (his enemy's) passions and/or intentions (lit., "their heart"—as if they act in unison) had been insensitive (HALOT, s.v. "טפשׁ," p. 379; very rare form) and "as fat [כַּחֵלֶב]" (but an alternative Hebrew ms. and the Greek and Syriac versions have the equivalent of כֶּחָלָב "like milk"). The NETS (cf. LXX) renders this, "Their heart was curdled like milk," but JPS reads, "Their minds are thick like fat."

119:70b. Either way, he boasted (v. 70b) that he had delighted (שִׁעֲשַׁעְתִּי) (in) God's law (תּוֹרָתֶךָ). The verb (II שׁעע) is the same verbal root used in verses 16 and 47.

119:71. He confessed that it (was) good for him to have been humiliated (pass. of II ענה) in order that he might learn (cohortative function not form; למד) God's statutes (חֻקֶּיךָ).

119:72. The "law [תּוֹרַת]" God spoke (lit., "from your mouth"; source/agency genitive) was better to him than thousands of gold or silver (coins). This suggests God's verbal revelation of his will or directives.

Disobedience Should Be Disciplined but God's Enemies Destroyed (יָדֶיךָ; "Your hands") (119:73–80 [י])

Yahweh is called upon to correct him, yet all the more crush his enemies.

119:73. Again, like a lament, the psalmist expressed his problem and prayed for help, as well as against his enemies with an imprecation.

Since God is his creator ("your hands made me and still prepare me"), he cried out for insight (impv. of בין) so that he might learn (cohortative) God's "commands [מִצְוֹתֶיךָ]." But what does this mean? How will he learn the commands since he already knows them? The point could be that he wanted to learn how to more wisely apply God's precepts.

119:74. He wished (jussive verbs) that those who fear God might observe him (the psalmist) and be glad (or rejoice when they see him) because he had put his hope (strengthened form of יחל) in God's "word" (MT sg., but this is plural in several variant Heb. and Gk. mss.), i.e., in God's revealed promises (see commentary on vv. 16, 27, 37, 65).

119:75. He had known (and still does) that Yahweh's judgments (מִשְׁפָּט) are just (צֶדֶק), therefore God was faithful (אֱמוּנָה) to have humiliated him (or to have allowed his humiliation; same verbal root in v. 71). The worldview of such ancient people was that God or gods were behind all that happened, but the ancients do not try to resolve all the logical, theological, or philosophical angles. A contrast between this Hebrew psalmist and his ANE neighbors is that he finds rest and trust in Yahweh while they tended to maintain a more constant fear as terror before the gods, whom they did not trust to act on their behalf for their good.

119:76. In line with the "declaration" (אמר; idiom for "promises" in some versions) that God had made to his servant (the psalmist or his people), he prayed "please may it be" (jussive יְהִי plus נָא) that God's loyal love (חַסְדְּךָ) lead to rest (לְנַחֲמֵנִי).

119:77. He asked God to let (jussive form) his compassions come to him "so I might live" (cohortative), because God's law (תּוֹרָה) is his delight (שַׁעֲשֻׁעָי, cf. vv. 16, 47, 70).

119:78a. Turning his attention to his foes, he asked God that these arrogant people might be shamed (jussive) because they "bent [the evidence against]" him falsely (lit., "for a lie" [HALOT, s.v. "עות," p. 804]).

119:78b. When this happens (implied), he vowed he would speak about (אָשִׂיחַ; or traditional "meditate on") God's precepts.

119:79. He then asked if those who fear "you" (= Yahweh) may turn (jussive) to him (the psalmist; v. 79a), meaning those who know God's decrees (עֵדֹתֶיךָ; v. 79b; the MT has a past tense form, but variant Hebrew mss., and Greek, Syriac, and Latin versions, suggest an original future/present form or ptc.).

119:80. In addition, he wished that his heart (attitude) might be (jussive mood for היה) blameless (i.e., that he might have a clear conscience) in regard to God's statutes (בְּחֻקֶּיךָ), so that he will not be shamed (future indicative).

Divine Promises Are Certain but Not Immediate (כָּלְתָה; "[I] have fainted") (118:81–88 [כ])

The poet complains about the time God is taking to avenge him.

119:81. The psalmist moaned (perhaps hyperbolically) that his "life force" (נַפְשִׁי) had faded (כָּלְתָה) for (i.e., while waiting on) God's deliverance (v. 81a), although in God's "word" (= past promises) he has placed his hope (strengthened form of יחל; v. 81b; same as v. 74). The term "word" is singular in the MT but plural in other mss. and versions. There is no conjunctive on the verb in verse 81b, but some transitional word is suggested. Still, the NIV's adversative "but" seems contrary to the flow of thought.

119:82a. He said he is fainting even though he is trusting God to act. His vision had become blurred because of God's promise (not coming to fruition [implied]; אמר here but דבר in previous verse).

119:82b. So, he asked (inf. of אמר), "When will you [God] comfort me?" (by answering his prayer for vengeance [implied]).

119:83a. Therefore (כִּי), he continued, "I have become like a wineskin in smoke." This image contextually is something negative, so the smoky wine probably refers to burned wineskins (cf. Job 30:30; Lam. 4:8; Anderson 1995, II:830).

119:83b. Even so, he has not forgotten God's statutes.

119:84. He then pleaded, (1) "How many days [does] your servant?" (have to wait?; implied; v. 84a); and (2) "[When] will you execute [תַּעֲשֶׂה] judgment [מִשְׁפָּט] against those chasing me relentlessly?" (ptc.; v. 84b).

119:85. He announced to God, as if he did not know, "These prideful men have dug ditches for me [to fall into; implied], which is against your law" (which law and how does he know about the pits?).

119:86. He recognized that all God's commands are sure (אֱמוּנָה), so he implored God to help him! (impv. verb) (because) they (the arrogant men) had pursued him falsely (cf. v. 78).

119:87. In fact, he claimed, they almost brought me (= my life) in the land to a complete end (strong form of כלה), yet I never abandoned your precepts.

119:88. Therefore, he pleaded with God, "Revive my life! [strengthened impv. of חיה for urgency] according to your loyal love [כְּחַסְדְּךָ], so I may keep [cohortative form of שמר] the decrees you spoke [lit., 'of your mouth']."

Divine Revelation Is Definitive (לְעוֹלָם; "Always") (119:89–96 [ל])

The poet praises God's verbal revelations in hope of quick rescue.

119:89. He began by declaring that Yahweh's "word [דְּבָרְךָ = your/God's communication]" is lasting (לְעוֹלָם), fixed firmly (pass. ptc. of I נצב) in the heavens.

119:90. Divine revelation is by definition secure, fixed like the stars in the sky. The "steadfastness [אֱמוּנָתֶךָ]" of Yahweh (is/remains) throughout the generations (v. 90a); "you [God] established [כּוֹנַנְתָּ] the land [= the psalmist's known world] and it stood [firm; past tense of עמד]" (v. 90b; however, the LXX has a pres. indicative διαμένει, "it endures").

119:91. He extolled God's "judgments [מִשְׁפָּט; sg. in LXX] that they have stood to this day" (v. 91a), "because everything [is] your [God's] servant" (v. 91b; but Jerome has the Latin equivalent of "they all have served you").

119:92. He claimed that apart from God's law or "torah" (תּוֹרָה) being his delight (again שׁעע), he would have perished (died?) due to his affliction (which apparently in light of previous verses is emotional), so the verb may be hyperbolic.

119:93. He said he will never (לְעוֹלָם) forget God's precepts (פִּקּוּדֶיךָ) because by them "you [= God] revived [strong form of חיה] me [the psalmist]."

119:94. Reflecting on God's promises gave him emotional strength during his ordeal. Still, he pleaded with God to save him (impv. verb) because (lit.) "to you I [am]," which is restated in the following parallel line as "I have searched for your precepts" (same word as in v. 93). The idea seems to be his proven commitment based on adherence to the divine laws.

119:95. His wicked (enemies) had waited (and still wait) to destroy him (strengthened inf. of purpose), (yet) he will (= is determined to) understand (strong form of בין) God's decrees (עֵדֹתֶיךָ).

119:96. This verse is difficult, literally, "For all completion/perfection [תִּכְלָה is a very rare form] I have seen an end; your commands [מִצְוָתְךָ] are very wide." The JPS is still a bit vague: "I have seen that all things have their limit, but Your commandment is broad beyond measure." The idea seems to be that unlike all human advice, God's directives are timeless. Human laws are relative/utilitarian, but divine law is absolute/universal (perhaps is the point).

Divine Revelation Leads to Skillful Reasoning (מָה; "How/What") (119:97–104 [מ])

The poet revels in how God's laws promote wisdom.

119:97. The psalmist exclaimed, "How I have loved [and still love] 'your law' [תוֹרָתֶךָ]" (v. 97a); "every day it [is] my 'meditation' [reflection]" (v. 97b).

119:98. Then he added, "Your commands make me wiser [strong form] than my enemies" (v. 98a); "because 'she [הִיא = these commands (are); collective singular]' is 'continually [לְעוֹלָם]' before me" (v. 98b; i.e., your directives help me outsmart my foes).

119:99. He admitted, "I have gained wisdom [causative form] more than 'all those trying to teach me' [strengthened ptc.]" (v. 99a), "because your decrees [are the source of] 'my ponderings' [שִׂיחָה לִי]" (v. 99b). He stated that the daily use of God's revelation enabled him to outwit these enemies, who keep trying to persuade him with their perspectives. He was not saying that he has become more insightful than all those who have guided him in the past or more than Israel's current sages (for they also meditate on

God's laws). Psalm 119:99a could be translated as well, "I have gained understanding from all my teachers." Interpreters differ on whether the prefixed preposition (מִן) is comparative or source (but the latter is proposed).

119:100. The next verse may be read differently than some traditional translations like the NIV (which pushes the "I am better than my teachers" idea). The psalmist next claimed, "I am determined to gain insight [strong reflexive of בִין ; same verb in vv. 95, 104] from the elders [old, experienced people], since I have followed your precepts." Alternatively, Psalm 119:100a could be translated, "I will gain insight beyond the old people [could this refer to his enemies?]." Regardless, the notion he was claiming, that God's commands make him smarter than the local academics, is contrary to the context, colored with modern bias, and ignores that the emphasis is on his obedience in contrast to his enemies.

119:101. Consequently, he then boasted that he had restrained his feet (from going in; i.e., has not followed) any wrong (רַע; not "evil") direction (morally) in order to keep God's "word[s]" (i.e., instructions; again, while the MT is sg., other mss. and versions are plural; see vv. 16, 27, 37, 65, 74, and commentary).

119:102. He then said he had not turned aside from God's rulings (מִשְׁפָּט) because God "has instructed him" (causative of III ירה).

119:103. Then he exclaimed, Oh, how his "saying[s]" (אמר; plural in other mss. and ancient versions) "have been sweet" (pass.) to his palate/taste (v. 103a); (have been sweeter) than (comparative [מִן]) honey (NETS [cf. LXX] adds "and honeycomb") to his mouth (v. 103b). Perhaps the original was "sweet like honey, (sweet) like honeycomb." The picture is that of verbal rehearsing God's laws being compared to eating candy.

119:104. They are sweet because, in verse 104a, from God's precepts (פִּקּוּד) he will seek insight (strong reflexive); and in verse 104b, he therefore hated (and still hates [past perfect]) every errant path (another case syntactically of the "perfect of experience"; Williams 2007, 68).

Obedience to God's Ways Increases Physical Safety (נֵר; "Lamp") (119:105–112 [נ])
The poet looks to Yahweh's laws as a means by which he may be kept from harm.

119:105. The psalmist next stated that God's "word[s]" (again, many MT mss. and some ancient versions have the plural form; see vv. 16, 27, 37, 65, 74, 101, and commentary), meaning God's laws, provide light like a lamp so he can stay on the right road.

119:106. In fact, he "made an oath" (pass.) and "then he took a stand" (past, sequential verb) "to keep" (inf. of purpose) God's "right rulings" (מִשְׁפְּטֵי צִדְקֶךָ). The root צדק basically concerns what is "right" in God's estimation. The current and frequent use of "righteous" can be misleading since contemporary use carries semantic baggage, and Christian usage emphasizes the NT idea of imputed sinlessness. In the OT context, the idea is about God's directives putting those who aspire to be obedient on the right path morally or theologically. "Upright" comes close in its use as "reputable" or "trustworthy."

119:107. The poet then explained that he "had been oppressed" (pass. of II ענה) greatly (v. 107a), so he cried out, "O Yahweh, revive me [impv.] in line with your [previous] promise [lit., 'word']" (v. 107b).

119:108. And he prayed, "please accept! [impv.], O Yahweh, [this] offering [i.e., prayerful lamentation] *from* my mouth" (construct genitive of source) (v. 108a); "and teach me! [impv.] your judgments" (v. 108b; i.e., act quickly so I can experience your answer and revenge on my oppressor).

119:109. He then said, "my life [נֶפֶשׁ; not "soul"] [is/was] in my hand [= hands; collective sg.] continually (v. 109a; although some older versions have "in *your* hands"). The JPS is best with, "Though my life is always in danger." Even though, "I have never forgotten your law" (v. 109b).

119:110. He pointed out that wicked people had set a trap for him, but he had not erred per God's precepts (פִּקּוּד).

119:111. He had (pluperfect) inherited God's enduring (לְעוֹלָם) decrees (עֵדוּת); for they [are] his "heart's joy" (i.e., they are his joyful passion).

119:112. Consequently, his "heart" (his intention or passion) had been inclined (and still is; past perfect) to follow God's statutes (חֹק) always, to the end.

God's Ways Trump All Other Ways (סֵעֲפִים; "Divided ones") (119:113–120 [ס])

The poet proclaims his preference for God's ways against ungodly ways.

119:113a. Next, the psalmist stated that he "has hated divided ones." The NIV (cf. NRSV) renders this "double-minded people" and the JPS, "men of divided heart"; but the NETS (cf. LXX) has, "Transgressors of the law" and Douay, "the unjust." The idea seems to be about those who are hypocritical, acknowledging God but breaking his laws.

119:113b. Unlike such people, the psalmist "has [always] loved" God's law (תּוֹרָה).

119:114. He then confided that Yahweh is his secret (place) and his shield (v. 114a; i.e., his hiding place for refuge and safety or protection), so

he "has placed his hope" (strong verb) in God's (previous) promise (lit., "word" [דבר]; v. 114b).

119:115. So, he ordered the "lawbreakers" (מְרֵעִים; not "evildoers," cf. v. 101) to "turn away!" (impv.), so that (resultative conjunction וְ) he "might be able to keep" (cohortative) his God's "commands [מִצְוָה]."

119:116a. Then the psalmist implored his God "Uphold me!" (impv.) according to what has been said/promised (כְּאִמְרָתֶךָ; but many alternate mss. and some versions reflect an original preposition [בְּ] "by" instead of [כְּ] "according to"), "and let me live" (cohortative).

119:116b. And he added, "May you not shame me" (jussive) from (the standpoint of) my hope." The JPS has, "do not thwart my expectation," and the NIV, "do not let my hopes be dashed."

119:117. Next, he called out, "Support me!" (impv.) "so that I may be rescued" (וְאִוָּשֵׁעָה); "so that I may be attentive" (וְאֶשְׁעָה) "to your statutes [בְחֻקֶּיךָ] always." These last two verbs have a cohortative mood.

119:118. The psalmist then observed that "you [Yahweh] have (always) rejected [experiential perfect] all who (habitually) ignore [ptc. of שגה] your statutes [חֹק] because their deceit (is) treachery" (HALOT, s.v. "שֶׁקֶר," p. 1647).

119:119a. He noted also that "you [Yahweh] have brought to an end [causative of שבת] all the wicked people in the land [the known world of the psalmist, as he would not know about the earth at large] (like) dross."

119:119b. "Therefore," he continued, "I have loved [and still do], your decrees [עֵדֹתֶיךָ]."

119:120. He (lit., "my flesh") had trembled in dread of God (v. 120a); and he has been afraid of

God's judgments (v. 120b). The proper parallel is dread // fear not fear // awe. He is not fearful of the regulations per se, but here the point is God as a judge, before whom all are anxious because all are guilty.

Obedience Gives Confidence in God's Care (עָשִׂיתִי; "I have done") (119:121–128 [ע])
The poet begged Yahweh to rescue his obedient servant from his tormentors before it is too late.

119:121a. The psalmist declared that he had done what is lawful (מִשְׁפָּט) and just (וָצֶדֶק), although a few variant mss. and the Syriac version use the second person pronoun on the verb ("you [Yahweh] have done"). The first object (action) has been a word for God's laws or judgments throughout the psalm, and the second term is often about justice or lawfulness (what is right) rather than personal holiness or righteousness.

119:121b. Therefore, due to his obedience, he asked God that he "may not leave" him (causative indicative form with precative/irrealis function; from I נוח) for his oppressors (or "to those oppressing me"; either a nominal or verbal ptc.). "To/for my oppressors" means "at the mercy of my oppressors."

119:122. He then pleaded for God to "make sure! [impv. of I ערב]" that his servant (is treated) well (לְטוֹב); (and) do not let them, those arrogant ones, oppress me (jussive form). Other Hebrew manuscripts have the conjunction (ו), "and," prefixed to the negative particle.

119:123. The psalmist claimed that his eyesight had failed from looking so long and hard for God's help, which help or salvation in the second line of the parallelism (the connective [ו] being appositional, "that is") is called (God's) "word [= 'promise'] of justice" (וּלְאִמְרַת צִדְקֶךָ), which is an attributive genitive construct meaning "just declaration."

119:124. He continued to implore God to help and cried out, "Treat! [impv. עֲשֵׂה] your servant according to your loyal love [כְחַסְדְּךָ]" (v. 124a); "teach me! [strong form, impv.] your statutes [חֹק]" (v. 124b, meaning, help me understand how to follow them). He believed he deserved God's covenant favor and assistance.

119:125. "Since I am your servant," he continued, "give me insight! [causative impv. of בִין] (v. 125a), "so that [resultative conjunction ו] I may know [cohortative] your decrees [עֵדוֹת]" (v. 125b).

119:126. Time was running out for him, so he next cried out, "(It is) time for (you) oh Yahweh to do (something), (because) they have broken (causative of I-פרר) your law (v. 126).

119:127–128. The poet ended this part by declaring, "Since I have loved your commands [מִצְוָה] more than gold, more than refined [gold; v. 127]; and because I have 'observed carefully' [strong form of ישר; all your precepts [פִּקּוּד], I have hated every false path [v. 128]." These false paths are moral misdirections.

Obedience Enhances the Odds of Divine Rescue (פְּלָאוֹת; "Wonders") (119:129–136 [פ])
The poet reaffirms his worthiness for deliverance from oppression based on his obedience.

119:129. He told God how wonderful (are) his decrees (עֵדוֹת), and that is why he (lit., "my soul") has kept them (and still does; past perfect).

119:130. Verse 130a is difficult. But the idea of this verse is that God's verbal revelation enlightens the understanding of those who are insufficiently informed.

119:131. Consequently, the psalmist admitted that he had opened his mouth and then "panted" (וָאֶשְׁאָפָה; consecutive action) because he had longed for God's "commands" (מִצְוָה).

119:132. Therefore, he begged God to "turn! [impv.]" to him and "be gracious! [impv.]" according to his "custom [מִשְׁפָּט]" for "those who continue to love [ptc.]" God's "name" (i.e., the character expressed by his name, on which his reputation is based).

119:133. He continued, "Fix! [impv.] my feet [i.e., set me on a certain path] by your saying [בְּאִמְרָתֶךָ; or "sayings/promises" in a number of mss. and versions], so that no iniquity may dominate [jussive use of שׁלט] me."

119:134. "Redeem me! [impv.]" from (this) man's oppression (perhaps he has the ringleader in mind; or he means "from man," meaning human opponents; v. 134a), "so that I may keep [cohortative] your precepts [פִּקּוּד]" (v. 134b).

119:135. He wanted God to "make shine! [causative impv.]" his face on this servant (v. 135a). In the ANE, the concept of the king's face being turned towards someone indicated the king's favor. Then he added, "and teach me! [strengthened impv.] your statutes [חֹק]" (v. 135b). The implication is "show me how to apply these statutes."

119:136. He ended this part by saying that he bawled because God's law (תּוֹרָה) has not been followed (the text is not clear if he meant by others or himself or both).

God's Laws and Loyalty Remain Despite Difficulties (צַדִּיק; "Just; Right") (119:137–144 [צ])
The poet praises Yahweh's laws and his loyalty to them despite his troubles.

119:137. The poet then declared that Yahweh and his judgments are just ("judgment" in a few mss., LXX, and Jerome).

119:138. He (Yahweh) has ordered (צוה) just and very trustworthy decrees (עֵדוּת).

119:139. The psalmist explained that he had been destroyed (strong form of צמה = consumed; exhausted) by his personal zeal (for God's laws, implied), meaning his outrage over the fact that his enemies ("your enemy" in the Syriac version) have forgotten God's words (= teachings; "word" in many Heb. mss. and the Syriac version).

119:140. He explained that God's "saying" (אמר; "promise"?) is being refined (pass. ptc.) very much (= as the JPS, "Your word is exceedingly pure"), so his servant has loved it.

119:141. The psalmist claimed he was "a little one" (= as the JPS, "belittled") and being despised (pass. ptc.; by his enemies, implied), but yet he had not forgotten God's precepts (פִּקּוּד).

119:142. God's justice is always (לְעוֹלָם) right (צֶדֶק) and his law (תּוֹרָה) is reliable (אֱמֶת).

119:143. The psalmist had been found in distress and anguish, yet God's commands (מִצְוָה) are a delight.

119:144. God's decrees (עֵדוּת) are always just/right (צֶדֶק), he said, so he called on God to "give understanding! [causative; impv.]" to him so that he might live (cohortative).

Longevity Is Opportunity for Obedient Service (קְרָאתִי; "I have cried") (119:145–152 [ק])
The poet prays for extended life so he can continue serving God obediently.

119:145. The psalmist cried out with all his desire (lit., "heart"): "Answer me! [impv.] Oh 'Yahweh' [יְהוָה] so that I may [be able to] keep [cohortative form] your statutes [חֹק]."

119:146. He also cried out: "Rescue me! [causative impv.] so that I might [be willing to] keep [cohortative form] your decrees [עֵדוּת]."

119:147. He told how he had risen to meet [God] before dawn and cried for help; he had placed his hope in God's words ("promises"?).

119:148. He had stayed awake all night in order to (inf. of purpose) "meditate" on (reflect on) God's saying (אמר; "promise"?; but plural in a few Heb. mss., LXX, and Jerome's Latin text).

119:149. So, he called on Yahweh to "Hear! [impv.]" his voice according to his "loyal love [חֶסֶד]" (v. 149a); "keep me alive! [strong form of impv.] according to your just judgment [מִשְׁפָּט]" (v. 149b).

119:150. He complained that his cunning (HALOT, s.v. "I זמה," p. 272) pursuers (nom. ptc. רֹדֵף) have gotten close to him, while they have moved far away from God's law.

119:151. Still, he asserted, Yahweh is near and his commands (מִצְוֺתֶיךָ) are trustworthy (אֱמֶת; not "true"; Marlowe 2010, 24–42).

119:152. The psalmist had known (and still knows; past perfect) that God, in ancient times, had prepared (pluperfect) lasting (לְעוֹלָם) decrees (עֵדֹת).

God's Reliable Revelation Gives Confidence of God's Help (רְאֵה; "See!") (119:153–160 [ר])
The poet asks to be avenged and kept alive as God has promised.

119:153. So, the psalmist requested, "Look! [impv.] at my suffering and deliver me! [strong form of impv.] because I have not forgotten your law [תּוֹרָה]."

119:154a. He demanded physical rescue based on his obedience. He adds, "Defend! [impv.] my defense and avenge me! [impv. of I-גאל, which may be "redeem" or "avenge"].

119:154b. In the following parallel line, the psalmist asked, as several times already, "Keep me alive! [impv.] in line with your [past] affirmation [אמר; "promise"?]."

119:155. He contended next that such physical "salvation" or "rescue" (יְשׁוּעָה) is far from wicked people (like his enemies) because they have not sought God's statutes (חֹק); i.e., they do not follow God's rules, so they do not deserve prolonged life.

119:156. But since Yahweh has great compassion (v. 156a), the psalmist asked again, "Keep me alive! [impv.] in line with your justice/judgments [כְּמִשְׁפָּטֶיךָ]" (v. 156b).

119:157. He explained, "Many adversaries are still chasing me [ptc.], but I have not turned from your decrees [כְּמִשְׁפָּטֶיךָ]."

119:158. He boasted, "I have looked at and loathed those who are treacherous [nom. ptc.]; they have not kept your "word" ("promise"?) [אִמְרָתֶךָ; 'sayings' in the NETS; cf. LXX]" (v. 158).

119:159. But by contrast, he cried out, "Observe! [impv.] that I have loved [and still love; experiential perfect or stative] your precepts" (v. 159a); "[so] keep me alive! [impv.] in conformity with your loyal love [כְּחַסְדְּךָ]" (v. 159b).

119:160. He acknowledged that whatever God says is trustworthy, and what he rules is just, from beginning to end.

Law-Keepers May Feel They Deserve Not to Suffer (שָׂרִים; "Rulers") (119:161–168 [שׁ])
The poet tries to prove that his suffering is undeserved and salvation from it is deserved.

119:161a. He next complained that people in power have pursued him for no good reason.

119:161b. Then came an odd phrase: literally, "and from your words my heart has trembled" ("word" in many other Heb. mss. and several ancient versions). He seems to be saying that he was being persecuted even though he has feared and followed God's laws. He seems to have thought that such obedience should make him immune to such trouble. He wanted to know why he is suffering since he has "kept his nose clean."

119:162. He then said, "I keep rejoicing [ptc.] over your promise [lit., 'saying'; 'words [promises?]' in a few other mss. and LXX], like someone who keeps finding [ptc.] great spoil [= amounts of lost bounty]."

119:163a. He boasted that he had (always) hated (past perfect) and wished he might abhor (in the future also; cohortative) falsehood (but the Hebrew verb form is similar to a past form, "I abhorred").

119:163b. Consistent with this or by contrast, he announced that he had (always) loved (past perfect) God's law (v. 163b).

119:164. In fact (but is this hyperbolic?), he claimed that he had the regular practice of praising (strong form of II הלל) God seven times each day for his just (צֶדֶק) judgments (מִשְׁפָּט).

119:165. He believed that great "peace [שָׁלוֹם]" is afforded "those who keep loving [ptc.]" God's law (v. 165a); and nothing is a stumbling block for them (v. 165b).

119:166. He professed that he had performed what has been commanded (מִצְוָה; v. 166b), so has unwaveringly hoped (strengthened verb)for Yahweh to rescue him (v. 166a).

119:167. Then with more passion he stated that "I" [נַפְשִׁי] have kept your decrees [עֵדֹתֶיךָ]" (v. 167a), "[because] I loved them [past tense] very much" (v. 167b).

119:168. This section ends with the psalmist's assertion that he has obeyed God's precepts (פִּקּוּד) and decrees (עֵדוּת), because God is aware of all that he does.

The Law-Keeper Expects God to Hear His Prayer (תִּקְרַב; "May it come near?") (119:169–76 [ת])

The poet makes a final urgent request for Yahweh to hear and answer his supplication.

119:169. The psalmist petitioned God, "Let my shout 'come close' [תִּקְרַב; jussive verb] before you, oh Yahweh (v. 169a); "give me insight [causative; impv.] according to your revelation" (v. 169b; lit., "word/speech"; but other mss. and the Syriac version reflect the preposition "in/by/with [בְּ]" instead of "according to [כְּ]."

119:170. He asked also, "May my supplication come [jussive mood] before you" (v. 170a); "deliver me! [impv.] according to your promise [lit., 'saying' from אמר]" (v. 170b).

119:171. And he prayed, "Let my lips overflow [causative/jussive of נבע] [with] praise" (v. 171a), "because you will teach me [strengthened future] your statutes [חֻקֶּיךָ]" (v. 171b).

119:172. Then the poet requested, "Let my tongue sing [jussive mood of desire] about your 'affirmation' [אִמְרָתֶךָ; plural in other mss. and versions; "promise"?] because all your commands [מִצְוֹתֶיךָ] are just [צֶדֶק]."

119:173. He also requested, "Let your hand be [jussive mood of desire] for my assistance, because I have chosen [to follow] your precepts [פִּקּוּדֶיךָ]."

119:174. And he agonized, "I have been waiting [a long time] for your rescue, oh Yahweh, [וְ; 'even though'] your law [וְתוֹרָתְךָ] is my delight."

119:175. And he also said, "Let me live [jussive verb] 'so that [וִ]' it [my נֶפֶשׁ or 'life force'] may praise you [jussive, strong form of II הלל], and may your decisions [or 'judgments'] help me [jussive]."

119:176. The psalmist concluded by confessing he had strayed like a lost sheep but still called for God to "seek!" (impv.) his servant (the psalmist) because he has not forgotten (to follow) God's commands (מִצְוָה). He had gone to great lengths in the psalm to convince God to rescue him from deadly enemies based on his not perfect but impressive obedience (at least as he saw it).

THEOLOGICAL FOCUS

The exegetical idea (this ancient Hebrew poet expressed his love for and loyalty to the laws of "Yahweh" [יְהוָה] with the hope that he would experience divine deliverance from a deadly foe) leads to this theological focus: A life regulated by, and devoted to, God's stipulations has the best chance for safety and success.

Psalm 119 is almost fanatical in the psalmist's frustration and fascination with his devotion to God's verbally revealed laws and his dumbfoundedness at God's delay in defeating his enemy, who is disobedient, while he obeys divine regulations. There is the unnuanced expectation that obedience should lead to prosperity and protection. Following God's ways is not easy and deserves rewards of success and safety (all things being equal; readers have to keep in mind that this poet writes with, and to an audience holding, an ancient Hebrew perspective and knowledge, a long time before God revealed all that current believers know). Of course, a number of principles are the same. Being a law-keeper still risks ridicule, even from fellow believers, yet it also invites God's gracious blessing. An experience of God's intervention and help fosters or strengthens future faithfulness. God's laws remain good despite his discipline for breaking them. God's enemies seem not to suffer at all or enough, but

God only disciplines those he loves. God's assurances of blessing for obedience or cursing for disobedience are carried out at his timing, not ours. Believers of all ages have found this irritating, but the need to trust God's wisdom is highlighted. God's ways are the way of wisdom. Law keeping does not guarantee complete safety but makes an early earthy death and destruction less likely. God's revelation remains reliable despite all circumstances. To think law keeping ensures health and wealth is presumption. God will hear the prayers of a righteous person, but God cannot be manipulated.

A Final Reflection

Christian readers of Psalm 119 may feel a bit uneasy appreciating the psalmist's great love for God's "law," especially because so much of OT law is distinctly Jewish, and even more so if they have been taught a strong Pauline perspective on freedom from law by being under grace (Rom. 6:14). God certainly has dispensed laws that Jews and Christians must obey, but what accounts for this poet's intense emotion? A Christian's emotional commitment is to Christ, so how to identify with and appropriate or apply (if indeed this is required) such a portion of OT Scripture?

In popular treatment this psalm is often described as if the author is excited about the privilege of having God's Word, as if he had access to written revelation as we do today. We forget that having a personal Bible is only a recent phenomenon in the history of God's work on earth through Israel and the church. We often act as if Bible reading is indispensable for spiritual growth; but for much of human existence, people were expected to become mature believers without having a Bible to read or memorize or study. Only certain leaders had access to Scripture. Lay people were dependent upon their teaching and interpretations and public readings for knowledge about divine revelation. This is why there is such emphasis on the importance of trained and trustworthy teachers in

Scripture. This power could be abused and eventually was misused by some.

Once Bible translation and printing was possible and began to flourish, many church leaders (rightly so) were afraid of uncontrolled opinions and increased division over doctrine. Some instituted harsh measures, unwisely, but the cat was out of the bag. Reformation leaders were beaming and sometimes not cautious enough with the idea that every person could engage in personal Bible study. But this could be and was, and still is, abused. Some publishers liked the profits and ignored the prophets. The church today is inundated with competing translations and trained as well as self-proclaimed and anointed untrained "teachers," among whom those with the most charisma and cash gain the largest audience. Having God's verbal revelation in print, online, and widely available is a double-edged sword: on the one hand, a delight; on the other, a danger. The answer of course is not elimination but education.

With great privilege comes great responsibility. Like a Formula One race car, God's Word in the hands of a novice is deadly. Psalm 119 is not about the joy of having a Bible but the privilege of learning God's revelation and wisdom and being obedient to it. The NT (when there still as yet was no Scripture as a Bible for lay people) emphasizes the importance of leaders learning to present (themselves) to God as approved workmen who do not need to be ashamed and who correctly handle the word of truth (2 Tim. 2:15). This calling continues for every believer who wants to read, research, and relate the Bible.

PREACHING AND TEACHING STRATEGIES

Exegetical and Theological Synthesis
Devotion to God's Word as the proper response to the challenges of life can be seen in

the salient features of the psalm. The psalmist's devotion can be seen in his terminology and in his artistry. Terminologically, Psalm 119 employs eight different Hebrew terms to relate to the Law (see "Preaching Pointers" above), or perhaps more generally instruction (i.e., the meaning of Torah), or the word of God. These eight terms are used 176 times, equaling the 176 verses of the psalm. The commitment of the psalmist towards God's instruction can hardly be missed by even a casual reader. But such devotion can also be seen in the creative structure of the psalm, which is an alphabetic acrostic in Hebrew. While acrostics can serve a variety of communicative purposes (see the discussion on Psalm 111), the A-to-Z effect likely expresses the comprehensiveness of the poet's devotion.

The fact that psalmist's devotion was not the product of idyllic sentimentalism but of the crucible of trials and tribulations is evidenced by a number of statements. He devotes himself to God's Word as he wrestles with temptation (vv. 9–11, 36–37, 67, 101), sorrow (vv. 28, 136, 147, 169, 170), personal hostility (vv. 23, 50, 61, 84, 86, 92, 95, 107, 117, 110, 121, 122, 134, 143, 150, 153, 157, 161), and faces criticism and rejection (vv. 42, 51, 69, 78, 85). So, for the psalmist, devotion to God's Word is indeed an appropriate response to the multifaceted challenges of life.

Preaching Idea
Devotion to God's word is the proper response to the challenges of life.

It should be pointed out that all 176 verses of Psalm 119 are rarely preached in total. As the longest psalm in the Psalter, it is typically broken down into sections for a preaching series. The acrostic structure makes the book fairly easy to divide. But if one decides to preach smaller sections, then it would probably be better to tweak the preaching idea, which is necessarily general and broad, to something that more clearly reflects the specifics of the smaller section. Assuming that we have the main subject correct (i.e., Devotion to God's Word . . .), then most likely what will be changed is the complement.

Contemporary Connections

What does it mean?
What does it mean to be devoted to God's Word? Devotion generally carries the idea of focused heartfelt commitment. It is focused in that it tends to be singular in its attention. It is heartfelt in that it involves emotional attachment. It is committed in that we are dedicating ourselves to something or someone. If you are devoted to your spouse, you are committed in a focused, heartfelt way to that person.

With that in mind, being devoted to God's Word means that one is focused on the Word of God, passionate in its appropriation, and committed to its incorporation into one's life. A quick perusal of just the first three acrostic letters and their twenty-four verses reveals that at least thirteen statements express these different facets of the psalmist's devotion to God's Law/Word. Consider the following: "Oh that my ways may be steadfast in keeping your statutes" (v. 5), "having my eyes fixed on all your commandments" (v. 6b), "when I learn your righteous rules" (v. 7b), "I will keep your statutes" (v. 8a), "with my whole heart I seek you" (v. 10a), "I have stored up your word in my heart" (v. 11a), "with my lips I declare all the rules of your mouth" (v. 13), "in the way of your testimonies I delight" (v. 14a), "I will meditate on your precepts and fix my eyes on your ways" (v. 15), "I will delight in your statutes" (v. 16a), "I will not forget your word" (v. 16b), "my soul is consumed with longing for your rules at all times" (v. 20), "I have kept your testimonies" (v. 22), "your servant will meditate on your statutes" (v. 23b), "your testimonies are my delight; they are my counselors" (v. 24), and there are 152 more verses to go.

As noted earlier, this devotion is not in the abstract but is expressed in the crucible of life's challenges. For examples of these challenges, see the list in the "Exegetical/Theological Synthesis" section above.

Is it true?
Is it really true that devotion to God's Word is the proper response to the challenges of life? The psalmist would certainly say yes. But how does that work exactly? The law/word of God helps to navigate the challenges of life in at least two ways.

First, God's Law/Word points to a God worth trusting during challenging times. The psalmist appeals to the Lord numerous times. One can note all the *lets* and *mays*. God is described as one who answers (v. 25), gives life-giving promises (v. 50), is steadfast (v. 88), faithful, (v. 90), a hiding place and shield (v. 114), and one who is near (v. 151). Ultimately, God's Law/Word would point to, and be incarnated in, Jesus of Nazareth who is now the way, the truth, and the life (John 14:6).

Second, God's Law/Word provides a source of truth to live by. While it might be culturally and intellectually fashionable today to deny that there is any absolute truth, life and pastoral experience has taught me (Charles) that personal crises hate uncertainty. The psalmist is absolutely committed to the proposition that the Law/Word is invaluable for navigating life's challenges, and many of the faithful throughout the ages would affirm that as well.

Now what?
If devotion to God's Word is the proper response to the challenges of life, how should we respond to this idea and apply it to our lives? One hundred seventy-six verses might be more of a bite than most people will want to chew, *so select three of the most meaningful verses to you and commit those to memory.*

For those that might be interested in more of a challenge, *make a commitment today to read the entire Bible in a year*. And before you consider that too great a task, consider Craig Keener, a former atheist but now a New

Testament scholar, who as a young Christian devoted himself to reading forty chapters a day (enough to finish the New Testament every week or the entire Bible every month!).[1] You can undoubtedly read the Bible in a year.

But memorizing and reading the Bible is not enough. Like the psalmist, *be hardcore in your commitment to its truth claims upon your life.* He declares nearly twenty times that life is to be lived "according to his word" (vv. 9, 25, 28, 65, 107, 169, 170), promise (vv. 41, 58, 76, 116, 133, 154), law (v. 85), steadfast love (vv. 124, 149a, 159), justice (v. 149b), and rules (v. 156). But be forewarned, while this concept is simple its implementation will not be easy. Nonetheless, I have yet to meet a Christ-follower on their death bed regretting that they had heeded God's Word too often.

Creativity in Presentation

Pastor and theologian James Montgomery Boice tells the story of "George Wishart, a Bishop of Edinburgh in the seventeenth century. Wishart was condemned to death along with his famous patron, the Marquis of Montrose, and he would have been executed, except for this incident. When he was on the scaffold, he made use of a custom of the times that permitted the condemned to choose a psalm to be sung. He chose Psalm 119. Before two-thirds of the psalm was sung a pardon arrived, and Wishart's life was spared. The story has been told as an illustration of God's intervention to save a saintly person. The truth is different. Wishart was more renowned for shrewdness than for sanctity. He was expecting a pardon, requested the psalm to gain time, and, happily for him, succeeded in delaying the execution until his pardon came" (Boice 2005, 970).

Take an old love letter that you have and use it as an illustration of how Psalm 119 is the psalmist's love letter to God and his Word. Search the internet for videos of believers receiving copies of the Bible and use them as an illustration for how people feel when they receive God's Word.

Use the 2021 film *The Map of Tiny Perfect Things* (directed by Ian Samuels) as an analogy of God's Word. In the film, Mark (played by Kyle Allen), one of the main teenage characters, is stuck in a time loop until he realizes that the way out is to be found in creating a map of tiny perfect things. Similarly, the Bible is like a map of tiny perfect things that offers a way to break the cycle of dysfunction that permeates our broken world.

There are numerous songs based on Psalm 119. A popular contemporary Christian song from 1984 was Amy Grant and Michael W. Smith's "Thy Word," which is built off of verse 105. A more recent one that I (Charles) like is on Psalm 119:33–40 by the Corner Room. Likewise, a fellowship of church songwriters named Cardiphonia Music, which crowd sources worship music for the joy and edification of the church, has produced an entire compilation of songs on each of the sections of Psalm 119, twenty-two artists in all. This fellowship has released various compilations featuring other groupings of the Psalms. Also, Exodus Music has released two of three albums with songs named after the successive Hebrew letters representing each stanza or section of Psalm 119, plus chord charts online.[2]

The key point to emphasize is this: A life regulated by, and devoted to, God's rules has the best chance for safety and success. Devotion to God's Word is the proper response to the challenges of life.

---

1   Craig Keener, "Why It Is Important to Study the Bible in Context," Bible Background (blog), February 25, 2013, https://craigkeener.com/why-it-is-important-to-study-the-bible-in-context.

2   Exodus Music is a ministry of Exodus Church of Belmont, North Carolina. Music resources available at http://theexoduschurch.org/music.

- Devotion to God's Word helps us to see God.

- Devotion to God's Word helps us to live right.

- Devotion to God's Word helps us to face wrong.

DISCUSSION QUESTIONS

1. Why did the psalmist think it necessary to construct such a long and redundant psalm or prayer?

2. Is the psalmist's claim to have earned salvation from his suffering, or not to deserve it, at odds with other biblical teachings about God's unmerited grace?

3. What does the psalmist have in mind when he mentions God's revelations or promises, either דבר or אמר?

4. Is "word" or "Word" ever a good translation for the Hebrew terms in question 3, for the current English audience? Why or why not?

5. What is the purpose of the alphabetic acrostic structure?

6. What in this psalm points toward the person and work of Christ?

FOR FURTHER READING

Bateman, Herbert W., IV, and D. Brent Sandy, eds. (2010). *Interpreting the Psalms for Teaching and Preaching.* St. Louis: Chalice Press.

Beisner, E. Calvin. (1994). *Psalms of Promise: Celebrating the Majesty and Faithfulness of God.* 2nd edition. Phillipsburg, NJ: P&R.

Boice, James Montgomery. (1994). *Psalms. Vol. 1: Psalms 1–41.* Grand Rapids: Baker.

_____. (1996) *Psalms. Vol. 2: Psalms 42–106.* Grand Rapids: Baker.

_____. (1998). *Psalms. Vol. 3: Psalms 107–150.* Grand Rapids: Baker.

Bridges, Charles. (1861). *Exposition of Psalm 119: As Illustrative of the Character and Exercises of Christian Experience.* 17th edition. New York: Robert Carter & Brothers.

Broyles, Craig C. (1999). *Psalms.* New International Biblical Commentary. Peabody, MA: Hendrickson.

Bullock, C. Hassell. (2015). *Psalms. Vol. 1: Psalms 1–72.* Teach the Text. Grand Rapids: Baker.

_____. (2017). *Psalms. Vol. 2: Psalms 73–150.* Teach the Text. Grand Rapids: Baker.

Byassee, Jason. (2018). *Psalms 101–150.* Brazos Theological Commentary on the Bible. Grand Rapids: Brazos.

Charry, Ellen T. (2015). *Psalms 1–50.* Brazos Theological Commentary on the Bible. Grand Rapids: Brazos.

Freedman, David Noel, with Jeffrey C. Geoghegan, and Andrew Welch. (1999). *Psalm 119: The Exaltation of Torah.* Winona Lake, IN: Eisenbrauns.

Futato, Mark D., and George M. Schwab. (2009). *The Book of Psalms, The Book of Proverbs.* Cornerstone Biblical Commentary 7. Carol Stream, IL: Tyndale House.

Sarna, Nahum M. (1993). *Songs of the Heart: An Introduction to the Book of Psalms.* New York: Schocken.

Stedman, Ray C. (1973). *Psalms of Faith: A Life-Related Study from Selected Psalms.* Ventura, CA: Regal.

Swindoll, Charles R. (2012). *Living the Psalms: Encouragement for the Daily Grind.* Brentwood, TN: Worthy.

REFERENCES

Abegg Jr., M., P. Flint,, and E. Ulrich. (1999). *The Dead Sea Scrolls Bible: The Oldest Known Bible Translated for the First Time into English*. New York: HarperCollins.

Allen, R. B. (1980). *Praise! A Matter of Life and Breath: Praising God in the Psalms*. Nashville: Thomas Nelson.

Alter, R. (1985). *The Art of Biblical Poetry*. New York: Basic Books.

Anderson, A. A. ([1981] 1995a). *Psalms I: 1–72*. Reprint, Grand Rapids: Eerdmans.

_____. ([1981] 1995b). *Psalms II: 73–150*. Reprint, Grand Rapids: Eerdmans.

Anderson, F. R. (2016). *Singing God's Psalms: Metrical Psalms and Reflections*. Calvin Institute of Christian Worship Liturgical Studies. Grand Rapids: Eerdmans.

Aquinas, T. (2012). "St. Thomas's Introduction to his Exposition of the Psalms of David." In *Commentary on the Psalms*. Kindle ed. Fig Classic Series on Medieval Theology. N.p., FigBooks. https://www.amazon.com/Commentary-Psalms-Thomas-Aquinas-ebook/dp/B00C46A78I.

Arnold, B. T., and J. H. Choi. (2003). *A Guide to Biblical Hebrew Syntax*. Cambridge: Cambridge University Press.

Arnold, B. T., and B. E. Beyer, eds. (2002). *Readings from the Ancient Near East*. Grand Rapids: Baker Academic.

Avishur, Y. (1994). *Studies in Hebrew and Ugaritic Psalms*. Publications of the Perry Foundation for Biblical Research in the Hebrew University of Jerusalem. Jerusalem: Magnes Press of the Hebrew University.

_____. (1984). *Stylistic Studies of Word-Pairs in Biblical and Ancient Semitic Literatures*. Alter Orient und Altes Testament 210. Kevelaer: Butzon & Bercker; Neukirchen-Vluyn: Neukirchener.

Bailey, C. W., director. (2012). *Psalm 1*. https://www.imdb.com/title/tt2319999. For more information about using this resource, contact the film director through Vimeo or his website at https://www.cbaileyfilm.com.

Baker, D. (1976). "Typology and the Christian Use of the Old Testament." *Scottish Journal of Theology* 29 (2):137–57. https://doi.org/10.1017/S0036930600042563.

Barr, J. (1962). *The Semantics of Biblical Language*. London: Oxford University Press. First published in English by Oxford University Press in 1961.

Bateman IV, H. W., ed. (2012). "Part 2: Expectations of a King." In *Jesus the Messiah: Tracing the Promises, Expectations, and Coming of Israel's King*, by H. W. Bateman IV, D. L. Bock, and G. H. Johnston, 211–330. Grand Rapids: Kregel.

Bateman IV, H. W. and D. B. Sandy, eds. (2010). *Interpreting the Psalms for Teaching and Preaching*. St. Louis: Chalice Press.

Beegle, Dewey M. (n.d.). "Moses: Hebrew Prophet." In *Encyclopaedia Britannica*, n.p. Accessed August 6, 2020.

Berlin, Adele. (1996). "Introduction to Hebrew Poetry." In *The New Interpreter's Bible*, 301–14. Edited by Robert Doran, Carol A. Newsom, J. Clinton McCann, Adele Berlin, et al., vol. 4. Nashville: Abingdon.

_____. (1985). *The Dynamics of Biblical Parallelism*. Bloomington: Indiana University Press.

Berlin, Adele and Marc Zvi Brettler, eds. (2004). *The Jewish Study Bible*. Oxford: University Press.

Biblia Hebraica Stuttgartensia, Tagged. (1997). Edited by Karl Elliger and Wilhelm Rudolph. Stuttgart: Deutsche

Bibelgesellschaft. OakTree Software, Accordance eBook. Version 1.6.

Blenkinsopp, Joseph. (1995). *Wisdom and Law in the Old Testament: The Ordering of Life in Israel and Early Judaism.* Oxford: University Press.

Block, Daniel I. (1998). *The Book of Ezekiel.* NICOT. Grand Rapids: Wm. B. Eerdmans.

Botha, P. J. (2005). "The Ideological Interface between Psalm 1 and Psalm 2." *Old Testament Essays*, 18:2, 189–203. Accessed August 12, 2019.

_____. (2012). "Interpreting 'Torah' in Psalm 1 in the light of Psalm 119." *HTS Teologiese Studies/Theological Studies* 68:1 (2012): 1–7.

Bouzard, Walter C. Jr. (1997). *We Have Heard With Our Ears, O God: Sources of the Communal Laments in the Psalms.* SBLDS 159. Atlanta: Scholars Press.

Brown-Driver-Briggs Hebrew and English Lexicon, The. (1907, 1974). Edited by F. Brown, S. Driver, and C. Briggs. Translated by Edward Robinson. Based on Gesenius's *Lexicon.* Reprint, Oxford: Clarendon.

Brown-Driver-Briggs Hebrew and English Lexicon Abridged, The. (1907). Edited by F. Brown, S. Driver, and C. Briggs. Translated by Edward Robinson. Based on Gesenius's *Lexicon.* Electronic text corrected, formatted, and hypertexted by OakTree Software, Inc., 2001. Version 3.7.

Brownlee, William H. (1971). "Psalms 1–2 as a Coronation Liturgy." *Biblica* 52:3 (1971): 321–36.

Brueggemann, Walter. (1980). "Psalms and the Life of Faith: A Suggested Typology of Function." *Journal for the Study of the Old Testament* 17 (1980): 3–32. [JSOT]

Bullock, C. Hassell. (1979). *An Introduction to the Old Testament Poetic Books.* Chicago: Moody.

_____. (2007). *Encountering the Book of Psalms: A Literary and Theological Introduction.* Revised and expanded, Grand Rapids: Baker.

_____. (2015). *Psalms. Vol. 1: Psalms 1–72.* Teach the Text. Grand Rapids: Baker.

_____. (2017). *Psalms. Vol. 2: Psalms 73–150.* Teach the Text. Grand Rapids: Baker.

Buszin, Walter E. (1946). "Luther on Music." *Musical Quarterly* 32:1 (1946): 80–97; citing Martin Luther (1538). Foreward [sic] to Georg Rhau's Collection, *Symphoniae iucundae.*

Calvin, John. (1556). "Author's Preface." In *Commentary on the Book of Psalms*, vol. 1, n.p. Translated by Reverend James Anderson. Grand Rapids: Christian Classics Ethereal Library. Edinburgh: Calvin Translation Society. Accessed 29 Nov. 2017. http://grace-ebooks.com/library/John %20Calvin/JC_Psalms_ Vol_1.pdf.

Carson, D. A. (1984). *Exegetical Fallacies.* Grand Rapids: Baker Book House.

_____., gen ed. (2015). *NIV Zondervan Study Bible.* Grand Rapids: Zondervan.

Charry, Ellen T. (2015). *Psalms 1–50: Sighs and Songs of Israel.* Grand Rapids: Baker/Brazos Press.

Childs, Brevard S. (1979). *Introduction to the Old Testament as Scripture.* Minneapolis: Fortress Press.

Cohen, A. (1945). *The Psalms.* Soncino Books of the Bible. London: Soncino Press.

Cooper, L. E. (1994). *Ezekiel.* New American Commentary. Nashville: Broadman & Holman.

Creach, Jerome F. D. (1999). "Like a Tree Planted by the Temple Stream: The Portrait of the Righteous in Psalm 1:3." *Catholic Biblical Quarterly* 61 (1999): 34–46.

Daffern, Mary. (2016). "Repeat the Song! The Psalms and the Eucharist." *Expository Times* 127:12 (May 2016): 573–84.

Dahood, Mitchell. (1966). *Psalms I: 1–50.* Anchor Bible 16. Edited by W. F. Albright and D. N. Freedman. Garden City, NY: Doubleday.

_____. (1968). *Psalms II: 51–100*. The Anchor Bible 17. Edited by W. F. Albright and D. N. Freedman. Garden City, NY: Doubleday.

_____. (1970). *Psalms III: 101–150*. The Anchor Bible 17a. Edited by W. F. Albright and D. N. Freedman. Garden City, NY: Doubleday.

De Claissé-Walford, Nancy L., Rolf A. Jacobson, and Beth LaNeel Tanner. (2014). *The Book of Psalms*. NICOT. Grand Rapids: Eerdmans.

De Claissé-Walford, Nancy L., ed. (2014) *The Shape and Shaping of the Book of Psalms: The Current State of Scholarship*. Ancient Israel and Its Literature (Book 20). Atlanta: Society of Biblical Literature.

Deißler, A. (1955). *Psalm 119 (118) und seine Theologie*. Ein Beitrag zur Erforschung der anthologischen Stilgattung im Alten Testament. Münchener Theologische Studien, 11. München: Karl Zink.

De Moor, J. C., ed. (1988). *The Structural Analysis of Biblical and Canaanite Poetry*. JSOT Supplement Series 74. Sheffield, UK: Sheffield Academic.

Duvall, J. Scott and J. Daniel Hayes. (2012). *Grasping God's Word: A Hands-On Approach to Reading, Interpreting, and Applying the Bible*. 3rd edition. Grand Rapids: Zondervan.

Ehrman, Bart D. (2008) *God's Problem: How the Bible Fails to Answer Our Most Important Question—Why We Suffer*. New York: HarperOne

Eiselen, F. (1918.) *The Psalms and Other Sacred Writings*. Philadelphia: Methodist Book Concern.

Eissfeldt, Otto. (1974). *The Old Testament: An Introduction*. Translated by Peter R. Ackroyd. Oxford: Basil Blackwell.

Encyclopaedia Britannica. https://www.britannica.com/topic/Septuagint. Accessed November 30, 2017.

Enns, Peter. (2005). *Inspiration and Incarnation: Evangelicals and the Problem of the Old Testament*. Grand Rapids: Baker Academic.

Evans, Craig. (2010). *Holman QuickSource Guide to the Dead Sea Scrolls*. Nashville: Holman.

Ferris, Paul W. Jr. (1992). *The Genre of Community Laments in the Bible and the Ancient Near East*. SBLDS. Atlanta: Scholars Press.

Flint, Peter W. and Patrick D. Miller, eds. (2005). *The Book of Psalms: Composition and Reception*. Leiden: Brill.

Fox, James. J. (2014). *Explorations in Semantic Parallelism*. Canberra, AU: ANU Press.

Fox, Michael V. (1997). "Ideas of Wisdom in Proverbs 1–9." *Journal of Biblical Literature* 116: 613–33. [JBL]

Freedman, David Noel (1985). "What the Ass and the Ox Know—But the Scholars Don't." *Bible Review* (February), 42–43.

Frei, Hans. (1974). *The Eclipse of Biblical Narrative: A Study in Eighteenth and Nineteenth Century Hermeneutics*. New Haven, CT: Yale University Press.

Geller, Stephen A. (1993). "Hebrew Prosody and Poetics: Biblical." In *The New Princeton Encyclopedia of Poetry and Poetics*, 509–11. Edited by Alex Preminger and T. V. F. Brogan. Princeton, NJ: Princeton University Press.

_____. (1979). *Parallelism in Early Biblical Poetry*. Harvard Semitic Monographs. Boston: Scholars Press.

Gesenius, W. (1859). *Hebrew and Chaldee Lexicon to the Old Testament*. London: Samuel Bagster & Sons. Digital access (2019): http://www.tyndalearchive.com/TABS/Gesenius/; or https://archive.org/details/GeseniusHebrewChaldeeLexiconOldTestamentScriptures.tregelles.1857.24/page/n4.

Getty, Keith. (2018). "How Singing the Psalms Provides a Fixed Point for Theological Expression and Growth," 3–5. Accessed March 21, 2019.

Gignilliat, Mark S. (2012). *A Brief History of Old Testament Criticism: From Benedict*

Spinoza to Brevard Childs. Grand Rapids: Zondervan. Accordance edition hypertexted and formatted by OakTree Software, Inc. eBook. Version 1.0.

Gillingham, Susan. (2012). "Entering and Leaving the Psalter: Psalms 1 and 150 and the Two Polarities of Faith." In *Let Us Go Up to Zion: Essays in Honor of H.G.M. Williamson on the Occasion of his Sixty-Fifth Birthday, 383–94.* Edited by Iain Provan and Mark J. Boda. Leiden: Brill.

_____. (2013). *A Journey of Two Psalms: The Reception of Psalms 1 & 2 in Jewish & Christian Tradition.* Oxford: Oxford University Press.

_____. (2002). "From Liturgy to Prophecy: The Use of Psalmody in Second Temple Judaism." *Catholic Biblical Quarterly* 64:3 (July 2002): 478.

Goldingay, John. (2006). *Psalms I: 1–41.* Edited by Tremper Longman III. Grand Rapids: Baker Academic.

_____. (2006). *Psalms II: 42–89.* Edited by Tremper Longman III. Grand Rapids: Baker Academic.

_____. (2006). *Psalms III: 90–150.* Edited by Tremper Longman III. Grand Rapids: Baker Academic.

Goppelt, Leonhard. (1977). "τύπος." In *Theological Dictionary of the New Testament*, 246–59. Vol. 8. Edited by Gerhard Kittel and Gerhard Friedrich. Translated by Geoffrey W. Bromiley. Grand Rapids: Eerdmans.

Green, Michael. (1981). *I Believe in Satan's Downfall.* Grand Rapids, MI: Eerdmans.

Gregory, Bradley. (2015). "The Value of Reception History for Theological Interpretation: Some Reflections on Susan Gillingham's *A Journey of Two Psalms,*" *Cithara* 55:1 (Nov. 2015): 41–46, 64. https://search. proquest.com/religion/ docview/1750209965/3433B2 DB97344 D0DPQ/8?accountid=31623. Accessed August 13, 2019.

Gunkel, Hermann. ([1933] 1998). *An Introduction to the Psalms: The Genres of the Religious Lyric of Israel.* Compiled by Joachim Begrich. Translated by James D. Nogalski. Reprint, Macon, GA: Mercer University Press.

_____. (1933). *Einleitung in die Psalmen.* Göttingen: Vandenhoeck and Ruprecht.

Haïk-Vantoura, Suzanne. (1976). *The Music of the Bible Revealed: The Deciphering of a Millenary Notation.* 1st French edition. Translated by Dennis Webber. San Francisco: Bibal.

Hebrew and Aramaic Lexicon of the Old Testament, The. (2000.) Edited by Koehler, Ludwig and Walter Baumgartner. Translated and edited by M. E. J. Richardson, et al. Leiden: Koninklijke Brill NV. OakTree Software, Accordance, eBook. Version 3.4.

Hennig, Kurt. (1990). *Jerusalemer Bibellexikon.* Stuttgart: Hänssler-Verlag.

Herdner, Andrée. (1963). *Corpus tablettes alphabetiques.* Paris: P. Geuthner.

Ho, Peter C. W. (2017). "The Design of the MT Psalter: A Macrostructural Analysis." Thesis submitted to the University of Gloucestershire, for the degree Ph.D.; supervisor Gordon McConville.

Holladay, William L. (1972). *A Concise Hebrew and Aramaic Lexicon of the Old Testament.* Grand Rapids: Eerdmans.

Houtman, Cornelis. (1993). *Der Himmel im Alten Testament: Israels Weltbild und Weltanschauung.* Leiden, NL: Brill.

Howard, David. (1999). "Recent Trends in Psalms Studies." In *The Face of Old Testament Studies: A Survey of Contemporary Approaches, 329–68.* Grand Rapids: Baker.

_____. (2005). "The Psalms and Current Study." In *Interpreting the Psalms: Issues and Approaches,* 23–40. Edited by David Firth and Philip S. Johnston. Downers Grove, IL: IVP Academic.

Kaiser, Walter C., Jr. (2010). "Psalm 73: The Prosperity of the Wicked and the Perspective of the Believer." In *Interpreting the Psalms for Teaching and Preaching*, 98–106. Edited by H. W. Bateman IV and D. B. Sandy. St. Louis: Chalice Press.

_____. (1981). *Toward an Exegetical Theology: Biblical Exegesis for Preaching and Teaching*. Grand Rapids: Baker.

Kautzch, E. (1920). *Gensenius' Hebrew Grammar*. 2nd edition. Translated by A. E. Cowley. Oxford: Clarendon Press.

Keel, Othmar, (1985). "Das sogenannte altorientalische Weltbild." *Bibel und Kirche* 40 (1985): 157–161.

_____. (1997). *The Symbolism of the Ancient World: Ancient Near Eastern Iconography and the Book of Psalms.* Translated by Timothy J. Hallett. Reprint, Winona Lake, IN: Eisenbrauns.

Kidner, Derek. (2009). *Psalms 1–72.* Tyndale Old Testament Commentary 15. Downers Grove, IL: IVP Academic.

_____. (1964). *The Proverbs: An Introduction and Commentary*. Tyndale Old Testament Commentary 17. Downers Grove, IL: Inter-Varsity.

King, Philip J., and Lawrence E. Stager. (2001). *Life in Biblical Israel.* Louisville: Westminster John Knox.

Kloos, Carola. (1986.) *Yhwh's Combat with the Sea. A Canaanite Tradition in the Religion of Ancient Israel.* Leiden: Brill.

Kondyuk, Denis. (2006). "The Themes of Flee/Exile and Return to the Land in the Psalter, and Their Relation to Its Literary Structure in the Context of Davidic Clusters (Psalms 3–14 and 138–145)." Thesis. Leuven: Evangelische Theologische Faculteit.

Koorevaar, Hendrik J. (2010). "The Book of Psalms as a Structured Theological Story With the Aid of Subscripts and Superscripts." In *The Composition of the Book of Psalms*, 579–92. Edited by Erich Zenger. Bibliotheca Ephemeridum Theologicarum Lovaniensium, 238. Leuven: Peeters.

_____. (2015). "David sang und sprach: Der Wert der Namen als historische Personen in den Überschriften der Psalmen im Rahmen der Struktur des Psalters." In *Die Königherschaft Jahwes*, 21–59. Festschrift zur Emeritierung von Herbert H. Klement. Edited by Harald Seubert & Jacob Thiessen. *Studien zur Theologie und Bibel* 13. Zürich, Wien: LIT.

Kraus, Hans-Joachim. (1960). *Psalmen.* Neukirchen-Vluyn: Neukirchener.

_____. (1988). *Psalms 1–59.* Continental Commentary, vol. 1. Translated by Hilton C. Oswald. Reprint, Minneapolis: Fortress.

_____. (1993). *Psalms 60–150.* Continental Commentary, vol. 2. Translated by Hilton C. Oswald. Reprint, Minneapolis: Fortress.

_____. (1992). *The Theology of the Psalms.* Continental Commentary. Translated by Keith Crim. Reprint, Minneapolis: Fortress.

Kugel, James L. (1998). *The Idea of Biblical Poetry: Parallelism and Its History.* Reprint, Baltimore: Johns Hopkins University Press.

Lambert, W. G. (1996). *Babylonian Wisdom Literature.* Winona Lake, IN: Eisenbrauns.

Lamsa, George M. (1933). *Holy Bible from Ancient Eastern Manuscripts.* Translated by George M. Lamsa. Reprint, San Francisco: HarperOne, 1985.

Leaver, Robin A. (2006). "Luther on Music." *Lutheran Quarterly* XX (2006): 125.

_____. (1989.) "The Lutheran Reformation." In *The Renaissance: From the 1470s to the End of the Sixteenth Century*. Edited by I. Fenelon. Englewood Cliffs, NJ: Palgrave Macmillan.

Leonard, Jeffrey M. (2008). "Identifying Inner-Biblical Allusions: Psalm 78 as a Test Case." *Journal of Biblical Literature* 127:2 (2008): 241–65.

Leroux, Neil R. (2007). *Martin Luther as Comforter, Writings on Death.* Leiden: Brill.

"Letter of Aristeas." (2012). *Encyclopedia Britannica Online.* https://www.britannica.com/topic/Letter-of-Aristeas. Accessed August 9, 2020.

Lewis, C. S. (1967). *Reflections on the Psalms.* Reprint, London: Fontana.

_____. (1958). *Reflections on the Psalms.* New York: Harper One.

Liddell, Henry George and Robert Scott. (1977). *A Greek-English Lexicon.* Revised by Henry Stuart Jones and Roderick McKenzie. Oxford: Clarendon Press.

Limburg, James. (1981). "Old Testament Theology for Ministry: The Works of Claus Westermann in English Translation." *Word & World* 1:2: 170. Accessed April 7, 2018.

Long, John D. (1998). *The Bible in English.* Lanham, MD: The University Press of America.

Longman, Tremper. (2005). "The Psalms and Ancient Near Eastern Prayer Genres." In *Interpreting the Psalms: Issues and Approaches*, 41–62. Edited by David Firth and Philip S. Johnston. Downers Grove, IL: IVP Academic.

Lowth, Robert. (1815). *Lectures on the Sacred Poetry of the Hebrews.* Boston: J. T. Buckingham. https://books.google.be/books?id= V0AAA AAAYAAJ&pr intsec=frontcover&source=gbs_ge_summary_r&cad=0#v=one page &q&f=false. Accessed November 29, 2017.

_____. ([1775]; 2011). *De sacra poesi Hebraeorum: praelectiones academicae Oxonii habitae, subjicitur Metricae Harianae brevis confutatio et oratio Crewiana.* Reprint. Oxford: Clarendon Press.

Luther, Martin. ([1538]; 1965). "Foreward [sic] to Georg Rhau's Collection, Symphoniae iucundae." Translated by Ulrich S. Leupold. In *Luther's Works. Vol. 53, Liturgy and Hymns.* Edited by Ulrich S. Leupold. Philadelphia: Fortress Press. Accessed November 29, 2017.

Margulis, B. (1969). "The Plagues Tradition in Ps 105." *Biblica* 50 (1969): 491–96.

Marlowe, W. Creighton. (2014). "A Spirit Chiasm in Isa. 11:2–3a." *Scandinavian Journal of the Old Testament* 28:1 (2014): 44–57.

_____. (2010). "In Tune with 'Truth': The Meaning of אמה in the Old Testament Psalter," 24–42. In *My Brother's Keeper: Essays in Honor of Ellis R. Brotzman.* Edited by T. J. Marinello and H. H. Drake Williams. Eugene, OR: Wipf & Stock.

_____. (2015). "The Meaning and Missional Significance of 'Call on the Name YHWH.'" *Asbury Journal* 70:2 (Fall 2015): 6–27. [AJ]

_____. (2007). "Meditation in the Psalms." *Midwestern Journal of Theology*, 6:1 (Fall 2007): 3–18.

_____. (2009). "The Wicked Wealthy in Isaiah 53:9." *Asbury Journal* 64:2 (Fall 2009): 68–81.

Martinez, Florentino Garcia, ed. and trans. (1994). *The Dead Sea Scrolls Translated: The Qumran Texts in English.* Translated by Wilfred G. E. Watson. Leiden: Brill.

Martinez, Florentino Garcia, and Eibert J. C. Tigchelaar, eds. (1997). *The Dead Sea Scrolls Study Edition.* Vol. 2: 4Q274–11Q31. Leiden: Brill.

Matthews, Victor H., and Don C. Benjamin. (1991). *Old Testament Parallels: Laws and Stories form the Ancient Near East.* New York: Paulist.

McCann, J. Clinton, Jr. (1996). "The Book of Psalms." In *The New Interpreter's Bible*, vol. 4, 751. Nashville: Abingdon.

_____. (1993). *A Theological Introduction to the Book of Psalms: The Psalms as Torah.* Nashville: Abingdon.

McCune, Rolland. (2009). *A Systematic Theology of Biblical Christianity*, vol. 1. Allen Park, MI: Detroit Baptist Theological Seminary Press.

Miller, Patrick D. (1993). "The Beginning of the Psalter." In *The Shape and Shaping of the Psalter*, 83–92. Edited by J. C.

McCann. https://search.proquest.com/religion/ docview/220239918/ fulltext-PDF/ 90D309EB97344CA1PQ/37?accountid=31623. Accessed August 13, 2019.

_____. (2012). "Who are the Bad Guys in the Psalms?" In *Let Us Go Up to Zion: Essays in Honor of H. G. M. Williamson on the Occasion of His Sixty-Fifth Birthday*, 423–30. Edited by Iain Provan and Mark J. Boda. Leiden: Brill.

Motyer, J. A., ed. (1994). *IVP New Bible Commentary*, n.p. University and Colleges Christian Fellowship. OakTree Software, Accordance eBook. Version 2.1.

Mowinckel, Sigmund. (1992). *The Psalms in Israel's Worship*, 2 vols. in one. Translated by D. R. Ap-Thomas. Sheffield: JSOT.

Muraoka, T. (2010). *A Greek-English Lexicon of the Septuagint*. Leuven: Peeters.

Nicol, Thomas. (1915). "Syriac Versions." In *International Standard Bible Encyclopedia Online*. n.p. https://www.internationalstandardbible.com/S/syriac-versions.html. Accessed July 18, 2020.

Nicoll, W. Robertson, ed. (1976). *The Expositor's Greek Testament*, vol. 2. Reprint, Grand Rapids: Eerdmans.

NIV Study Bible. ([1985]; 2015). "Introduction to the Psalms." *NIV Study Bible Online*. Revision. Grand Rapids: Zondervan. Accessed October 19, 2019.

Noth, Martin and D. Winton Thomas, eds. (1955). *Wisdom in Israel and in the Ancient Near East*. VT Supp. 3. Leiden: Brill.

O'Connor, Michael Patrick. (1997). *Hebrew Verse Structure*. Winona Lake, IN: Eisenbrauns.

O'Neill, J. C. (1991). *The Bible's Authority: A Portrait Gallery of Thinkers from Lessing to Bultmann*. Edinburgh: T&T Clark.

Pardee, Dennis. (1988). *Ugaritic and Hebrew Poetic Parallelism: A Trial Cut ('nt I and Proverbs 2)*. *Vetus Testamentum* Supplement 39. Leiden: Brill.

Pelikan, Jaroslav, and Helmut Lehman, eds. (1955). *Luther's Works: American Edition*. Vol. 49: 427–28. St. Louis/Philadelphia: Concordia/Fortress. Accessed November 29, 2017.

Pietersma, Albert. (1980). "David in the Greek Psalms." *Vetus Testamentum* 30 (April 1980): 219–26.

_____, ed. (2000). "Psalms: to the Reader." In *A New English Translation of the Septuagint: The Psalms, 542–47*. New York: Oxford University Press. http://ccat.sas.upenn.edu/nets/edition/24-ps-nets.pdf. Accessed November 30, 2017.

Pope, Marvin H. (1973). *Job*. AB 15. Reprint, Garden City, NJ: Doubleday.

Prinsloo, G. T. M. (1991). "Analysing Old Testament Poetry: Basic Issues in Contemporary Exegesis." *Skrif en Kerk* 12:1 (1991): 64–74.

Pritchard, James B., ed. (1969). *Ancient Near Eastern Texts Relating to the Old Testament*, 3rd. edition. Princeton, NJ: Princeton University Press.

Rahlfs, A. ed. (1935). *Septuaginta*, 2 vols. 9th edition. Stuttgart: Würtembergische Bibelanstalt.

Ramantswana, H. (2011). "David of the Psalters." *Old Testament Essays* 24:2 (2011): 431–63.

Ringgren, H. (1963). *The Faith of the Psalmists*. Minneapolis: Fortress.

Robertson, O. Palmer. (2015). *The Flow of the Psalms: Discovering Their Structure and Theology*. Phillipsburg, NJ: P & R.

Rochford, J. M. (2013). "Did the Ancient Jews Believe in Life after Death?" In *Evidence Unseen: Exposing the Myth of Blind Faith*, Columbus, OH: New Paradigm Publishing, Accessed July 9, 2020.

Ross, Allen P. (2011). *A Commentary on the Psalms (1–41)*, vol. 1. Grand Rapids: Kregel.

Schoors, A. (1973). *Jesaja II*. De Boeken van het Oude Testament Deel IXB. Roermond: J. J. Roman & Zonen, Uitgevers.

Sheehan, Donald. (2013). *The Psalms of David Translated from the Septuagint Greek*. Eugene, OR: Wipf & Stock.

Schiffman, L. H. (2010). *Qumran and Jerusalem: Studies in the Dead Sea Scrolls and the History of Judaism*. Studies in the Dead Sea Scrolls and Related Literature. Grand Rapids: Eerdmans.

_____, and J. C. VanderKam, eds. (2000). *Encyclopedia of the Dead Sea Scrolls*. 2 vols. Oxford: University Press.

Silva, Moisés. (1983). *Biblical Words and Their Meaning: An Introduction to Lexical Semantics*. Grand Rapids: Zondervan.

Singer, Isidore, and George A. Barton. (1906). "MOLOCH." In *Jewish Encyclopedia.com*. http://www.jewishencyclopedia.com/articles/10937-moloch-molech. Accessed August 10, 2020.

Schökel, Luis Alonso. (1988). *A Manual of Hebrew Poetics*. Translated by Adrian Graffy. Subsidia Biblica 11. Rome: Biblical Institute Press.

"Solomon, Psalms of." (1911). In *Encyclopaedia Britannica Online* 25: 365–366. 11th edition. https://www.britannica.com/topic/Psalms-of-Solomon. Accessed July 18, 2020.

Sparks, Kenton L. (2005). *Ancient Texts for the Study of the Hebrew Bible*. Grand Rapids: Baker Academic.

Stamm, J. J. (1940). *Erlösen und Vergeben im Alten Testament*. Bern: A. Francke.

Tanner, Beth and Rolf A. Jacobson. (2014). "Book Four of the Psalter." In *The Book of Psalms*, 90–106. *NICOT*. Edited by E. J. Young, R. K. Harrison, and Robert L. Hubbard Jr. Grand Rapids: Eerdmans.

Taylor, J. G. (2010). "Psalms 1 and 2: A Gateway into the Psalter and Messianic Images of Restoration for David's Dynasty. In *Interpreting the Psalms for Teaching & Preaching*, 47–63. Edited by H. W. Bateman IV and D. B. Sandy. St. Louis: Chalice Press.

Toorn, Karel van der. (2018). "Three Israelite Psalms in an Ancient Egyptian Papyrus." *Ancient Near East Today* VI:5 (2018), n.p. Accessed August 20, 2020.

VanderWeele, Tyler J. (2017). "On the Promotion of Human Flourishing." *Proceedings of the National Academy of Sciences* 114, no. 31: 8148–56. https://doi.org/10.1073/pnas.1702996114.

von Rad, Gerhard. (1972). *Wisdom in Israel*. London: SCM Press.

_____. (1975). *Old Testament Theology*, vol. 1. London: SCM Press.

Waltke, Bruce K. (1995). "The Book of Proverbs and Ancient Wisdom Literature." In *Learning from the Sages: Selected Studies on the Book of Proverbs*, 39–41. Edited by Roy B. Zuck. Grand Rapids: Baker.

_____, and M. O'Connor. (1990). *Introduction to Biblical Hebrew Syntax*. Winona Lake, IN: Eisenbrauns.

Walton, John H. (1989). *Ancient Israelite Literature in Its Cultural Context*. Grand Rapids: Zondervan.

_____, Victor H. Matthews, and Mark W. Chavalas, eds. (2000). *IVP Bible Background Commentary: Old Testament*, n.p. OakTree Software, Accordance eBook. Version 2.1.

Watson, Wilfred G. E. (2005). *Classical Hebrew Poetry: A Guide to Its Techniques*. Revised, London: T&T Clark.

Weber, Beat. (2007). "Psalm 78 als 'Mitte' des Psalters?—ein Versuch." *Biblica* 88 (2007): 305–325. https://www.bsw.org/biblica/vol-88-2007/psalm-78-als-mitte-des-psalters-ein-versuch/75. Accessed February 13, 2018.

Weeks, Noel K. (2006). "Cosmology in Historical Context." *Westminster Theological Journal* 68 (2006): 283–93.

Weiser, Artur. (1962). *The Psalms*. 5th edition. Translated by Herbert Hartwell. Old Testament Library. English reprint, London: SCM.

Westermann, Claus. (1977). "Comments by Westermann at the Sprunt Lectures, Union

Theological Seminary in Virginia," 169–75. Unpublished lecture. Accessed April 7, 2018.

_____. (1968). *Das loben Gottes in den Psalmen.* Reprint, Göttingen: Vandenhoeck & Ruprecht.

_____. (1964). *Forschung am Alten Testament. Theologische Bücherei, Bd. 24.* München: C. Kaiser.

_____. (1981). *Praise and Lament in the Psalms.* Translated by Keith R. Crim and Richard N. Soulen. English reprint, Atlanta: Westminster John Knox Press.

Westermeyer, Paul. (1998). *Te Deum: The Church and Music.* Minneapolis: Fortress Press.

Williams, Donald. (1986). *Psalms 1–72.* Mastering the Old Testament 13. Dallas: Word.

Williams, Ronald J. (2007). *Williams' Hebrew Syntax.* 3rd edition. Revised by John C. Beckman. Toronto: Toronto University Press.

Wilson, Gerald H. (2014). *NIV Application Commentary: Psalms I.* Grand Rapids: Zondervan. https://www.biblegateway. com/passage/?search =Psalm +151 +1&version=CEB. Accessed November 27, 2017.

_____. (2002). *Psalms,* vol. 1. *New International Version Application Commentary.* Grand Rapids: Zondervan.

_____. (1993). "Shaping the Psalter: A Consideration of Editorial Linkage in the Book of Psalms." In *The Shape and Shaping of the Psalter,* 72–82. Edited by J. C. McCann. JSOT Supp. 159. Sheffield, UK: JSOT Press.

_____. (2004). *The Editing of the Hebrew Psalter.* Society of Biblical Literature Dissertation Series 76. Reprint, Chico, CA: Scholars Press.

Wilson, R. D. (1926). "The Headings of the Psalms." *The Princeton Theological Review* 24:1 (1926) 380–91.

Wise, M., M. Abegg Jr., and E. Cook. (1996). *The Dead Sea Scrolls: A New Translation.* San Francisco, CA: Harper.

Wolff, H. W. (1974). *Anthropology of the Old Testament.* London: SCM.